The Inheritance
of Economic Status

Studies in Social Economics
TITLES PUBLISHED

STUDIES IN SOCIAL ECONOMICS

John A. Brittain

The Inheritance
of Economic Status

THE BROOKINGS INSTITUTION
Washington, D.C.

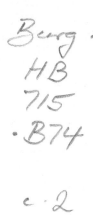

Copyright © 1977 by
THE BROOKINGS INSTITUTION
1775 Massachusetts Avenue, N.W., Washington, D.C. 20036

Library of Congress Cataloging in Publication Data:

Brittain, John A
 The inheritance of economic status.

 (Studies in social economics)
 Includes bibliographical references and index.
 1. Inheritance and succession. 2. Social status.
I. Title. II. Series.
HB715.B74   301.44′1   76-56369
ISBN 0-8157-1082-8
ISBN 0-8157-1081-X pbk.

9 8 7 6 5 4 3 2 1

THE BROOKINGS INSTITUTION is an independent organization devoted to nonpartisan research, education, and publication in economics, government, foreign policy, and the social sciences generally. Its principal purposes are to aid in the development of sound public policies and to promote public understanding of issues of national importance.

The Institution was founded on December 8, 1927, to merge the activities of the Institute for Government Research, founded in 1916, the Institute of Economics, founded in 1922, and the Robert Brookings Graduate School of Economics and Government, founded in 1924.

The Board of Trustees is responsible for the general administration of the Institution, while the immediate direction of the policies, program, and staff is vested in the President, assisted by an advisory committee of the officers and staff. The bylaws of the Institution state: "It is the function of the Trustees to make possible the conduct of scientific research, and publication, under the most favorable conditions, and to safeguard the independence of the research staff in the pursuit of their studies and in the publication of the results of such studies. It is not a part of their function to determine, control, or influence the conduct of particular investigations or the conclusions reached."

The President bears final responsibility for the decision to publish a manuscript as a Brookings book. In reaching his judgment on the competence, accuracy, and objectivity of each study, the President is advised by the director of the appropriate research program and weighs the views of a panel of expert outside readers who report to him in confidence on the quality of the work. Publication of a work signifies that it is deemed a competent treatment worthy of public consideration but does not imply endorsement of conclusions or recommendations.

The Institution maintains its position of neutrality on issues of public policy in order to safeguard the intellectual freedom of the staff. Hence interpretations or conclusions in Brookings publications should be understood to be solely those of the authors and should not be attributed to the Institution, to its trustees, officers, or other staff members, or to the organizations that support its research.

Foreword

It is common knowledge that income and other elements of economic status are unequally distributed among the American population. Economists have traditionally attributed such inequality to differences in productivity associated with unequal accumulations of property and skill. In this study, however, John A. Brittain weighs the extent to which economic status tends to be inherited, that is, determined by the advantages or disadvantages conferred by one's family. Since children are born with the economic status of their parents, it is important to appraise the effect of unequal starts in life on chances of economic success. Insofar as children tend to remain in the same economic rank as their parents, a lack of equality of opportunity is implied, and policies to increase vertical economic mobility are in order.

This inquiry reflects statistical data on the intergenerational economic relationships revealed by a sample of families in the Cleveland area in the mid-1960s. The data allowed Brittain to study the effects of family status on the educational attainment, occupational status, income, and residence quality of sons and daughters. He relates these dimensions of children's status to explicit parental characteristics, including their own education and occupation.

Brittain's main finding is that one's economic status at birth and in maturity tends to be the same. His analysis shows that the degree of inequality of economic status among brothers is substantially less than that among all males. Because women usually marry men with family backgrounds similar to their own, the influence of parents on the economic status of daughters tends to be as strong as their corresponding influence on sons. In Brittain's view, these observations constitute impressive evidence of the effect of family background on a man's chances for economic success; they imply that inherited advantage, over which the individual has no control, is important; and they bolster the case for a public policy aimed at redistribution of income and wealth.

The author is most grateful to Marvin B. Sussman, Judith N. Cates, and David T. Smith, authors of *The Family and Inheritance,* who made the Cleveland data available, and to the Russell Sage Foundation, which sponsored their original research.

He is also grateful to Henry J. Aaron, Edward M. Gramlich, Gerald R. Jantscher, Christopher S. Jencks, Marc L. Nerlove, Guy H. Orcutt, Joseph A. Pechman, Paul J. Taubman, and others who offered criticism and comments on the manuscript. He acknowledges essential research assistance provided by William Perkins and, for lesser periods, by Tun A. Wai, Barrington Brown, K. Wendy Holt, and Andrea Mills. The Brookings Social Science Computation Center supplied programming advice. The manuscript was checked for accuracy and consistency by Evelyn P. Fisher and Brookings staff members under her direction; it was edited by Ellen Alston. The manuscript was typed by Charlotte Kaiser, and the index was prepared by Frank Sokolove.

Mr. Brittain is a senior fellow in the Brookings Economic Studies program. His study was supported by a grant from the Ford Foundation; it is the fourteenth in the Brookings series of Studies in Social Economics, a program of research on selected problems in the fields of health, education, social security, and welfare. The views expressed in the study are the author's and should not be ascribed to the Ford Foundation or to the staff members, officers, or trustees of the Brookings Institution.

GILBERT Y. STEINER
Acting President

January 1977
Washington, D.C.

Contents

Text Tables

Text Figures

xiii

chapter one **Introduction**

Americans exhibit an ambivalent attitude toward the inequality of income, wealth, and other badges of economic success in our society. On the one hand we tolerate the substantial inequality of individual rewards that results from differences in endowments and accumulation of property and skills. We rationalize this by the belief that the greater the variation in attainable rewards, the greater the competitive effort and productive efficiency of individuals will be. On the other hand, there is a persistent suspicion that the inequality generated by the American economic system could be substantially reduced without a great loss of efficiency.[1] Moreover, it has been shown that one cause of the inequality of property and skills is the degree of privilege conferred by one's socioeconomic background and other parental influences.[2] Thus, the inequality of material wealth and even of "human wealth," or earning power, may be due in large part to the process of inheritance, both explicit and implicit.[3]

Our competitive and individualistic society places a high value on self-reliance. But even the rugged individualist knows that the struggle for success is an unfair competition, and the greater the influence of socioeconomic origins, the more unfair is the race for success in life.[4] Individuals

1. For an elegant analysis of this relationship, see Arthur M. Okun, *Equality and Efficiency: The Big Tradeoff* (Brookings Institution, 1975).

2. See the national studies discussed in chapter 3. It should be noted, however, that specific background characteristics may, in part, be proxies for other parental influences, including genetic endowments, birth order, and upbringing.

3. Inheritance is conceived of here as measured by the overall statistical association between the economic status of children and characteristics of their parents. It includes not only the directly observable inheritance of material wealth but all causes underlying the intergenerational economic relationship, known and unknown. That is, it includes all influences of parents on their children.

4. Insofar as these background characteristics are proxies for latent parental influences on the ability and productivity of their children, they do not constitute "unfair" privilege in the usual sense. Even so, they represent variations in life chances over which children have no control.

1

in this race inevitably have different head starts and handicaps, since every child starts with the economic status of his parents. Ability, upbringing, initiative, and luck affect the outcome of the race, but the influence of an individual's starting position persists throughout his life. It is the effect of these head starts and handicaps on the individual's economic success that is the primary subject of this study. Two other key, and related, influences—educational attainment and the marital selection process—will also be considered.

This inquiry is, however, limited in at least two significant respects. First, the sample used here does not make possible effective separation of the genetic and environmental components of parental influence. This means that the implications of the findings for public policy are less apparent than they might be if the effects of nature and nurture could be separated. Tax policies, for example, can more directly affect environmental transmission of earning capacity than genetic transmission. On the other hand, whether policy should interfere more or less with inherited advantages due to parental investment than those due to genetic endowments is a value judgment in any case.[5]

The second qualification has to do with the roles of education and marital selection. There is no way to separate here the effect of educational attainment on economic status as a screening or signaling device to employers from its productivity in terms of human capital. Analogously, education may also serve as a screening device in the marital selection process, helping to transmit economic status across generations. The role of the daughter's education in status transmission via marriage is considered in chapter 4, but again, there is no way to distinguish its screening and productive functions.

Despite our inability to separate genetic and environmental background effects, the relative importance of family background, intermediate factors (such as education), and sheer luck as determinants of individual economic success is relevant to any policy toward inequality. The findings to be presented here may be placed in perspective by contrasting them with the results of three earlier studies. Blau and Duncan found a relatively weak influence of socioeconomic background on chances of success and a strong effect of educational attainment independent of family background (that is, a strong effect of variations in education not explainable by back-

5. It could, of course, be argued that social attempts to offset the advantage of inherited educational opportunity will tend to discourage parents from investing in their children. No such effect would result from attempts to offset genetic advantages.

ground).[6] Bowles shows a stronger family background influence and a relatively weak independent effect of education.[7] Jencks and collaborators found a strong effect from neither, implying economic success to be primarily a random or unexplainable phenomenon.[8]

The present study concludes with the only other combination of answers. The findings indicate a strong influence of socioeconomic background on the economic status of both men and women, *and* a substantial effect of educational attainment that is independent of background.[9] These two factors account for as much as two-thirds of the variation of some measures of success. This remains a significant result, even when it is acknowledged that the measured effect of formal education exaggerates its independent role.[10]

Insofar as the present results have general validity, they have two very general implications for public policy. The strong role of inherited advantage and disadvantage bolsters the case for the redistribution of rewards to moderate that component of inequality which is due to circumstances over which the individual has no control. Second, the indicated independent effect of education, though subject to more qualifications, suggests that policies to equalize educational attainment may yet prove more effective in reducing inequality than indicated by recent experience.[11]

6. Peter M. Blau and Otis Dudley Duncan, *The American Occupational Structure* (Wiley, 1967).

7. Samuel Bowles, "Schooling and Inequality from Generation to Generation," *Journal of Political Economy,* vol. 80 (May–June 1972, pt. 2), pp. S219–S251.

8. Christopher Jencks and others, *Inequality: A Reassessment of the Effect of Family and Schooling in America* (Basic Books, 1972).

9. These findings are based on a particular sample at a particular time and are subject to other qualifications to be discussed. The result for socioeconomic background is more strongly established and of more general validity than that for formal education.

10. Marital selection is a supplemental factor also found to have great importance for the perpetuation of inequality. It is interpreted in chapter 4 as the key avenue through which the influence of parental economic status is transmitted to daughters; the relationship between the economic status of daughters and their parents is almost as close as if they had married their brothers.

11. While educational attainment appears to have a strong independent influence, it is also to some extent inherited. Equalizing educational attainment would thus tend to neutralize this factor in the maintenance of inequality. All findings concerning the role of formal educational attainment in determining economic status must be carefully qualified, however, because unmeasured background factors may play important roles; for instance, ability is usually emphasized, but what goes on in the home may be even more important. The importance of parental education found in the present analysis is highly consistent with this possibility.

Inheritance, Opportunity, and the Durability of Inequality

Before outlining the empirical findings of this study, it seems appropriate to face some general questions that inevitably arise. They concern different types of inheritance, the observed inequality of rewards, and the kinds of roles played by inheritance and inequality of opportunity in maintaining these differentials. In particular, we should consider the extent to which inherited advantage reflects an "unfair" inequality of opportunity.

What Types of Inheritance Generate Inequality?

In economic studies the concept of inheritance has generally been confined to the explicit inheritance of property. Certainly bequests of material wealth do play a major role in the persistence of economic inequality, especially in the maintenance of the wealth and income shares of the very wealthy.[12] However, the present analysis embraces a more general definition of inheritance as "the acquisition of a possession, condition or trait from past generations." Thus the productivity or "human wealth" of an individual is considered a heritable "condition or trait," along with all other heritable influences on one's economic status.[13]

The fact that human wealth and earning power tend to be transmitted across generations by some not necessarily observable, often implicit, conditioning process does not make this type of inheritance any the less real or important. This is especially true when the entire range of the wealth and income distribution is under consideration. In the across-the-board sample studied here, the wealth and bequests of the decedent parent showed much less influence on the economic status of heirs than the collective effect of other parental characteristics. Other background factors had more influence on education, income, occupation, and residential status of sons and daughters.[14] This is not surprising, since, for example,

12. Of course, some wealthy persons are self-made. For a discussion of the relative importance of inherited and created wealth in the generation of fortunes, see Lester C. Thurow, *Generating Inequality: Mechanisms of Distribution in the U.S. Economy* (Basic Books, 1975), chap. 6.

13. Examples of other heritable influences on a person's economic status are parental "pull," and the tendency for patterns of speech, dress, and motivation to be transmitted from one generation to the next.

14. The material wealth of the children themselves was not known, and bequests and parental wealth might well have a greater effect on that dimension of economic

removal of property income from income distributions reduces standard inequality measures by only about 15 or 20 percent. So an explanation of the persistence of overall inequality calls for consideration of all aspects of inheritance, and especially the inheritance of human wealth or capital. This amounts to evaluation of the influence of all known and unknown background factors on the economic status of an individual. Whether these are explicit or implicit and represent material or human wealth, they are all inherited influences over which the individual has no control.

Different policies are required to affect the two types of wealth inheritance—material and human. For example, part of the influence of family background on economic status is transmitted via material gifts and bequests; many would favor stronger tax policies to reduce the special advantage generated by such inheritances. On the other hand, there appears to be no serious proposal that we try to equalize the inheritance of mental or physical ability. Even so, both types of inheritance have something in common: they confer on the recipient a relative advantage unrelated to any independent initiative, effort, or contribution by him.

Most observers would probably view inequality generated by *either* material or genetic inheritance as a more fitting target for redistributive policies than inequality due to independent individual performance. For example, inequality generated by varying diligence among otherwise identical individuals is obviously less troubling than that due to varying material inheritances, or even that due to variations in inherited ability.[15] In other words, the extent to which success is inherited and beyond the independent control of the individual is relevant to policy, whether it reflects parental "connections," material bequests, or the inherited productivity of the individual.

Inequality and Tax Policy

The facts about inequality itself are far better established than the extent to which it is caused by inheritance and unequal opportunity. It is well known that the degree of inequality of income and other measures of economic success achieved by individuals has persisted over time at a high

status. However, the income, occupation, and residential status measures, especially when combined, probably offer a better overall indication of economic status for the entire range of the distribution.

15. Even diligence, of course, may be inherited or transmitted, to some extent, within the family.

and rather stable level. Through New Deal, Fair Deal, New Society, Great Society, and the War against Poverty, the relative gap between rich and poor in America has remained substantially impervious to egalitarian public policy.

Though income tax rates on very high incomes have ranged from 70 to 91 percent during the last generation, and low-income families are completely exempt from income taxes and also benefit from public transfers (and, in the longer run, from public education), the money income of the top tenth of the population, even after the income tax bite, consistently averages around twenty times that of the lowest tenth. Similarly, when very wealthy people die, their estates are taxed at rates up to 77 percent. Yet famous family fortunes have survived generation after generation, and the top 1 percent of wealth-holders continues to hold about one-quarter of all personal wealth decade after decade.[16]

Why is it so difficult to reduce the inequality of economic success among individuals? The reason usually emphasized for the persistence of such a high degree of inequality is that the equalizing effect of progressive public policies is not nearly as strong as it appears on paper.[17] This is undoubtedly true, but more attention is needed to the strong underlying forces that transmit a high degree of inequality from generation to generation. It will be shown here that these forces—especially the advantages or disadvantages conferred by one's family of origin—are so strong that the relative ineffectuality of contemporary redistributive policies is not surprising.

Why Focus on Inheritance as a Cause of Inequality?

There are many factors involved in the generation of unequal rewards, including individual effort that is independent of any inherited advantage. Yet inheritance invites attention, because it may create an "unfair" head start or handicap. The extent to which inherited competitive advantage

16. See, for example, James D. Smith and Stephen D. Franklin, "The Concentration of Personal Wealth, 1922–1969," *American Economic Review*, vol. 64 (May 1974, *Papers and Proceedings, 1973*), pp. 162–67. (Shares of the very wealthy are understated in these estimates, owing to exclusion of wealth held in trusts not subject to estate tax.)

17. The ineffectuality of income redistribution has been demonstrated in many studies. The impotence of estate taxation as an equalizer of the wealth distribution has received less attention, but this aspect of the problem is being treated in a current detailed study by Gerald R. Jantscher and George Cooper for the Brookings Institution.

is perceived as unfair varies across a wide spectrum. Four distinct types of inheritance may be easily ranked on that dimension. As an example of the most blatantly unfair, "success that depends on whom you know rather than what you know is a clear case of inequality of opportunity. And it seems particularly unfair when the real issue is whom your father knows."[18] Also generally accepted as unfair is the disadvantage due to discrimination against inherited traits like race and religion. This type of discrimination has attracted more attention than more subtle forms of favoritism because it can be tackled effectively by public policy.

A second type of inheritance is the bequest of material wealth, which has long been a target of reformers. Economists in the early quarter of this century often complained about it as a clear-cut case of something for nothing. Even the orthodox marginal-productivity theorist did not feel comfortable with the transmission of rewards so totally unrelated to the recipient's own contribution. That part of inequality due to inheritance seemed unfair and intolerable, and offered some hard-nosed "objective" theorists an outlet for humanitarian expression. Furthermore, it appeared that this inequity could be struck down with ease. It seemed likely to economists that there would be stronger public support for very progressive inheritance taxes than for progressive taxes on earned income.

Recent adverse public reactions to inheritance tax proposals have cast doubt on the sagacity of economists as public opinion analysts. Even so, the United States has had a seemingly very progressive estate tax since the rates were greatly increased in the thirties. On paper, it appeared in tune with the earlier views of Andrew Carnegie, who feared the stultifying effect of a silver spoon in the mouth of the rich man's son. In practice, however, the low effective rates under this tax law would have satisfied Andrew Mellon, who feared that heavy taxation of inherited capital would wipe out private property in two or three generations. Whether the head start due to inherited capital is judged as fair or not, its effects *could* be readily modified by taxation.[19]

A third form of parental influence on children's status is more subtle. Superficial characteristics such as styles of speech and dress tend to be

18. Okun, *Equality and Efficiency*, p. 76.
19. High estate taxes may, of course, discourage bequests and encourage investment instead in a son's education and the intergenerational transmission of human capital. Given the major role found here for human capital in the generation of inequality, such a tax policy might even aggravate the problem. At the same time, the social gain from rapid accumulation of human wealth could be an offsetting factor.

transmitted from one generation to the next. In most cases these have no fundamental effect on a son's productivity, but they may affect his marketability or earning power, tending to place him in a particular occupational track. Insofar as these traits are inherited, this process reduces intergenerational economic mobility and helps perpetuate inequality. Unlike parental pull or connections, this type of background influence looks innocent, but it yields unfair head starts and handicaps.

Finally, the most vexing question is raised by the tendency of real productivity also to be inherited by children from their parents. Here again, the distinction between genetic and environmental determinants of children's economic status should be emphasized, even though the data in this study do not permit quantitative separation. For example, both natural ability and educational opportunity are to some extent inherited. Furthermore, parental attention and preschool training are more likely to speed the development of a child in an advantageous environment. How should we react to such inherited advantages that clearly manifest themselves in actual productivity differentials? Certainly no one believes it is "unfair" for parents to develop the productivity of their children. Still, the fact that these competitive advantages or disadvantages are inherited makes them relevant to an evaluation of the whole process.

Suppose a given degree of inequality within a generation emerged entirely by chance, as though generated by a lottery. Society might view it as excessive and attempt to moderate it by public policy. But this should be compared to the same degree of inequality generated substantially by inheritance. Even if it reflected actual productivity rather than mere favoritism, it would be more intolerable than inequality due to chance. Under a fair lottery, a poor man would at least know his son had the same chance for success as anyone else. But in the real world he knows the son of a rich man has a better chance. This aspect of inequality is reflected in the concept of an intergenerational poverty trap: "It would be one thing if poverty hit at random, and no one group were singled out. It is another thing to realize that some seem destined to poverty almost from birth— by their color or by the economic status or occupation of their parents."[20] The hypothesis that poverty tends to be inherited or self-perpetuating is persuasive. Neither government policy nor public scolding can quickly eliminate such contributory factors as early marriages and large families. Alvin Schorr sees the family life of the poor as a series of stages of ever-

20. Mollie Orshansky, "Children of the Poor," *Social Security Bulletin*, vol. 26 (July 1963), p. 3.

increasing financial strain, often leading to a break-up of the family;[21] at the same time the husband tends to be without an opportunity to accumulate the skills with which to break out of the poverty trap.[22] More relevant to the present study is the fact that the *children* of the poor, having been raised under these unfavorable conditions, often find themselves in the same bind.

It is true, of course, that the jaws of the poverty trap do not have an invincible grip. Millions of children of the poor have escaped from it, just as the silver spoon is no guarantee of success at the top. But it remains important to compare the life chances of those who start life at the top with those who start at the bottom. Even though many of those who inherit a position in the poverty trap remain there because of an actual disadvantage in productivity, the unequal starts are troublesome. Inherited disadvantage, even more so than inequality due to pure chance, invites after-the-fact redistribution of rewards; chance, at least, does not tend to assign families to the same slot generation after generation.

Inheritance and "Inequality of Opportunity"

We can easily agree that some types of inherited advantage are far more intolerable than others. Unfair advantage is apparent if a corporation president makes his incompetent, indolent son vice-president at ten times the average wage of his workers. But neither capitalist nor socialist society objects to a high salary for a productive son. That is true even if he has simply been lucky enough to have "inherited" real ability and productivity from his parents. Can the concept and goal of "equality of opportunity" help us evaluate these different varieties of inheritance? Unfortunately, the concept itself is a fuzzy one, but it is so prominent in the literature on inequality that it cannot be dismissed.[23] Despite the ambiguity of the concept, it seems useful to consider the following question: To what extent can inequality of opportunity be attributed to the inequality generated by inheritance?

21. It is often charged that public welfare policy is not without responsibility for this. For a discussion of this question, see Heather L. Ross and Isabel V. Sawhill, *Time of Transition: The Growth of Families Headed by Women* (Washington, D.C.: Urban Institute, 1975).

22. Alvin L. Schorr, "The Family Cycle and Income Development," *Social Security Bulletin*, vol. 29 (February 1966), pp. 14–25.

23. See, for instance, Kurt Klappholz, "Equality of Opportunity, Fairness and Efficiency," in Maurice Peston and Bernard Corry, eds., *Essays in Honour of Lord Robbins* (International Arts and Sciences Press, 1972), pp. 247–56.

Clearly, inheritance generates inequality of opportunity according to at least one standard definition. If the son of a poor black man has a relatively low probability of success for that reason alone, he does not have "a good chance for advancement or progress" (one conventional definition of opportunity). On the other hand, if his poor prospects are due solely to his productivity rather than racial discrimination by employers, he is disadvantaged, but is he denied equality of opportunity? The answer depends on the side of the market from which one views the question. A color-blind employer would assume he has not denied equal economic opportunity if he takes account only of productivity. But insofar as the job-seeker believes his low productivity is inherited and beyond his control, he could reasonably hold the opposite view.

The inheritance of status takes place in its most extreme form in a rigid caste society. Under any reasonable definition, such confinement of individuals to one track for life constitutes a denial of equal economic opportunity. But how are we to interpret a tendency for economic status to be inherited within an economic system characterized as "democratic capitalism"? Presumably, in terms of the economic dimensions of the system, the term "democratic" refers to the effective pursuit of a goal—the assurance to each individual of an equal opportunity to attain the good life.

In its narrowest sense equality of opportunity refers to nondiscrimination in hiring and wages between, for example, two persons who (in the eyes of the employer) are equal in productivity and other respects, but differ only in one characteristic such as race. Whatever his definition of equality of opportunity, practically anyone other than the avowed racist would agree that nondiscrimination on the basis of race would be a step toward that goal. However, the goal itself remains arbitrary; it depends on the particular characteristics that an individual or society wishes to bar as criteria for hiring, wage determination, and so on. Equal opportunity is achieved by definition when the specified types of discrimination are eliminated. The problem is that, for perfectly rational reasons, no society bars productivity as a criterion. If racial discrimination in the legal sense is eliminated, equality of opportunity will theoretically be achieved for blacks. However, as long as the black man's productivity tends to be negatively affected by a disadvantaged background, he will not have equal opportunity in any practical sense.

While discrimination on the basis of race was one of the first official targets of the drive for equal opportunity, the list of characteristics prohibited as labor market criteria has grown in recent years. In October 1975, the District of Columbia ordered employers to post notices forswearing discrimination on the basis of any of thirteen characteristics: race, color, religion, national origin, sex, age, marital status, personal appearance, sexual orientation, family responsibilities, physical handicap, matriculation, and political affiliation. Suppose, by some miracle, employers could be induced to ignore these characteristics and make decisions solely on the basis of productivity. Even then, the prospects for a blind, sixty-four-year-old black woman caring for ten grandchildren would not be good; her age, race, and sex would tend to give her an inherited disadvantage in education and other determinants of productivity.[24] It is difficult to look upon her as having equality of opportunity,[25] even though she has been assured the same consideration under the law as that accorded a handsome, thirty-year-old, straight, white, Protestant American male in perfect physical condition.

The struggle for success in life is often compared to a foot race with head starts and handicaps. This analogy is ambiguous, because the implied legal definition of head starts and handicaps varies with the given definition of equality of opportunity. Yet the analogy is of some help in clarifying the role of inheritance in perpetuating inequality. The current District of Columbia criteria imply that contestants in the race have no "unjust" handicaps or head starts if discrimination is avoided with respect to the thirteen characteristics: blacks and whites, men and women, old and young, all then have the same starting position. The contestants obviously differ in "productivity" as runners, but, according to the traditional view, that is what the race is all about. With arbitrary discrimination ruled out, the race is said to be fair, and the strongest contestants get the biggest prizes.

Reasoning of this kind can be questioned at several levels. First, even if the thirteen specified types of discrimination are apparently excluded, invisible head starts and handicaps will continue to persist. The "pull" of a father may give an invisible head start to a son, just as a depressant injected into a rival horse afflicts him with an invisible handicap. The formal

24. Her disability and responsibilities may also weigh against her productivity, though they are not necessarily inherited.

25. This depends, of course, on one's definition of this elusive concept. She may well have an equal chance to use her own capacities to the fullest, but that is a narrow concept. Insofar as capacities are low because of an underprivileged environment, this would seem to deny equality of opportunity.

assurance of equality of opportunity (even if accomplished) leaves intact inherited influences on life chances.

Second, while some of these invisible head starts and handicaps derive from the true strength or productivity of the contestants, some, like the handicap of the drugged horse, do not. The effects of four types of inherited head starts in life that exhibit varying degrees of unfairness have already been mentioned—pull or connections, material wealth, superficial characteristics, and actual productivity. The appropriate policy toward each obviously varies with the extent to which it is believed to confer unfair advantage. Whether fair or unfair, handicaps and head starts, even though invisible, can be offset by tax policy after the rewards are distributed.

Finally, instead of thinking of an apparently equal race with invisible head starts and handicaps, it may be more realistic to view the head starts and handicaps in real life as visibly present at the start of the race. The economic status of children at birth is identified with that of their parents. Therefore, some clearly start the race for success far behind, others far ahead. The policy implication of this depends, of course, on a value judgment; many individuals probably believe that equal opportunity to seek rewards for a person's *given* capacities is enough. Nonetheless, whatever the mixture of fairness and unfairness in these differential life chances, the mere fact of their existence invites some kind of policy intervention; the minimum called for is after-tax redistribution of rewards to modify the influence of these head starts and handicaps over which the individual has no control.

The Inheritance of Economic Status

Obviously a son or daughter from an affluent family has a better chance of economic success than a person born in poverty. The key question is how much better? The first objective, therefore, is to evaluate the overall strength of the tendency for economic status to be transmitted from one generation to the next. Assume that it is agreed that the inequality of rewards is greater than necessary to provide adequate incentive effects. If we believe that economic success is a matter of pure chance—the outcome of a giant lottery—the only appropriate policy is to redistribute the rewards after the fact. If we conclude instead that success in life is to a substantial degree inherited, we will be inclined to look for specific policy levers to reduce the overall role of inheritance in perpetuating inequality. The closest thing to a lottery interpretation of the income distribution is that of Jencks and colleagues. One of their two key findings was that a man's socioeconomic background has little influence on his chances for success in life. Their study relied on an analysis of brothers, and began with the plausible assumption that a strong socioeconomic or family background effect would reveal itself in the form of homogeneity of economic status (relatively low inequality) among brothers from the same family. Their startling conclusion was that "there is nearly as much economic inequality among brothers raised in the same homes as in the general population."[26] The study was hampered by the absence of any actual data on brothers and by some questionable inferences as to what data on brothers might have shown if available. In contrast, the appraisal here of the overall effect of socioeconomic background on economic status is based on an actual sample of brothers.[27]

The Sample

The empirical base of this analysis is an admirable and painstaking survey of 659 persons who died in the Cleveland metropolitan area during 1964–65, and a follow-up survey of their survivors.[28] The data analyzed were first restricted to families for which information on economic status was available for two or more brothers. In 1965–66, different variants of the sample covered from 115 to 231 brothers. The measures of son's economic status provided were a residential quality rating, occupational classification, and the son's family income.[29]

The sample of brothers is fairly representative of the 1966 U.S. male labor force in many respects, as will be detailed in chapter 2. The average age of forty-two was about five years above the national average, and the median income of about $8,500 and educational attainment of about

26. Jencks and others, *Inequality*, pp. 7–8.
27. The findings highlighted in this section are backed up in detail in chapter 2, where the results are compared to recent findings for other samples of brothers. The emphasis on brothers is purely pragmatic; it is more difficult to measure the economic success of sisters, especially the 85 percent of the sample who were housewives.
28. Results of this survey were generously made available by Marvin B. Sussman, Judith N. Cates, and David T. Smith, authors of *The Family and Inheritance* (New York: Russell Sage Foundation, 1970).
29. The son's educational attainment was also included, but it was generally interpreted as an intermediate influence standing temporally between family background and ultimate economic status.

twelve years appear close to those for northern metropolitan areas at that time. The median wealth and education of their decedent parents also agreed closely with national estimates. On the other hand, taken collectively, the men surveyed departed substantially from the national profile in three related ways. Over half were from Roman Catholic families— about double the national ratio; half of their decedent parents were foreign born—perhaps three times the national figure for persons born about the same time (the mid-nineties); and the average number of children in the family of origin was also rather high at about 4.4.

Is it risky to try to reach any general conclusions from this ethnically atypical sample? Given the present objective, there is one very encouraging indication on this score. We are trying to measure the strength of the *relationship* between the economic status of sons and their parents. Estimates of the intergenerational correlations between the education and occupation of fathers and sons are available from a large national survey conducted by the Bureau of the Census only a few years earlier. The correlations for the Cleveland sample are lower, although not significantly so. In any case, this comparison suggests that findings based on the Cleveland sample are highly unlikely to *over*state the effect of inheritance on economic status. At the same time, the Cleveland sample contains much valuable information not available in the national sample, including explicit information on the economic status of brothers.

Approaching the Analysis of Brothers

The sample of brothers offers important methodological advantages. It permits analysis of the effects of family background on the son's economic status without resort to explicit (often unreliable or unavailable) data on the parents themselves. Parental influences are held constant to a substantial degree when variation among brothers is measured. The degree of inheritance of son's economic status can be approximated through a comparison of the variation among brothers to the variation among all men. The less the variation among brothers relative to that among all men, the stronger the role of inheritance in determining outcomes; the greater the variation among brothers, the weaker is inheritance as a determinant of economic status.

The analysis of brothers covers more parental influences than even a detailed specification of socioeconomic background characteristics, such as parental education and occupation, that are usually identical for brothers.

This is because brothers also tend to be more alike with respect to unmeasured characteristics such as ability and environment than unrelated men. An analysis of brothers offers a measure of the effect of all influences shared by brothers as members of the same family. However, even brothers vary in genes, birth order, and upbringing.[30] For that reason, the measure of family effects derived from the sample of brothers must be viewed as a first approximation—a conservative estimate of the overall degree of parental influence on economic status. On the other hand, insofar as brothers influence or emulate each other, the same measures may overstate parental influence.[31]

Subject to these qualifications, two measures of the degree of inheritance were defined on the basis of the above reasoning. The first measure $\overline{R}_i^2$—the "intraclass correlation coefficient"—is an estimate of the fraction of variation in the economic status of these men that is due to family effects, that is, the fraction explained by all characteristics, known and unknown, that brothers have in common as members of the same family. So, without benefit of explicit background information, it measures the overall effect of shared parental influences, including the most conventionally recognized source of inheritance, material wealth. The second measure is the estimated ratio of standard deviations within and between families, s_w/s_b. The lower this ratio, the greater the influence of factors affecting brothers in common.

To What Extent is Economic Status Inherited?

For the three measures of son's economic status (residence, occupation, and income), as well as composite measures combining them, both inheritance measures show a strong tendency for brothers to achieve similar status. Depending on the criteria and sample, the measure $\overline{R}_i^2$ showed between 34 and 67 percent of the variance of economic status explained by family effects. The standard deviation ratio s_w/s_b ranged from 0.47 to 0.67, indicating that the standard deviation of brothers' economic status averaged somewhat over half the same measure applied to family means.

It is possible to impart a more concrete meaning to these rather abstract measures of inheritance. First, we can compare the predicted family incomes of sons with advantageous backgrounds to those of sons who are

---

30. Only in the case of identical twins are brothers' genes identical.
31. These opposing biases are considered later, along with other qualifications such as the age-homogeneity of brothers.

less fortunate. Adjusting the incomes to a 1976 basis, a son who ranks 10 percent from the top in background is predicted to have an income of $25,200, while his opposite number with background rank 10 percent from the bottom has a predicted income of $11,500—less than half that predicted for the advantaged son. For sons with background ranks in the middle of the top and bottom 5 percent, respectively, the predictions are $30,900 and $9,400.[32]

Even more striking than these differentials are the chances of a son's earning a given income or higher. Consider the same two contrasts in background rank specified above. The estimate (more speculative than those above) is that the son ranking 10 percent from the top in background had a 51 percent chance of having a 1976 family income of $25,000 or more, compared to a 2 percent chance for his disadvantaged opposite number. The son from the middle of the top 5 percent in background rank had nearly a 40 percent chance of achieving an upper-middle-class income of $35,000 or more. The chance for the son with the poor background is negligible. Even a more fortunate son who starts life in the middle of the pack had only a 2 or 3 percent chance of reaching the $35,000 income level in 1976.

The discussion so far has dealt with the inheritance of ultimate economic status. One factor helping to explain the differentials discussed is the tendency for the intermediate factor, educational attainment, also to be inherited. For example, consider again the men with backgrounds in the middle of the top and bottom 5 percent, respectively. The number of years of educational attainment predicted for the advantaged son is sixteen to seventeen, compared to about nine years for his opposite number. This estimate suggests that the disadvantaged son tends to go to school only slightly more than half as long. This inherited differential in expected schooling is one factor underlying the tendency for economic status to be inherited.

These predictions and probabilities are, of course, highly speculative estimates based on a particular sample; they are subject to many qualifications such as the representativeness of the sample and possible effects on sons that may be independent of parental socioeconomic status.[33]

---

32. The scaling of incomes to a 1976 basis is for illustrative purposes only, and does not represent a forecast of 1976 incomes for these men on the basis of the 1965–66 sample. The data and income distribution of that time are taken as given.

33. These are discussed in detail in chapter 2 and are generally found to be of minor importance.

However, even the most cautious interpretation rules out the conclusion that individual incomes are essentially the result of a gigantic game of chance.

Since there is a large chance component in the distribution of income, some characteristics of a lottery are indeed present. Unlike the state lotteries of today, however, this one is rigged in favor of those with advantageous backgrounds. It is as though the lottery gave discounts to participants with privileged socioeconomic backgrounds. And if the most privileged were given the largest discounts, the state lottery would begin to resemble the one that generates our income distribution today.

Predicting Son's Status from Specific Parental Characteristics

The overall degree of inheritance of economic status—the collective effect of *all* background characteristics—was found to be very substantial. But what can be said about the influence of known parental characteristics as determinants of son's economic status? An attempt was made first to gauge the strength of individual background influences, without yet speculating as to the mechanism through which the parental influence is transmitted across generations.

The effect of material bequests is transmitted directly, while other determinants operate indirectly, as through parental investment in a son's education. Environmental influences, such as those affecting speech and dress, fall between these clear-cut extremes and simply "rub off" on the son in unspecified ways. All affect his ultimate economic status, but no distinction is made at this stage between direct and indirect effects. All that can be said for certain about these background determinants is that they are almost entirely predetermined (given) influences on the current generation. However the effect of parental education is transmitted, and even if it is proxying in part for parental ability and home environment, we know at least that the causation is temporally forward.[34]

The available background variables are not causal in the same sense as a bequest that directly affects the son's wealth. Most simply represent, or are proxies for, various dimensions of parental economic status. The high occupational status of a corporation president does not ordinarily directly cause his son to rank high in occupation, but a statistical tendency for such

34. Details of the estimates to be summarized here are presented in chapter 3.

a relationship to hold can be observed. This could be due in part to provision of an advantageous environment (including education); it could also be due in part to unmeasured genetic endowments to which background characteristics are related. The relationship is a predictive or probabilistic one, rather than a causal one in any mechanistic sense. Even so, a high probability of success for the son of a corporation president would be clear evidence of inherited inequality of life chances, whatever the reasons for it.

Background Characteristics and Hypotheses

The characteristics for which data were available ranged from the directly causal (material bequest), to a pure proxy for parental economic status (whether the decedent left a will). Although some important parental characteristics are unknown, the set of known characteristics available for this study is unusually rich.

The consistently strongest measured background influence was the educational attainment of the decedent parent.[35] The inverse relationship between the decedent's age and educational attainment led to a joint treatment of these two factors. The basic hypothesis is that parental education is generally favorable to a son's chances for success. But the older the parent at death in 1964–65, the greater the influence of a given number of years of education; that is, a college education amounted to a *relatively* higher educational standing for a man born in 1875 than for a man born in 1915. In other words, a year's differential in education provided a greater competitive advantage for men born in the early year than for those born later.

Ultimately, the explanatory model to portray these tendencies was designed to allow the relationship between son's economic status and parental education to vary with the parent's age. However, it was not because of any independent influence on the son's economic status that parent's age was included as an explanatory variable.[36] Its basic function was to

35. The education of only one parent—the decedent—whether father or mother, was included in the analysis. The education of the second parent was not available in enough cases to warrant inclusion.
36. No independent effect of age via a contribution of on-the-job training to the stock of human capital was found. Although stressed in the literature, it may have been missed here because most earners were on the flat portion of the age-income profile.

allow for the decline over time in the influence of a given education differential.

Five additional family background characteristics were included in the statistical model as explanatory variables: father's occupation, family size, race, religion, and wealth. The interpretation and treatment of these five characteristics was more routine. A high parental occupational status was assumed to confer a competitive advantage on sons, either directly or through the environment in which the sons mature. A large family was presumed to be disadvantageous to the children competing for its resources.[37]

Race and, usually, religion are directly inherited characteristics. They can directly influence the son's economic status insofar as there is discrimination in education, employment, and so forth. These categories also serve as proxy variables to portray the effect of historical differentials among these groups. Finally, son's economic status was assumed to be favored by family wealth. This dimension of parental status was represented by two indicators: the decedent's estate size and the existence of a will.[38]

The Strength of Background Influences

Before considering statistical estimates of specific background influences, their collective effect on son's economic status can be evaluated. This is best done by a comparison with the more general explanatory approach in the last section (based on brothers). That analysis measured the total influence on economic status of all factors, known and unknown, that affect brothers in common as members of the same family. For example, these background factors explained 57 percent of the variation in the three-variable composite index of son's status (based on residence, occupation, and income); this result can be viewed as a rough upper limit to the explanatory potential of explicit family background characteristics. The model discussed here used the six available general background characteristics to explain 44 percent of the variation in the same economic status measure. Given the various inadequacies of the background information available, the model's estimate of the effect of inheritance seems

37. The measured family size effect may reflect in part birth-order effects, but it was not possible to disentangle these factors empirically.

38. Some other hypotheses were tested, but unsupported; they included birthplace, birth order, material inheritance, and a distinction between male and female decedents. However, the test of birth-order effects was empirically inadequate and inconclusive.

remarkably close to the more generally based earlier figure.[39] Although the explanation of the three separate measures of son's status was less satisfactory, the 44 percent performance of the model is stressed as one clue to the reliability of estimates of specific background influences.

Estimated Effects of Parental Education

Having weighed the overall explanatory power of the model against the previous results for brothers, it is appropriate to move on to other samples more than double in size. In these samples the intergenerational relationships were more frequently significant, and in all such cases the effect on son's economic status was in the expected direction.

The parent's education had a very strong measured influence on the son's income and occupation. For a decedent of given age, his educational attainment had the expected positive effect on the son's income. But there was also a corollary finding: given the decedent's education, the greater his age, the greater the son's predicted income. This second result supports the hypothesis that the influence of a given parental education differential on son's income has declined over time.

The average age of the parents at their death was seventy-one. It is useful to summarize the estimated effects of the educational attainment of parents with age held constant at that level. The model predicts that the son of a parent of that age who went to college will have a 71 percent higher income than the son of a parent of the same age who did not go to high school. As a partial explanation of this large predicted differential in income, the same comparison can be made for the son's expected educational attainment. The son with the more educated parent is predicted to have completed nearly three more years of school.[40] The measured effect of parental education on occupation is also very high.

The contrast in predicted incomes is greater when there is also a substantial difference in the year of birth of the parents. Consider two sons with rather extreme contrasts in parental education: one whose decedent parent went to college, even though born in 1877, and another whose parent did not go to high school, even though born much later, in 1909. They are assumed to be alike in all other measured respects. The model

39. The sample provides no data on family income or the other parent's education, the wealth and occupation variables are defective, and most of the background information depends on recollections of the sons.

40. Put another way, the expected education of the first son is one standard deviation higher than that of the second son.

predicts a 119 percent higher income for the son of the more educated parent.

More speculative estimates are available of the contrasting income prospects of advantaged and disadvantaged sons. Consider the same two sons just discussed. Assume that the model predicts that the disadvantaged son's income, adjusted to a 1976 basis, is at the lower quartile, or about $13,000. Under conventional assumptions, the model implies that he had a 7 percent chance of actually attaining a family income of $25,000 or more. But the same probability for the son who differed from him only with respect to the more favorable parental age-education combination was 62 percent. So the son of the more educated parent, other things being equal, had nine times as great a chance to achieve that income status.

These differing income prospects due to contrasting age-adjusted education of only one parent are so striking as to suggest the probability that the case for education is being overstated owing to lacunae in the model. Parental education could be a proxy for missing variables such as parental income and ability or home environment. Thus, the measured effects of parental education may (although there is no proof of this) reflect substantial genetic influences. If so, education could be deriving some of its statistical credit from its relationship to these other unmeasured influences. The information available does not permit evaluation of this possibility, but two points can be made. Five other major background characteristics are included, which also may be correlated to the missing influences. The indicated effect of parental education survives with flying colors their inclusion as competitors in the explanatory model. In fact, education is so highly significant that it is difficult to conceive of its being supplanted statistically by any rival influences, even if they could be measured and included.

Effects of Other Background Factors

The son's economic success was much less strongly associated with father's occupation than with parental education. On the other hand, family size had a significant negative effect on all success measures for the sons except occupational status. The association of son's status with religious background was also fairly consistent. According to the model, even if their backgrounds were alike in all other measured respects, sons from Jewish families generally fared better than the sons of Protestants, who in turn were better off than those from a Catholic background. The weakest background effects were registered by the two parental wealth indicators; the indicated effects of both were overshadowed by the effects of parent's education.

Race was a significant factor: for example, a white son identical to a nonwhite in all five other respects is predicted to have a 75 percent higher income. The number of nonwhites in the sample was so very small, however (only five), that the relationship between economic status and race could not be accurately estimated, and the results must be regarded skeptically. Even so, the indicated racial differentials were so great that they were highly significant for all success indicators except the intermediate indicator—education in years. As discussed later, this result may be misleading because of the lower quality of education experienced by nonwhites.

Intergenerational Economic Mobility

The foregoing discussion was based on equations relating son's success to socioeconomic background characteristics. An alternative approach was to construct single measures or indexes of the son's success and his socioeconomic background. The sons were then ranked according to both measures—their success and their backgrounds. These ranks were used to construct mobility tables portraying the success ranks achieved by sons of given background ranks. Sons were divided into tenths according to both background and success ranks. The most homogeneous sample considered was that of married sons of male decedents. Seven of the 14 sons who came from the top tenth in background ended up in the top tenth themselves, and none fell farther than the fourth tenth.

Greater mobility was observed from the bottom tenth in rank. Only 5 of the 14 sons who started out in that rank remained there, but not one of them managed to escape the bottom half of the economic ladder. The striking thing about this sample is that there is not a single case of overlap of the success measures of the sons from the top and bottom tenth; all 14 of the former were better off than all 14 of the latter. That indicates a sharp contrast between the life chances of sons of upper and lower socioeconomic background ranks.

These mobility tables point to the powerful influence of head starts and handicaps on the outcome of the race for economic success. Differential starting positions reflect only in part an inequality of opportunity in the narrow sense discussed earlier. However, they represent entirely real differentials at birth. The 14 most advantaged sons may be viewed as *starting* the race for success with a position in the frontrunning tenth, while the other 14 started with a handicap that placed them at the back of the pack of about 140 starters.

It is true in a literal sense to say that the sons started life in these contrasting positions. As children, their economic status was that of their family, and the variables used to rank their family backgrounds (except the generally insignificant wealth indicators) were already fixed when the sons in the race were born. Some of the children are far behind when we take the first snapshot of their starting position at birth; some are far ahead. Not one son among the 14 lagging farthest behind at the start caught up with the slowest of the 14 with the greatest head start. In this particular sample, it appeared almost as though there were two entirely separate fields in the race.

Larger samples and a broader status index for sons and daughters were also available. In the sample of 253 sons, 25 out of 50 starting in the top fifth ended up in that position themselves, versus two who rose to that rank from the lowest fifth. The largest sample was that combining a total of 430 sons and daughters. Of the 21 ranking in the top twentieth, 13 ended up there themselves and 20 finished in the top fifth. Among the 21 most disadvantaged, none reached the top fifth, only 3 achieved the top half, and only 1 succeeded in overtaking the slowest of the 21 who had the greatest head start among the 430.

The analysis yielded at least one mildly encouraging indication. All samples analyzed show a significant contrast in the incidence of upward and downward economic mobility. Disadvantaged children overcame their initial handicap more frequently than those with a head start slipped downward. For example, in the largest sample, 55 out of 86 sons and daughters rose from the bottom fifth, compared to the 33 who fell from the top. Overall, however, these mobility patterns confirm the earlier indications of a strong degree of inheritance of economic status—that is, a low degree of intergenerational vertical mobility.

The Process of Inheritance: The Roles of Education and Marital Selection

The empirical analysis has thus far dealt with the extent to which economic status is inherited and the indicated influence of specific parental characteristics. It showed that a man's chances of economic success are strongly influenced by his start in life, as provided by his parents. In fact, his economic status at birth may be defined as identical to that of his parents, or completely inherited. But what is the working mechanism that maintains a close relationship between the son's ultimate economic status and that of his parents, with which he started? This is a more difficult question, and the answers to be suggested should be treated with caution.

The mechanisms through which economic status tends to be transmitted across generations are much more difficult to isolate than an obvious, direct effect such as the bequest of material wealth, which did not play a consistently significant role in the intergenerational relationships found here. A father's occupation, for example, does not ordinarily "cause" a son's occupation to be what it is. How then does inheritance, broadly interpreted, influence the occupational, income, and residential status of sons?

The most obvious way in which status is transmitted is through the inheritance of educational opportunity. The information available, however, permits only an incomplete and tentative analysis of the part played by education in this process. The analysis is incomplete because no information is available in this sample on factors such as ability, home environment, and motivation, which are undoubtedly correlated with educational attainment. If these correlations are strong, the analysis will tend to credit education with an influence on son's economic status that is due in part to earlier factors in the causal chain. Despite these difficulties, it is worth asking what the information available can tell us. The tentative conclusions are that the inheritance of educational attainment is a significant factor in economic status transmission, and that education also has a strong influence on a man's status over and above that associated with socioeconomic background.

Also considered as a mechanism for transmitting economic status across generations is the marital selection pattern. Having concentrated for pragmatic reasons on the inheritance of economic status by sons, it is time to consider inheritance by daughters. The strongly supported conclusion is that parents' economic status was transferred to daughters almost to the same extent as it would have been if they had married their brothers.

Educational Attainment and Other Intermediate Factors[41]

The first objective was to separate from the *total* effect of socioeconomic background on economic status the *indirect* effect transmitted via

41. The estimates to be mentioned here are discussed in detail in chapter 4.

the inheritance of educational attainment. This task was facilitated by the plausibility of an assumed temporal chain of causation. For example, the simplest model assumed the following causal order: socioeconomic background to son's educational attainment to son's economic status. Each variable is assumed to depend on the variable before it, and not vice versa.

Depending on the criterion of son's economic status, the analysis suggests that 25 to 40 percent of the effect of socioeconomic background was conveyed indirectly through its effect on the son's education. Highly tentative interpretations of these results may be suggested, subject to later qualifications. A typical estimate can be illustrated in terms of predicted effects on income. One model predicted that a son ranking 5 percent from the top in socioeconomic background would have an income 38 percent above the median. If the relationship between education and socioeconomic background were eliminated by the effects of public policies, the remaining effect of background would forecast an income only 23 percent above the median. This model shows a weaker background effect than the more comprehensive brother analysis, which predicts a 174 percent income advantage for a son 5 percent from the top in background over a son starting in a position 5 percent from the bottom. If we assume that 35 percent of the family effect is indirect via education, elimination of the inherited differential in education would cut the expected income differential from 174 to 92 percent.

These reductions in predicted income differentials associated with elimination of the inherited component of education differentials should be regarded as upper limits. They take no account of omitted partially inherited factors such as ability and motivation. So these estimates almost certainly exaggerate the effect of simply breaking the link between son's educational attainment and his socioeconomic background.

Independent Effects of Educational Attainment

In addition to conveying indirectly the effect of family background through its tendency to be inherited, educational attainment has an independent effect on son's economic status over and above that due to its association with background. Subject to the same qualifications as before, this independent effect was found to be highly significant. As a practical illustration, consider a man who was average in all respects covered by the model, except that he ranked 5 percent from the top in education; he would have a 30 percent chance of ending up in the top tenth in economic status. But a second man identical in all respects except that he ranked 5 percent from the bottom in education, would have only about one chance in 120 of making it into the top tenth, as measured by the three-variable composite economic status criterion. For sons born in 1925 (about average in the sample), the predicted income for a son with a college diploma was 24 percent higher than that for a high school graduate with the same background (and the same number of earners in the family). The predicted income differential attributed to a single extra year of education was 5.3 percent, according to the model. Finally, consider two men born in 1925 who were identical in measured background characteristics except with respect to education. Assume also that if they were average in years of schooling, the model would predict that they would have average incomes. However, one is a grade school graduate, and the other has some graduate school. According to the model, the more educated man has about fifteen times as great a chance to achieve an income double the average.

These are striking differentials for men whose backgrounds are held constant to a substantial degree. They must again be qualified to the extent that they reflect (take statistical credit for) ability, motivation, and other prior causes that have a component independent of background.

Unexplained Background Influence

Finally, it should be noted that even though the role of inherited education is important, it accounts for only 25 to 40 percent of the influence of socioeconomic background on economic status of sons in this sample. Nothing in the literature suggests that inclusion of all known intermediate factors could come close to accounting for the strong effects of background on economic success. How, then, is this unexplained background influence transmitted? Ability and home environment are two hidden factors in the intergenerational status link. Environment, for example, has to do with the tendency for unmeasurable characteristics like speech and dress to be transmitted across generations. The family situation also affects diet, health, and other conditions of the child. There may also be a tendency for parents to mold children in their own image and to influence their aspirations. All in all, there seem to be ample reasons to expect a strong family effect that simply rubs off on the child and cannot be accounted for by measurable factors like the provision of education.

The Role of Marital Selection

A very much neglected factor in the maintenance of inequality is the tendency for individuals to marry others of similar socioeconomic background. That appears to be the primary avenue by which parental economic status is transmitted to daughters. For pragmatic reasons, the economic status of married daughters is defined as that of their husbands.[42] If daughters married randomly the fraction of variation in economic status of sons and daughters combined that could be explained by background would be only about half that found for sons only. Such a finding would weaken substantially the role of inheritance in perpetuating inequality.

In practice, mating is far from random, and its role in maintaining inequality is almost as strong as if daughters married their brothers. The first evidence of this was the fact that a given differential in wives' background carried almost as much weight in predicting the success of a son-in-law as is the case in the relationship between sons and their own parents. Moreover, part of the total effect of daughter's background on son-in-law's status was conveyed through daughter's education. When the lower education of daughters was allowed for in the analysis, the net relationship between sons-in-law and parents-in-law was virtually identical to that between sons and parents.[43]

Mobility tables can also be used to compare the intergenerational relationships for sons and sons-in-law. Forty of the wives of the latter group came from the top fifth in socioeconomic status, and 15 of those 40 married men who ranked in the top fifth. This is nearly as high a ratio as the 19 out of 46 sons from the top fifth who clung to that position themselves. Greater mobility was apparent from the bottom rank, but again there was little difference between sons and sons-in-law.

These findings are surprising. Marital selection, like education, has an intermediate role in transmitting the force of family background as a perpetuator of inequality. Since married daughters' status is pragmatically defined as that of their husbands, it is reasonable to expect a looser rela-

42. Since most daughters were housewives, no satisfactory measures of their occupational status and earning capacity were available.

43. In other words, the slightly lower originally estimated effect of background on sons-in-law was entirely attributable to the lower education of the daughters. More generally, daughter's education may be acting as a screening device helping to link the economic status of son-in-law and parent-in-law.

tionship between daughters and parents than between sons and parents. However, the model using explicit background factors also showed the daughter-parent relationship to be only slightly weaker than for sons, and there was no difference in the case of incomes. The slightly weaker relationship for daughters may again be due to their lower educational level. Presumably educational attainment functions as a screening device, as people tend to choose mates of similar education. The lower education of daughters in the sample helps explain the fact that the average economic status of their husbands is lower than that of their brothers, and could also account for the slightly weaker intergenerational relationship found for in-laws.

Finally, it was even more surprising to find that the relationships of economic status with the individual background characteristics were generally very similar for sons and sons-in-law. The signs in the regression models were the same and few coefficients differed significantly. In sum, "assortative" mating was so strong that there was little attenuation of the intergenerational link from randomness in the marital selection process.

Only with respect to the overall economic status levels attained by daughters and sons was there a consistent difference. The evidence in this sample suggested that, given family background (and even daughter's education), daughters tended to end up with a lower economic status than sons. This finding is interesting but implausible in the aggregate, since every son-in-law is also a son; it may well be due to a tendency for the interviewed daughters to underestimate the economic status of their husbands, especially their incomes.

Some Policy Implications

Evidence has been summarized showing the strong influence on economic status of socioeconomic background, education (independent of background), and marital selection. The policies called for by these findings depend more heavily than usual on value judgments. This is especially true of formulating policy toward competitive advantage due to the inherited productivity of an individual.

Even if it is agreed that the degree of inequality attributable to inheritance is excessive, it is not necessarily feasible to attack the problem at its roots. For example, no one proposes that the influence of parents over the speech and dress of their children be reduced, or that parents be discouraged from developing the motivation and productivity of their children; nor does anyone suggest that free choice be eliminated from marital selection, with mates to be paired on a random basis. In practice, the effects of these sources of inequality can probably be modified only by after-the-fact redistribution.

So a discussion of policy implications in this area is hampered by the importance of nonobjective considerations and by untouchable institutions. Still, specific policies may be implied under given assumptions, even though the breadth of their acceptability varies substantially. Also, the implications of inheritance for redistributive policy should be made explicit.

Policies toward Inheritance

It has been stressed that some forms of inheritance of economic status are more intolerable than others. Four ways in which success tends to be inherited were mentioned to illustrate this range of tolerability: pull, material wealth, superficial characteristics, and productivity. Potential policies toward each of these types of inheritance may be considered in turn.

Practically everyone would agree that inherited advantage based on parental pull represents an unfair head start, and it can exist even though equality might be formally assured under the law. Every effective effort to diminish the effects of this type of favoritism is assured of wide support, but the fact that it can never be completely eradicated speaks in favor of a progressive income tax. Such taxation is also a convenient policy approach toward competitive advantage or disadvantage associated with the inheritance of superficial characteristics like speech and dress.

The advantage conferred by the inheritance of material wealth is less generally frowned upon. However, many economists still find it difficult to justify the reward to material inheritance, since it represents no effort on the part of the owner of the capital and he has made no contribution to its accumulation. It affects the heir's money-making capacity and the productivity of his investments, but not the productivity of his labor. Classical rationales for the return to the owner of capital, such as "abstinence," seem inapplicable.[44] This head start, however, does not violate the standard conception of equality of opportunity: no antidiscrimination rule is

---

44. It is difficult to argue that an heir may appropriately enjoy the rewards associated with his forebear's abstinence even if the latter intended just that; the forebear has already been rewarded once.

being broken. Even so, a stronger tax policy to alleviate this officially un-recognized form of inequality of opportunity seems in order.[45]

For years many economists have taken it for granted that inequality due to material inheritance without any productive contribution of one's own would be regarded by the public as a more justifiable target of public policy than inequality due to variations in the actual productivity of individuals. This does not seem to be supported by recent experience. People with no expectations of inheritance seem to support intensely the right to bequeath. This attitude found recent expression in the national cry of outrage that greeted the proposal of Senator George McGovern during the 1972 presidential campaign to place much stiffer taxes on inheritances. This reaction may have reflected an impression that the right to bequeath itself was challenged by the confiscatory rates in an early McGovern proposal. If the proposals could be presented as a progressive tax on inheritances and compared to taxes on earned incomes, the reception might be more favorable. An heir continues to receive his bequest from the donor, just as a wage-earner receives his pay from his employer, and both flows are objects of taxation. In that context it seems highly likely that the public would accept much higher tax rates on completely unearned inheritances than on earned incomes.

Policy toward the inheritance of real productivity is a more difficult issue. For various known and unknown reasons, the sons of able and affluent parents tend to achieve a relatively high level of productive ability and skill. Although this ability and skill are in part inherited, insofar as the productivity is utilized, the social product is enhanced by the individual's own effort. Our economy is not entirely successful at rewarding labor according to its productivity, but that is the professed goal of the system, just as it is in socialist economies. Certainly no one has proposed seriously that parents be discouraged from the productive development of their children.

What, then, is the appropriate policy toward the inheritance of productivity? The question calls for answers at two levels. First, a good economic case has been made for rewarding labor as closely in proportion to its true productivity as possible. The tendency to do so undoubtedly promotes efficiency, and it carries the appearance of equity. It is widely held that the purpose of the race for success in life is to stimulate the productive

45. As mentioned earlier, however, increased estate taxation may lead to off-setting effects on inequality by stimulating intergenerational transfers of human capital.

performance of the contestants by awarding the biggest prizes to the most productive. Such an outcome is generally accepted even though the most productive contestants may have inherited an effective head start.

In this connection, Okun remarks that "in real track meets, no official has ever disqualified a runner for having 'fast genes'."[46] This may be literally true, but it should be added that one form of horse race—the handicap—uses varying weights to moderate the inequality of chances for victory. This is done to stimulate wagering enthusiasm, but it obviously reduces the expected reward to the owner of the best horse and moves generally toward equality of outcomes. That is exactly what the progressive income tax structure tries to accomplish, although with an intermediate step. The nominal pretax reward of labor in proportion to productivity is justified on the grounds of efficiency, but the results are moved toward equality after each year's race is over. Income taxation, like the procedures in a handicap race, reduces the inequality of expected returns, and in both cases, the loss of incentives must be weighed against the alleviation of inequality.[47] There is, of course, wide disagreement over the terms of trade-off between equality and efficiency. Not surprisingly, the haves tend to evaluate efficiency very highly, while the have-nots would generally favor a move toward equality. But an overwhelming majority of the population appears to favor at least some moderation of the inequality that emerges in the marketplace. And it seems plausible that the stronger the role of inheritance in generating it, the greater the degree of equalization that will be acceptable.

This equalizing of rewards from racing purses and the incomes from productivity is also relevant to interpretation of the returns from inherited productivity. Even though the productivity differentials are real, an equalizing of the ultimate rewards has been found acceptable. But, in addition, there is a hierarchy of targets among the different types of inheritances. It would probably be generally agreed that the inherited effects of pull should be wiped out as far as possible. Among the four types of inheritance mentioned earlier, the advantages of inherited material wealth would be the next candidate in line for redistribution; they can be reduced in a capitalist economy either by preinheritance wealth and estate taxes or by inheritance taxation. The rewards to inherited superficial characteristics

46. *Equality and Efficiency*, p. 43.
47. Relative losses by owners of the best horses may, of course, be offset by a general rise in purses financed by increased wagering. Unfortunately, there seems to be no analogue to this in economic races contested by human beings.

can be equalized by after-the-fact redistribution. The returns to inherited real productivity are also equalized by taxation, but it seems appropriate that this equalization be less severe than for the other types of inheritance.

The distinction between inherited productivity and that resulting from independent effort remains significant. As an entirely hypothetical illustration, consider two men of equally high productivity. A comes from a highly advantaged background, and his productivity is as high as would be predicted on the basis of his background. B comes from a disadvantaged background, but he has attained the same high level of productivity as A through diligence and independent effort that raised him above the average level predicted by his background. Both will be taxed heavily on the basis of their ability to pay, but it would seem appropriate to assess a lower tax on B, whose independent effort played a large role, than on A, whose performance is no more than that predicted by his background (and, in that sense, inherited). A lower tax rate for B would thus be a reward for extra effort. A's productivity is no less real, but the fact that it is derived in part from inherited advantage makes a higher tax rate appropriate.[48]

This hypothetical tax rate differential is not suggested as a feasible policy; inherited productivity is admittedly a hypothetical concept, and it is difficult to distinguish the results of independent performance from those of luck. A differential tax rate on income from the inheritance of material wealth would be a less utopian notion and has a precedent in the differential rates imposed in some countries against unearned income. However, even there, an inheritance tax is a simpler alternative. The purpose of speaking of the inheritance of productivity as if it were taxable is simply to buttress a general, aggregative argument: the greater the role of inheritance of all kinds in determining economic rewards, the stronger the case for progressive taxation. In particular, if there is a very strong tendency for productivity to be inherited, there is less reason to fear tax-induced disincentive effects on independent effort.[49] At the same time, a high tax rate on high incomes, including earned incomes, appears more justified, the greater the extent to which they are the result of inherited advantage.

48. This tax rate should, however, be lower than the tax rate on the inherited effects of parental connections and other advantages having nothing to do with productivity.

49. Parents could, of course, respond by investing less in their children, but this seems a less probable reaction than the response of a son to a tax on rewards to his independent effort.

Whether fair or not, the head starts and handicaps in life are nonetheless real and beyond the control of the individual. At the start of the race for economic success, the child has no independent position. His status is that of his parent. Thus some start from behind and others are frontrunners. The causes underlying these head starts and handicaps are, of course, relevant to policy. But, in general, the more influence they have on the outcome, the stronger the case for redistribution of rewards by various policies, including taxation.

Education and Marital Selection

Fairly strong evidence will be presented of an independent effect of variations in educational attainment of sons from a given socioeconomic background.[50] This suggests that public policy to foster education may not be doomed to impotence because of overriding effects from socioeconomic background.

One of the most encouraging findings in this study is a strong effect of parent's education on the son's income. Coupled with the indicated effect of the son's own educational attainment on his economic status, this suggests the highly constructive influence of education in the long run.[51] Not only does a man's education give a strong boost to his own chances for success, but it also has an impressive effect on his son's chances, even when all other measured influences are held constant.

The strong effect of education on success independent of family background is encouraging for the efficacy of educational policy, but it should not be allowed to obscure the fact that education also tends to be inherited; in that sense it also contributes to the role of socioeconomic background in perpetuating inequality. The same is true of the encouraging effect of parental education on son's income. The general point that can be made about these relationships is that equalization of educational attainment not only promotes economic equality directly; it also has a constructive influence by reducing the differentials due to inheritance.

The influence of educational attainment on ultimate economic status

50. Unfortunately, no evidence is available in this particular sample on the extent to which the indicated effect of education is independent of variations in ability not related to measured family background.

51. William H. Sewell, Robert M. Hauser, and coworkers have concluded otherwise on the basis of a larger sample, but the men studied were so young that their current income may not predict well their ultimate economic status. See *Education, Occupation, and Earnings: Achievement in the Early Career* (Academic Press, 1975).

has clearly varied over time, but in the case of this particular sample, it appears to have had a strong positive effect. Whether the results of special programs to educate the disadvantaged can be accurately predicted from estimated relationships based on earlier experience is, of course, unknown. But the apparent effect of schooling—both "inherited" and independent— is strong enough (despite many qualifications) to suggest that it would be premature to write an epitaph on education policy as an effective tool for the reduction of inequality.

During or after the educational experience comes the marital decision. There is evidence that this process is so assortative that it does little to weaken the intergenerational economic link between parents and their own children. Clearly, if marital selection became more random with respect to economic status, it would contribute to a reduction of inequality over time. Since public policy aimed at randomizing or generating an inverse correlation in mating is obviously unacceptable, there seem to be two clear policy implications. First, the strong relationship between the socioeconomic background of husbands and wives is simply one more feature of the inheritance of economic status that can be included in the case for progressive taxation. And second, insofar as education does serve as a screening criterion in the marital selection process, a move toward equalizing educational attainment would tend to reduce assortative mating and thereby decrease inequality.

chapter two **An Analysis of a Sample of Brothers**

This chapter is an attempt to assess the degree to which the economic status of individuals is transmitted from one generation to the next and to define the role of this process in the perpetuation of economic inequality.[1] In particular, the homogeneity of economic status achieved by brothers, revealed by a sample of brothers in the Cleveland metropolitan area, is examined as evidence of the influence of parents on the success of their sons.

The degree of economic inequality among individuals (and families) has been found to be remarkably stable over many decades in many countries. One factor accounting for this is the tendency for economic status to be transferred from parents to children. For example, some 34 to 67 percent of the inequality among the male younger generation in the sample studied here is explained statistically by their membership in a given family—that is, primarily by the characteristics of their parents. If the overall intergenerational influence is as consistently strong as it has been found to be here, it is clear that the tendency for status to be inherited has been a major factor in the long-term persistence of a relatively stable degree of inequality. Correspondingly, a loosening of this intergenerational status link would tend to favor a trend toward equality.

The analysis in this chapter is based on a comparison of the variation of economic status among brothers to its variation among all men.[2] This approach has been rare in the literature until recently, presumably because

1. The phrase "economic status" is used here to indicate that several dimensions of economic condition, rank, or position are being considered, not income alone; neither does it refer to prestige in noneconomic terms.

2. Although daughters are considered later, the emphasis here is on brothers, since the economic status of males is more precisely and meaningfully measurable than that of females. This is because most of the married women in this sample were housewives, and the money income attributable to a housewife is no more than the crudest measure of her economic status, potential income, or productivity.

of a lack of information. Most of the earlier intergenerational studies relied on explicit background variables, as is the case of the well-known sociological studies referred to in chapters 3 and 4. Conveniently, this study of brothers avoids the need for parental data.

The best-known analysis of brothers' status is contained in the recent work of Jencks and others, even though they possessed no actual data linking brothers.[3] One of their most startling findings is set forth as follows: "Poverty is not primarily hereditary. While children born into poverty have a higher-than-average chance of ending up poor, there is still an enormous amount of economic mobility from one generation to the next. Indeed, there is nearly as much economic inequality among brothers raised in the same homes as in the general population."[4] This downgrading of the role of family background in the perpetuation of inequality surprised many.[5] The Cleveland area data source used here, which includes information on brothers, permits a detailed and more direct consideration of this question.

The tendency for the economic status of children to depend on their family of origin has many explanations. The policies, if any, to be adopted toward it ultimately depend on the explanation considered to be crucial. For example, a strong influence of parental wealth would suggest a policy different from that called for if inherited educational opportunity were a key factor in economic success. Nevertheless, the first step here is to assess the overall extent to which economic status tends to be inherited. The effect of specific parental characteristics on the status of their children will then be considered in detail in chapter 3, and the mechanism by which their influence is transmitted will be taken up in chapter 4.

3. Christopher Jencks and others, *Inequality: A Reassessment of the Effect of Family and Schooling in America* (Basic Books, 1972). The authors used intergenerational correlations obtained by others to speculate on inequality among brothers. For subsequent studies using samples of brothers, see, for example, Mary Corcoran, Christopher Jencks, and Michael Olneck, "The Effects of Family Background on Earnings," *American Economic Review,* vol. 66 (May 1976, *Papers and Proceedings, 1975*), pp. 430–35; Zvi Griliches, "Errors in Variables and Other Unobservables," *Econometrica,* vol. 42 (November 1974), pp. 971–98; Gary Chamberlain and Zvi Griliches, "Unobservables with a Variance-Components Structure: Ability, Schooling, and the Economic Success of Brothers," *International Economic Review,* vol. 16 (June 1975), pp. 422–29; and Paul Taubman, "The Determinants of Earnings: Genetics, Family and Other Environments, A Study of White Male Twins," *American Economic Review,* vol. 66 (December 1976). Unpublished studies of other samples of brothers are currently being conducted by Zvi Griliches and by Robert Hauser.
4. Jencks and others, *Inequality,* pp. 7–8.
5. The basis of these implausible inferences is examined in appendix B.

Approaching the Analysis of Brothers

The methodology will be outlined briefly here, and the source is described in appendix A.

What Can be Learned about Inheritance from a Sample of Brothers?

The question of the extent to which the economic status of sons is inherited from their parents clearly depends on a conception of inheritance broader than the receipt of property.[6] In the words of one dictionary variant, we are concerned with "the acquisition of a possession, condition or trait from past generations"—in this case, the extent to which a son tends to acquire his economic condition from his parents. But since the mechanism of the intergenerational transmission of economic status cannot be completely specified, the present conception of inheritance refers to the statistical relationship between successive generations, as evidenced by the homogeneity of economic status of brothers.

Information on brothers is a valuable, but not perfect, tool for assessing the extent to which sons inherit their economic condition. The data offer estimates of the fraction of inequality that is due to all factors, known and unknown, affecting brothers in common as members of the same family.[7] No single term describes these background influences perfectly. They will be designated here as "family effects," but it should be emphasized that the measured effects do not include all influences of parents on children.

The potential value of an analysis of brothers may best be clarified by contrasting three levels of generality in specifying the influences of family background: (1) socioeconomic characteristics of parents, (2) family effects experienced in common by brothers, and (3) inheritance, in the sense of all effects of parents on children. Brothers clearly have the same socioeconomic background in the sense described.[8] However, the effects

6. It differs also from the reception of genetic qualities, such as IQ. It also departs from the interpretation of "heritability" in the genetic literature as the fraction of the variance of a characteristic, such as IQ, explained by genes.

7. In the words of Ronald A. Fisher, the statistic to be emphasized here measures "the fraction of the total variance due to that cause which observations in the same family have in common." *Statistical Methods for Research Workers* (12th ed., London: Oliver and Boyd, 1954), p. 224.

8. Though the socioeconomic background of brothers may differ in particular cases: for example, the effective background of a younger brother may be more closely identified with a stepfather than that of his older brother.

on them as members of the same family are more inclusive. For example, the genetic endowments, parental care, educational support, and material inheritance of brothers, although not identical, are likely to be more alike than among the general population. So family membership exerts influences over and above those derived from socioeconomic background alone. But the family effects on brothers do not include all components of inheritance (or parental influence). Brothers may inherit different genes, experience a different order of birth, different parental care, educational support, and even receive contrasting gifts and bequests.[9]

In sum, the family effects experienced in common by brothers probably account for a substantial part of their inheritance of economic status. But the adopted measure of family effects clearly understates the overall parental influence. Insofar as brothers differ with respect to parental influences such as those mentioned, the extent of inheritance of economic status is even greater than reported here. On the other hand, it should also be noted that the available measure of family effects includes the influence of brothers on each other, which does not fall within the usual conception of inheritance. Insofar as brothers tend to follow each other, this type of family effect would exaggerate the estimated degree of inheritance. Unfortunately, the present sample offers no clue as to the extent to which such a tendency may offset the underestimate of inheritance.

A final qualification should be mentioned. The estimates here may embrace extraneous factors as evidence of the intergenerational transmission of economic status—for instance, the age homogeneity of brothers who may tend to have similar incomes for that reason alone. The available data make it possible to show that this is of minor importance for the relatively homogeneous age group studied here.

In sum, a comparison of the degree of inequality among brothers to the inequality among all men is a pragmatically promising initial approach to the appraisal of effects of inheritance. This is true even though it cannot capture all parental effects. Status information is needed for the younger generation only; the analysis is not dependent on specific parental characteristics that may be based on the memory of the children and are often poorly measured or unavailable. The overall family effects on sons

---

9. Only identical twins necessarily have the same genetic endowments and essentially the same birth order. The medical and psychological literature also stresses that even the environment of twins is not identical, but this seems a minor consideration for the determination of economic status.

will be explained at the most general level by their membership in family categories.

The Sample of Brothers

The primary 5 percent sample of 659 estates closed in Cuyahoga County, Ohio, Probate Court during 1964–65 led to a secondary sample of surviving sons and daughters. The data analyzed in this chapter cover only families for which information is available on the economic status of at least two brothers. Three basic measures of the economic status of surviving sons are available from this sample: residential quality rating, occupational status, and family income. Information on educational attainment is also available, but it is generally interpreted as a temporally intermediate influence between family background and ultimate status, and is generally reserved for special analysis in chapter 4.[10]

The residence, occupation, and income status criteria may be described briefly. The first two measures consist of qualitative categories, ranging from one (lowest) to seven (highest). The seven residence rating categories range from "poorest . . . easily judged substandard . . . slum areas . . . industry present" to "best . . . own grounds . . . two or more car garage . . . well kept." The occupation categories run from "unskilled labor" to "executive, proprietor of large firm, or major professional." The value of these two qualitative variables is represented by the category number.[11]

There are nine annual family income brackets, ranging from the lowest

10. Less frequently, educational attainment will be combined with the three indicators of ultimate status to form a broader status index to be explained by family background.

11. Assigning the category number as the numerical value of these qualitative variables is arbitrary. In the case of the occupation variable, not enough detail was available to permit utilization of the Duncan scale (Otis D. Duncan, "A Socioeconomic Index for All Occupations," in Albert J. Reiss, Jr., and others, *Occupations and Social Status* [Free Press, 1961], pp. 109–38). However, the frequency distributions suggest that these code numbers provide an informative description of the variation in each characteristic: the distributions are approximately normal, with means of about four, about half-way between the extremes of one and seven. Since they are dependent variables with more than two categories, they could not be represented by dummy variables, even in the regression analysis applied later; so these measures of the categorical variables were adopted for simplicity. It should be noted, however, that more elaborate techniques for analysis of qualitative variables have been developed in recent years. See Yvonne M. M. Bishop, Stephen E. Feinberg, and Paul W. Holland, *Discrete Multivariate Analysis: Theory and Practice* (M.I.T. Press, 1975).

(below $1,500) to the highest (above $18,000) in 1965–66. Since this is a quantitative variable, each bracket was represented by its estimated mean, rather than by the category number.[12] The logarithmic transformation was adopted to approximate normality and to focus on relative income differences. The most plausible hypothesis is that *relative* income differences among brothers (measured by the difference between logarithms) are generally less than those among all men. For example, this is likely to be true of the incomes of the Rockefeller brothers, even though one would not expect to find small differences among their absolute incomes.

In addition to the three individual economic status indicators, several composite variables or status indexes were devised by combining two or more of the basic variables. They were derived as a weighted average of the standardized values of the basic variables. The "first principal component" was adopted as status index in each case.[13]

How Representative Is the Sample?

Before considering the extent to which economic status characteristics were inherited by these men, it would be helpful to construct a profile of the available sample. All are sons of decedents in the primary sample of 659. These decedents represented a 5 percent systematic sample; every twentieth probate record was drawn for study. Each son was included in the present basic sample only if he was one of at least two brothers who cooperated with the original project interviewers. This yielded a maximum basic sample of 128 brothers from 55 families.[14] However, larger samples were available. When questionnaire results were included, the maximum was 163 brothers from 71 families; and the residence rating was available

12. The estimated mean is an imperfect representation of the incomes in a bracket, especially given the ultimate adoption of the logarithmic transformation. However, no markedly superior alternative was apparent for these data, and at least this choice appeared superior to use of the income category number.

13. This method of deriving composite variables is discussed in the next section (see, for example, table 2-2, note f). It may be prudent to mention at this point that the particular weighting scheme emerging from the principal component model did not play a crucial role in the findings to be reported. The weights for each status indicator were nearly equal, and substitution of equal weights made little difference.

14. This is the set of interviewed brothers for whom the education observation was available. Slightly smaller basic samples of brothers were available when other status criteria were considered; the smallest was for the income category, available for 120 brothers from 52 families.

for 231 brothers from 95 families.[15] Since at least one parent of each man had already died, and their average age at death was seventy-one, the brothers were considerably older on the average than the general population. However, their average age of forty-two was not far from the median age of thirty-seven of the male labor force in 1966.[16] The age distribution of these brothers was much less spread out than the ages of the overall work force; this was fortuitous, since practically all were old enough to have meaningful occupation and income characteristics, but were not yet retired. The standard deviation of the brothers' ages was less than ten years. Among the 128 in the largest basic sample, two were under twenty-five, and only two were over sixty-five.[17]

It is interesting to compare the sample brothers to national statistics for men in the same age groups. There are two obvious and significant ways in which this sample of brothers is not representative of the population of U.S. males of the same age. First, the requirement that at least two brothers had been interviewed in each family yielded a high average total number of brothers and sisters per family. This average, including non-respondents, was 4.36, compared to a 3.59 average for the sample of all sons analyzed in chapter 3. An average of 4.36 children per family was obviously well above the national average for this age group, even considering that the mean year of birth of these brothers was 1923.[18] As will be discussed later, large families tend to have relatively low economic status. However, as it happened, the selectivity leading to large family size did not yield significantly lower average status in the sample of brothers than for all sons.[19] The second and perhaps more significant atypical fea-

15. These "extended" samples, defined in table 2-2, yielded markedly narrower confidence belts for the statistics reported there. The basic sample is stressed here, because more characteristics of these individuals are available.

16. U.S. Bureau of the Census, *Statistical Abstract of the United States, 1967* (SAUS) (Government Printing Office, 1967), p. 222, table 316. All average age figures for the present sample are adjusted for the presumed half-year downward bias due to the convention of stating age as of the last birthday. Given the seasonality of births, this procedure embraces some minor error.

17. Although the men in this sample are relatively homogeneous with respect to age, the greater age homogeneity of brothers could account for some of the closeness of their economic status. Analytical provision for this possibility is reported later, but it did not materially affect the basic conclusions.

18. Even the 3.59 children per family ,in the sample of all sons is itself above average, since families are represented only if at least one son was interviewed.

19. The standard deviation of each status measure was considerably less for the sample of brothers than for all sons. The hypothesized homogeneity among brothers probably contributed to this result.

ture of the sample is its overwhelmingly metropolitan and midwestern quality. This characteristic has consequences that will be apparent when the sample is compared to the national population.

The mean logarithm of income can be translated roughly into dollars. The median family income reported in the sample of brothers was about $8,500 at the time of the interview in 1965–66.[20] This may be compared to the estimated median money income of all U.S. families headed by males of about $7,500 in this period.[21] The sample figure would be expected to be higher because it represents almost exclusively metropolitan incomes; furthermore, Ohio incomes are higher than the national average.[22] The earners are also concentrated in the thirty-five to fifty-five age group, for which incomes are slightly above average. On the other hand, the sample median is reduced by a 10 percent representation of unrelated men (not covered by the $7,500 national estimate), and by the heavy representation of brothers from large families, who tend to have lower incomes. All in all, the sample median seems plausible for what it represents, although no claim can be made that the sample is accurately representative of the national population. In any case, these brothers do appear to have had incomes typical enough to be of more than local interest.

The occupational classifications in the sample do not permit useful comparisons with the national statistics. However, a comparison of years of educational attainment is available. The mean educational attainment of brothers in the sample was about 12.4 years. The national median for males age twenty-five and over was put at 11.8 years as of March 1966, and at 10.8 years for nonmetropolitan areas (age fourteen and over).[23] Again, the sample appears plausible for a metropolitan area—slightly higher in educational attainment than the national average.

Various demographic characteristics of the sample can also be com-

20. The 95 percent confidence interval for the median is about $7,800–$9,300. Since the distribution of the logarithm of income is approximately symmetrical, its mean was taken here as an approximation of the logarithm of the median. The confidence interval was inferred on the assumption of log-normality.

21. This estimate is an interpolation of the 1965–66 estimates from Bureau of the Census, *Current Population Reports,* series P-60 (reported in SAUS [1968], table 478, p. 328) to cover the sixteen-month period included in the Cuyahoga County survey.

22. For example, the median money income of Ohio families was 9 percent higher than the national average in 1959 (SAUS [1968], table 475, p. 326).

23. SAUS (1967), table 156, p. 114, and table 159, p. 116. For all persons twenty-five and over the median was 12.1 years in metropolitan areas and 10.7 years for other areas (ibid., table 159, p. 116).

pared to the national average. Only about 32 percent of the brothers came from a Protestant background, and 5 percent had Jewish parents. Most of the remaining 63 percent came from Roman Catholic families. This differs sharply from a 1957 national survey showing nearly 66 percent of U.S. males over fourteen as Protestant, 3 percent Jewish, and only about 26 percent Roman Catholic.[24] Thus, the Roman Catholic majority in the sample is in sharp contrast with the national majority of Protestants. The relatively heavy representation of Roman Catholics in the sample was probably due in part to the exclusion of small families by the selection process. The simple correlation between the primarily Roman Catholic and family size variables (discussed later) was 0.31 (easily significant at the 1 percent level). A related indication is that about one-half of the decedent parents of the brothers in the sample were foreign born. This is clearly very high even for a set of parents whose average year of birth was about 1894. For example, in 1920, the ages of the decedent parents were concentrated in the fifteen to thirty-four year range. At that time only about 15 percent of the entire U.S. population in that age range was foreign born.[25] Finally, there were only two nonwhite brothers in this sample of 128. This small representation was to be expected in a group selected from parents, half of them foreign born, who died in a northern metropolitan area in 1964–65 at an average age of seventy-one.

Two specifically parental characteristics of the sample should also be mentioned. The median estate size left by the parent was about $11,000. This seems plausible for the entire range of the wealth distribution. Only about 7 percent of U.S. decedents filed federal estate tax returns showing gross estates over the $60,000 minimum in 1965. More specifically, a December 31, 1962, survey shows a median wealth of about $10,000 for consumer units headed by individuals over sixty-five.[26] Finally, the educational attainment of the decedents was very consistent with the national data. Only 24 percent were high school graduates and 8 percent had finished college. This may be usefully compared to data for metropolitan

24. U.S. Bureau of the Census, *Current Population Reports,* series P-20, no. 79 (reported in SAUS [1967], table 44, p. 41).

25. U.S. Bureau of the Census, *Fourteenth Census of the United States Taken in the Year 1920,* vol. 2, *Population* (Government Printing Office, 1922), p. 155.

26. See Dorothy S. Projector and Gertrude S. Weiss, *Survey of Financial Characteristics of Consumers* (Federal Reserve Board, 1966), p. 30. Marvin B. Sussman, Judith N. Cates, and David T. Smith, *The Family and Inheritance* (New York: Russell Sage Foundation, 1970), p. 175, also show a fairly close similarity between the top of their estate size distribution and the data in federal estate tax returns.

residents over sixty-five in 1966; about 28 percent of them had finished high school, and 6 percent were college graduates.[27]

To sum up, there is substantially higher representation of large families, foreign-born parents, and Roman Catholic heritage among these brothers than in the male society as a whole. On the other hand, the economic and educational characteristics of the sample brothers appear sufficiently typical to justify inferences about broader groups of the population. In fact, such inferences would be warranted if the sample were even less representative, provided that the *relationships* among the variables in the sample were similar to those within broader groups. Several such comparisons are available.

How representative are the intergenerational relationships in the Cleveland area of those in the nation as a whole? Multiple relationships estimated from the Cleveland area sample will be compared in chapter 3 to the findings of other studies. However, a useful comparison can also be made between a few simple relationships found here and earlier results from the massive survey "Occupational Changes in a Generation" (OCG).[28] Five of the variables in the present study are approximated by those in the OCG survey. The set of correlation coefficients from this survey presented in table 2-1 is derived from a nationwide sample of over 14,000 native, non-Negro men twenty-five to sixty-four years old in the experienced civilian labor force; the occupation of the parent is that of the father. Although the Cleveland sample includes the mother's education where the father's is not available, the variables covered by the two samples are otherwise closely comparable.

It has been stressed here that the sample of brothers derived from the Cleveland area decedents has demographic characteristics departing substantially from the national profile. A comparison of selected economic relationships found in this relatively small, local sample to those derived from the large national survey is extremely valuable, therefore, as an indicator of the reliability of the local sample for inferences concerning nationwide relationships. There were four comparable status variables—occupation and education for each generation. The six simple correlations between them in the Cleveland sample are all positive, as expected, and

27. U.S. Bureau of the Census, *Current Population Reports,* series P-20, no. 158 (reported in SAUS [1967], table 159, p. 116).

28. Adjunct to the Current Population Survey of the Bureau of the Census (conducted in March 1962; available on tape).

Table 2-1. Correlation Matrices of Selected Economic Status Variables for Brothers in Cleveland Area, 1965–66, and National Sample, 1962

Variable	Variable				
	Education of son	Occupation of son	Education of parent	Occupation of parent[a]	Number of siblings
	Cleveland area sample[b]				
Education of son	1.000	0.758	0.285	0.394	−0.168
Occupation of son	...	1.000	0.244	0.414	0.010
Education of parent	...	...	1.000	0.505	−0.105
Occupation of parent	...	...	...	1.000	−0.027
Number of siblings	...	...	...	...	1.000
	National sample				
Education of son	1.000	0.606	0.418	0.432	−0.351
Occupation of son	...	1.000	0.321	0.404	−0.261
Education of parent	...	...	1.000	0.494	−0.292
Occupation of parent	...	...	...	1.000	−0.278
Number of siblings	...	...	...	...	1.000

Sources: Cleveland area sample, see appendix A; national sample, Otis Dudley Duncan, David L. Featherman, and Beverly Duncan, *Socioeconomic Background and Achievement* (Seminar Press, 1972), especially pp. 261–63.

a. For the Cleveland area variable for female decedents, values are represented by the mean of the values for male decedents. For the national sample, only male decedents are included.

b. Correlations with son's occupation were done with 125 observations; all others were done with 128 observations.

significant at the 1 percent level or better.[29] The agreement of these six correlation coefficients with those in the large sample is remarkable. The six Cleveland area coefficients average 0.43, about the same as the average in the comprehensive national survey. The two intragenerational coefficients are higher than the four intergenerational ones in both samples, as might be expected. The intragenerational coefficients are higher in the Cleveland sample, and the four intergenerational coefficients are higher in the national sample; the intergenerational relationships average 0.334 in the Cleveland sample and 0.394 in the national, but in no case do the two sample estimates differ significantly.[30]

29. The critical level for significance at the 1 percent level is about 0.23 for the sample sizes available.

30. Assuming the large sample estimates to be virtually free of sampling error (although not necessarily free of reporting error), the significance of the departure of the Cleveland estimates from them was considered. The greatest difference between samples was in the estimated correlation between the education of parent and son, but even there the large-sample test, based on a standard error of 0.08, showed the Cleveland estimate to be not significantly lower—not even at the 10 percent level.

The last column shows no significant correlation between the number of siblings and the status measures in the Cleveland sample, despite fairly high correlations in the national survey.[31] Nevertheless, the number of siblings becomes important in the multiple regression analysis of brothers described in chapter 3, and more so in the analysis of the sample of all sons in which the families are smaller. In any case, the initial irrelevance of the number of siblings in the Cleveland sample poses no methodological problem. The purpose of the statistics summarized in table 2-1 is to show that no atypically high intergenerational status association exists in the Cleveland sample. On the contrary, the relationships are slightly less strong, as might be expected from its suspected inferior measurement of status, especially in the case of occupation. This is important, since the results to be reported showed much stronger overall intergenerational relationships than those based on only a few variables.

The value of the comparisons in table 2-1 is not only that they generally bolster the credentials of any relationships inferred from the Cleveland sample; they also suggest that such inferences are extremely unlikely to exaggerate the tendency for economic status to be transmitted across generations. At the same time, the Cleveland sample offers considerable information not available in the national OCG sample, including data on daughters, additional status variables such as income and residence rating, and more explanatory variables such as estate size and religion. More important for the present purposes, the Cleveland sample, like the previously mentioned samples being studied by others, offers explicit data on brothers. This makes possible an overall assessment of the degree of inheritance of economic status, as measured by the fraction of the inequality among these men that is explained by factors they have in common as brothers.

Measuring the Degree of Inheritance of Economic Status

For each of the status indicators a classical approximation of the degree of inheritance was derived: the fraction of the variation in status accounted for by membership in a given family. Although known in the literature as the "intraclass correlation coefficient," it will be labeled here

31. This is probably due to the selection process in the Cleveland sample, in which the requirement of two interviewed brothers per family led to a high average of 4.36 children per family. This reduced the variance of the siblings variable and may, therefore, have reduced its association with the four status measures.

$\bar{R}_i^2.$[32] This statistic, a standard measure in genetics, may be approximated by the $\bar{R}^2$ derived from a regression of economic status on dummy variables representing families. Under the most extreme pattern of inheritance, brothers would have identical economic status; that is, there would be no variation within families, and the inheritance measure $\bar{R}_i^2$ would equal one. This classical statistic is thus a direct measure of the degree of inheritance. At the other extreme, the estimate of $\bar{R}_i^2$ may be negative.[33] The more intuitively congenial estimate of zero for $\bar{R}_i^2$ is obtained when the estimated between and within variances are equal. In other words, the family effect is estimated to be zero when the estimated inequality of economic status within families is the same as the inequality among families.[34] A second measure of the degree of inheritance to be reported here is the ratio of the within-family standard deviation to the between-family standard deviation. A ratio of zero would indicate the maximum degree of inheritance, while a ratio of one would indicate no family effect.[35]

Results of Analysis of Brothers

The inheritance of status by various sets of brothers in the sample is portrayed in table 2-2. For every status criterion, the intraclass correlation

32. The subscript i indicates that this statistic is the classical "intraclass correlation coefficient" emerging from the analysis of variance. In the present case, this may be interpreted as the first-order correlation coefficient measuring the association between pairs of brothers. However, it is also analogous to the conventional $\bar{R}^2$ in regression analysis. Under certain assumptions, $\bar{R}_i^2$ in the $\bar{R}^2$ obtained in a regression on dummy variables representing families. For details, see table 2-2, note c, and appendix B.

33. Under the analytical treatment of degrees of freedom consumed in estimation, the "between," "within," and "total" variances are no longer additive. The estimation of $\bar{R}_i^2$ depends on between and within variances. See appendix B, relation B-2.

34. Negative intraclass correlations are to be found occasionally in the literature. Marc Nerlove recalls, for example, a discussion of litters of armadillos. The intraclass correlation of weights of baby armadillos tends to be negative because some babies in the litter apparently got much more milk than others, making for relatively greater weight inequality within litters. An analogous problem could arise in the analysis of the status of brothers. For example, families of limited resources may put most educational and other resources into one son, thus tending to produce relatively high inequality among brothers and a negative intraclass correlation. The present data offer no test of this possibility, but the high positive correlations actually found suggest that any such tendency must be of minor importance.

35. A ratio greater than one would indicate negative intraclass correlation.

Table 2-2. Measures of the Inheritance of Economic Status by Brothers, Cleveland Area Sample, 1965-66[a]

Economic status measure[a]	Coverage[b]	Sample Size: Number of families	Number of brothers	Mean status	Intraclass correlation coefficient, $\bar{R}_i^2$[c]	Confidence interval[d]	F	s_w/s_b[e]
RATE	Basic	54	126	4.20	0.525	0.33–0.68	3.58	0.53
	Extended	95	231	4.04	0.438	0.27–0.58	2.89	0.59
OCC	Basic	54	125	3.93	0.342	0.12–0.54	2.20	0.68
	Extended	70	159	4.21	0.407	0.23–0.56	2.56	0.62
LOGY	Basic	52	120	0.93	0.404	0.18–0.59	2.56	0.63
	Extended	66	151	0.95	0.436	0.26–0.58	2.76	0.60
Coy^f	Basic	50	115	0.00	0.521	0.31–0.68	3.50	0.53
	Extended	63	143	0.00	0.586	0.40–0.73	4.21	0.49
Cry^f	Basic	50	115	0.00	0.508	0.30–0.67	3.38	0.54
$Croy^f$	Basic	50	115	0.00	0.573	0.38–0.72	4.09	0.50
(ED)	Basic	55	128	4.21	0.383	0.17–0.57	2.44	0.64
	Extended	71	163	4.45	0.502	0.34–0.64	3.31	0.55
$(Coye)^f$	Basic	50	115	0.00	0.533	0.33–0.69	3.62	0.53
	Extended	63	143	0.00	0.606	0.43–0.74	4.49	0.47

Source: See appendix A.

a. The measures of economic status are defined as:

$RATE$ = Residential quality rating on scale of one (low) to seven (high)

OCC = Occupational classification on scale of one (low) to seven (high)

$LOGY$ = Common logarithm of annual family income measured in thousands of dollars

Coy = Composite (first principal component) variable: a weighted average of the standardized values of OCC and $LOGY$

Cry = Composite (first principal component) variable: a weighted average of the standardized values of $RATE$ and $LOGY$

$Croy$ = Composite (first principal component) variable: a weighted average of the standardized values of $RATE$, OCC, and $LOGY$

(ED) = Educational attainment on a scale of one (low) to seven (high); to approximate education in years, this variable is doubled and four is added. This variable is differentiated in this table by parentheses, since it is generally interpreted as a means of achieving economic status, rather than a measure of it.

$(Coye)$ = Composite (first principal component) variable: a weighted average of the standardized values of OCC, $LOGY$, and (ED)

b. The basic sample includes all sets of two or more brothers who were successfully interviewed; the extended $RATE$ sample includes all sets of two or more brothers available when residence ratings are included for those who refused interviews; the extended OCC, $LOGY$, Coy, (ED), and (Coye) samples include all sets of two or more brothers who were interviewed or returned a questionnaire.

c. This is an estimate of the fraction of the variance in status accounted for by family effects. Intuitive benchmark values—though not limits—are zero (no inheritance) and one (complete inheritance). For the computational formulas, see Ernest A. Haggard, *Intraclass Correlation and the Analysis of Variance* (Dryden Press, 1958), pp. 13–15. This statistic is analogous to $\bar{R}^2$ rather than R (as suggested by its traditional label). Thus, Ronald A. Fisher interprets it as "the fraction of the total variance due to that cause which observations in the same family have in common" (*Statistical Methods for Research Workers* [12th ed., London: Oliver and Boyd, 1954], p. 224). It may be approximated by the R^2 value obtained from the least-squares regression on dummy variables representing each family; this differs only through its slightly different treatment of variations in family size. The two approaches give identical answers under certain circumstances, as indicated in appendix B.

d. These 95 percent confidence intervals are derived as shown by Haggard, *Intraclass Correlation*, pp. 22–24.

e. The estimated ratio of within-family and between-family standard deviations. See Haggard, ibid., for source. Benchmark values—though not limits—are one (no inheritance) and zero (complete inheritance).

f. The first principal component is a composite variable: a weighted average of the standardized values of the specified variables, with weights chosen so as to maximize the variance of the derived variable. See M. G. Kendall, *A Course in Multivariate Analysis* (London: Griffin, 1957), chap. 2. Observations are included only if values of each variable are available for at least two brothers.

coefficient suggests a strong tendency for brothers to achieve similar status. The inheritance measure $\bar{R}^2_i$ shows that 34–61 percent of the variance of economic status is explained by family effects, even though background effects that may differ among brothers are not fully covered.[36] All values of $\bar{R}^2_i$ are easily significant at the 1 percent level on the F-test, and it is clear from the 95 percent confidence intervals in table 2-2 that most of the estimates are quite accurate. For each of the composite variables, the lower limit of the interval is at least 30 percent. In the case of the extended samples, the 95 percent confidence intervals are only about 30 percentage points wide.

A direct comparison of the inequality within families to inequality among them is available in the ratio s_w/s_b. These ratios range from 47 percent to 68 percent, suggesting that inequality among brothers averages just over one-half the inequality across sets of brothers. The more variables included in the status index, the lower the relative degree of inequality among brothers, and the higher the indicated degree of status inheritance.[37]

Before taking up specific results, a potential qualification should be considered. The indicated tendency for brothers to be alike in economic status could be due in part to their being close in age, which does not represent inheritance in any socioeconomic sense. To guard against this, the economic status variables were transformed to remove the effects of age; the inheritance measures were virtually unaffected.[38]

Residential Quality Rating and Occupational Status of Brothers

The availability in this sample of residence rating as an indicator of economic status may be unique for studies of this kind. It has been sug-

36. For example, a greater measured background effect would be expected for identical twins, whose genetic endowments are equal.

37. It should be noted that this inheritance measure, like the first, includes only those influences affecting brothers in common as members of the same family.

38. One approach was to use the residuals from the regression of economic status on age. However, the overall sample was relatively homogeneous with respect to age. The result was that there was no appreciable relationship, linear or quadratic, between any of the economic status variables and age, except in the case of education. Even in the latter case, the estimate of the degree of inheritance was not appreciably affected (although, surprisingly, it rose slightly). In chapter 3, where many more observations are available, another approach was utilized. The estimates were derived for more homogeneous age groups, but the conclusions were still not materially influenced.

gested that housing quality is one plausible proxy for "permanent" or life-time income; as such it is a useful supplement to the income information in the sample, which applies to one point in time only. It should be emphasized also that these residence ratings are based on a carefully constructed ranking of seven quality categories with accompanying photographic illustrations for the guidance of the investigator.[39] In fact, these attempts at objective housing ratings (specified independently by the interviewer) seem likely to be at least as reliable as the oral responses they obtain on family income and occupation.

The data in the basic sample (cases with completed interviews) show an impressive homogeneity in the quality of housing occupied by brothers. The estimated standard deviation of the residence rating of brothers is just over half that among families; on this criterion the data show brothers more alike in housing than in any of the other single-variable status indicators. Similarly, the 52 percent variation in housing quality explained by family effects is exceeded in the basic sample only in the case of the three-variable status indicator *Croy* (of which housing is one component).[40]

Assuming residential status to be closely related to permanent income, it is not surprising that there is more homogeneity among brothers on this criterion than is the case for reported family income in a single year. The latter may be rather roughly estimated and subject to considerable short-term variation, as well as to age-induced trends. It is also possible that residence quality, as a highly visible badge of status, tends to be maintained through thick and thin in accordance with long-run expectations and concern for reputation.

The 34 percent explanation of variation in occupational rank for brothers in the basic sample is the lowest encountered in this study, and the within-family standard deviation ratio is, correspondingly, the highest. It is difficult to account for the greater predictability of residential quality from family affiliation than the predictability of occupational status. Occupation, like residence quality, should be a better long-run indicator of status than current income, but it is quite possible that the seven-category occupation classification in the survey was not flexible or specific enough to permit an accurate measurement of the son's occupational ranking. For example, within any one of the seven categories there is a very wide variation in the incomes typically associated with the occupations included.

39. See appendix A.
40. The explanation of housing quality by family effects is significantly greater than that of occupation (at the 5 percent level), and nearly so in the case of income.

Even so, the far greater predictability of residence quality—a subjectively assigned variable—remains impressive.[41]

Family Income and Education of Brothers

In the case of family income, the intergenerational relationship appears slightly stronger than for occupation.[42] The basic sample shows family effects explaining about 40 percent of the variance of the logarithm of income. The within-family standard deviation of the logarithm of income is about 60 to 63 percent of the standard deviation across families.[43] Although the latter result is not directly comparable with the Jencks conclusions concerning incomes, the two results do differ strikingly. In one of the most widely publicized findings in the Jencks study, the average difference between the incomes of pairs of brothers is estimated as at least 90 percent of the average difference among all men.[44] Even though the authors possessed no data on the incomes of brothers and were forced to derive their estimates of average income differences indirectly, the contrast of their finding with the 60–63 percent ratio calls for an explanation. This disparity is considered in appendix B.

Educational attainment may be considered here as a means toward ultimate economic status. Family effects explained 38 percent of its variation among men in the basic sample and 50 percent in the extended sam-

41. It is, of course, possible that some aspect of the interviewing process contributed to this. For example, if all siblings were generally called on by the same interviewer, and if there were a substantial variation across interviewers in the "liberality" of their grading tendencies, a relatively small within-family variation would be expected. There might also be an inadvertent tendency to assign similar ratings to members of a family, but there seems to be no a priori reason to suspect this.

42. It would be more appropriate to consider the income of the brothers themselves, rather than family income, but no breakdown was available. In any case, the correlation between these two income variants is undoubtedly very high.

43. The logarithmic transformation leads to a comparison of the *relative* variation in income among brothers. This seems appropriate, since the hypothesis that variation among brothers is less than that among all men clearly refers to relative differences. For example, no one would presume that absolute differences in income among wealthy brothers average less than for all men; the hypothesis asserts only that the relative differences among them will tend to be less.

44. *Inequality*, p. 220, pp. 239–40, note 36. This estimate depends on an assumed 20 percent explanation of income variance by family background. The authors appear to regard this figure as about the highest plausible. They infer that a 15 percent explanation would yield an average difference ratio of more than 92 percent.

ple.[45] The ratios of within-to-between standard deviations in the two samples were 64 percent and 55 percent, respectively.

Composite Status Indicators

The broadest status index included in table 2-2 is the composite variable *Croy,* which combines residence quality, occupational status, and income. In the Cleveland area basic sample, family effects account for about 57 percent of the variation of this status variable, and the standard deviation among brothers on this criterion is only about 49 percent of the standard deviation across families. Taking these two inheritance measures together, the background effect on this indicator of economic status appears very strong, and the 95 percent confidence interval of 0.38–0.72 for $\bar{R}_i^2$ indicates an accurate statistic.[46]

Inclusion of education in the composite measure of status led to only slightly stronger estimates of the degree of inheritance. However, there is reason to believe that if the status indicator *Croy* were available in the extended sample, it would have shown somewhat stronger evidence of inheritance. For example, in table 2-2 the measure *Coy* combining occupation and income alone shows family effects explaining 52 percent of status in the basic example; when the sample is extended to include questionnaire results, the fraction rises to nearly 59 percent. The same is true when education is added to form the composite variable (*Coye*). Inclusion of the questionnaire results raises the sample size to 143 brothers and the fraction of status variation explained to 61 percent. The confidence interval of 0.43–0.74 also attests to the accuracy of this estimate.

It is useful to look at this sample of brothers from one more viewpoint. In studies of income distribution it is a common practice to separate single and unrelated individuals from others because of their markedly different characteristics. The economic status of unmarried men in this sample, as in the case of most income distributions, was considerably lower and more

45. This is *not* due to the potentially misleading association of education with age. The brothers were much more homogeneous with respect to age than the group as a whole. However, this age effect was eliminated in a supplementary test by considering residuals from the overall regression of education on age. The value of $\bar{R}_i^2$ measuring the fraction of these residuals ("relative education," given age) explained by family effects was even higher at 0.42 than the original 0.38 result in the basic sample.

46. It was to be expected that the averaging process would tend to reduce the erratic or random noise found in the component variables and yield a composite that is more predictable from family background.

erratic than that of the 91 percent who were married. When the extended sample is restricted to married brothers, the predictability of economic status by family background becomes appreciably stronger. For example, for the 124 observations available for the variable *Coy,* combining only occupation and income, the variance explained by family background rises to 63 percent. When education is included in the status index, the fraction of variance explained becomes 67 percent. The latter figure and its 95 percent confidence interval of 0.51–0.79 are the highest measures of status inheritance found in this study. On the other hand, if residence rating and other measures of son's economic status could have been included in the index, the evidence of intergenerational status transmission would probably have been even stronger. Furthermore, these results for a broader status index would still be understated because parental effects such as genetic endowments are not identical for brothers.

The discovery of closer intergenerational relationships in the extended sample is an important one. The regression analysis described in chapter 3 can be applied to the basic sample only, since the detailed characteristics of the decedents available from completed interviews were not sought in the mailed questionnaires. So there is no basis for adding the questionnaire results to the basic example for purposes of regression analysis. It should be stressed, therefore, that comparison of the analysis of brothers in the two samples suggests that the later regression estimates may be considered as conservative estimates of the strength of the intergenerational relationship.

Comparison with Other Studies of Brothers

The above results for income only can be compared to the findings of others. Table 2-3 reports the intraclass correlations of family income found in various studies of samples of brothers. The first three samples show much less homogeneity of brothers' income than the second three. However, the explanatory power of explicit background characteristics in the first three was also consistently lower than that found in several national samples, suggesting that the NORC, Talent, and Olneck intraclass correlations may be lower than would be found in national samples.[47]

47. See Corcoran, Jencks, and Olneck, "Effects of Family Background," p. 431. It should also be noted that the Project Talent respondents were only twenty-eight years old, perhaps too young for observed earnings to be a good measure of economic status. Moreover, the standard deviation of the logarithm of earnings in the NORC sample is suspiciously high.

Table 2-3. Intraclass Correlations for $\bar{R}_i^2$ for Earnings or Income, Six Studies of Brothers, Various Dates

Survey and year of earnings data	Sample size	Standard deviation of common logarithm of earnings	Intraclass correlation coefficient, $\bar{R}_i^2$
National Opinion Research Center (NORC), 1973	300	0.378	0.129
Project Talent, 1971–72	198	0.176	0.207
Olneck, 1973	692	0.194	0.220
Chamberlain and Griliches, 1927	312	0.20[a]	0.37[a]
Taubman, 1974	2,000	0.13	0.30
Cleveland area, 1965–66[b]			
Basic sample	120	0.209[c]	0.404[c]
Extended sample	151	0.211[c]	0.436[c]

Sources: First three studies, Mary Corcoran, Christopher Jencks, and Michael Olneck, "The Effects of Family Background on Earnings," *American Economic Review*, vol. 66 (May 1976, *Papers and Proceedings, 1975*), p. 431; Chamberlain and Griliches study, Gary Chamberlain and Zvi Griliches, "Unobservables with a Variance-Components Structure: Ability, Schooling, and the Economic Success of Brothers," *International Economic Review*, vol. 16 (June 1975), pp. 422–49; Taubman study, Paul Taubman, "The Determinants of Earnings: Genetics, Family and Other Environments, A Study of White Male Twins," (*American Economic Review*, vol. 66 (December 1976); Cleveland area study, table 2-2 above.
a. Estimated from results reported in Chamberlain and Griliches, "Unobservables," p. 430.
b. See table 2-2, note b.
c. The variant is family income, rather than individual earnings.

The present income variant is broader than those analyzed in the other five samples. The Cleveland area sample covers all family income, including property income. However, the earned income of the male earner tends to predominate in family income, suggesting a high correlation between the two. The most accurate estimate of the intraclass correlation in the present study is 0.436, with a 95 percent confidence interval of 0.26–0.58. This is significantly higher than those found in the first three samples, but not inconsistent with those derived by Taubman and Griliches. The more conservative of the present results for each status variant will be used in the next section to illustrate the effects of this degree of inheritance of economic status.

Practical Interpretation of Findings

The measures in table 2-2 give a first approximation of the degree to which economic status is inherited—that is, determined by family circumstances over which the individual has no control. These ratios can usefully be supplemented by concrete illustrations of the importance of family effects as causes of inequality.

The Relation of Son's Income to Family Background Rank

One economic status measure portrayed in a familiar unit is family income, measured in dollars per year.[48] It is desirable to go beyond the unitless ratios of table 2-2 and ask just how family income tends to vary with family background. The first step is to compare the predicted incomes of sons with advantaged backgrounds to those of sons from disadvantaged origins.

The Jencks study concedes that sons from well-off families tend to fare better than those from poor families, but it finds the difference unimpressive. This judgment, like one's reaction to the ratios of table 2-2, is a subjective matter; some may belittle an indicated income advantage while others will be shocked by the same differential. For example, Arthur Okun writes: "As Christopher Jencks and his associates report, the sons of families in the top fifth of the socioeconomic pyramid have average incomes 75 percent higher than those coming from the bottom fifth. The authors of that study insist that the difference amounts to *only* 75 percent, stressing that the differential is a rather small fraction of the total variation among family incomes. But I would emphasize that it amounts to *as much as* 75 percent—by any reasonable standard an enormous differential."[49]

The $\bar{R}_i^2$ value for the logarithm of income in table 2-2 is utilized, along with the mean and variance of the variable, to construct table 2-4. It may seem adventurous at best to construct so detailed a table from three summary statistics, so the assumptions entailed at each stage of its construction are specified in the table.

Jencks has been chided for "not understanding the distinction between goodness of fit and importance."[50] The apparent import of this distinction is that the slope of a relationship may be more important than the correlation.[51] The view here is that the "goodness of fit" of the intergenera-

---

48. The other indicators are measured in terms of numbered classes or standard deviations, except for the "intermediate" variable—education—to be considered next.

49. Arthur M. Okun, *Equality and Efficiency: The Big Tradeoff* (Brookings Institution, 1975), pp. 74–75.

50. C. Russell Hill and Frank P. Stafford, "Family Background and Lifetime Earnings," in National Bureau of Economic Research, forthcoming volume of the Conference on Research in Income and Wealth.

51. This distinction is really more apparent than real. If the effect of the units of measurement in a bivariate relationship is neutralized by standardization of the variables, the slope and correlation coefficient become identical. It remains true, of course, that the original units may impart a more practical flavor to the relationship.

tional relationship in table 2-2 needs no apologies; even so, anything that can be said about the meaning or importance of the relationship, as, for instance, in terms of contemporary dollars, may prove more illuminating. In this spirit, table 2-4 moves on from measures of the *degree* of inheritance of economic status to consider the expected or average levels of income for sons of varying background ranks. This focus on the slope of the relationship is then extended to a comparison of the (conditional) income distributions of sons from high and low ranks. It should be stressed that in both these exercises the point estimates of $\bar{R}_i^2$ are relied upon; the more conservative of the two estimates is used. The 95 percent confidence belt for the higher estimate in table 2-2 is based on a larger sample, but even so it is 32 percentage points wide. This should be kept in mind as a qualification of the results in table 2-4. For this reason, estimates are given in table 2-8 that show how the estimated conditional distribution for son's status varies with the $\bar{R}_i^2$ assumed. Conditional distributions are also presented in the form of transition matrices in chapter 3; these simply describe the data without making the assumptions (such as normality) to be relied upon here.

Table 2-4 accepts from table 2-2 the estimate that 40.4 percent of the variation of the logarithm of son's income is explained by all (unspecified) characteristics brothers share as members of the same family. The single linear combination of these background factors that would explain 40.4 percent of *LOGY* is the implied measure of family background;[52] so a simple correlation coefficient of 0.636 between *LOGY* and this implied background variable follows from table 2-2. Then the only assumptions needed to derive the *expected* incomes in table 2-4 are normality of the background variable and *LOGY*, and the validity of the linear relationship.

The classic "regression toward the mean" is illustrated by the son's expected income rank expressed in percentiles.[53] A son from a family ranked at the tenth percentile from the top will tend to slip from that rank and is predicted to end up at the 20.8 income percentile; but his expected income

52. See table 2-2, note c, and table 2-4, note a. If all these background characteristics were known and could be measured, a regression of income on them would have yielded an $\bar{R}^2$ of 0.404. Although these background factors are not specified, a background variable is defined as the linear combination of factors that would explain 40.4 percent of the logarithm of income—that is, the predicted value of *LOGY*.

53. The classical statement of this tendency related the successive generations with respect to a *single* characteristic such as height.

Table 2-4. Relation of Predicted Incomes of Sons to Family Background Rank, Cleveland Area Sample, 1965–66

Background rank		Expected income			Probability (percent) that 1976 income (thousands of dollars) is greater than:[e]					
Percentile (from top)[a]	Group represented[b]	Percentile rank[c]	1965–66[c] (thousands of dollars)	1976[d] equivalent (thousands of dollars)	50	35	25	15	10	5
2.5	Top twentieth	10.6	15.5	31.0	9.8	36.7	71.6	97.4	99.9	f
5.0	Top tenth	14.8	14.1	28.2	6.2	28.1	62.6	95.5	99.7	f
10.0	Top fifth	20.8	12.6	25.2	3.3	18.9	50.8	91.9	99.4	f
50.0	Median	50.0	8.5	17.0	0.2	2.6	14.9	63.3	92.4	f
90.0	Bottom fifth	79.2	5.8	11.5	g	0.1	1.8	23.6	64.8	98.8
95.0	Bottom tenth	85.2	5.1	10.3	g	g	0.8	15.6	53.2	97.4
97.5	Bottom twentieth	89.4	4.7	9.3	g	g	0.4	9.9	42.3	95.3

Source: Basic sample data underlying table 2-2.

a. For example, rank 2.5 indicates background rank of son is 2.5 percent below the top background rank for all sons. Background rank is defined as the predicted rank of each brother on the basis of all factors that brothers in the same family have in common; this follows from the interpretation of R_i^2 in table 2-2, note c.

b. In the computations each of these groups is "represented" by its median percentile (in the previous column). This yields an understatement of the difference between the expected incomes of upper and lower groups.

c. The estimate of the sons' expected income in 1965–66 may be illustrated by the 2.5 percentile. Assuming normality of the implied background variable, this family ranked 1.96 standard deviations above the mean. The expected value of $LOGY$ (defined in table 2-2) was computed on the basis of $R_i^2 = 0.404$ (from table 2-2), indicating a simple correlation of 0.636. Assuming validity of the linear relationship, the expected value of $LOGY$ is (0.636) (1.96) = 1.247 standard deviations above the mean; assuming a normal distribution of $LOGY$, this is the 10.6 percentile. From mean $LOGY$ of 0.930 and standard deviation 0.209, the expected value of $LOGY$ is 1.189, implying an annual income of $15,500.

d. For illustrative purposes, the 1965–66 data were doubled to yield an approximate 1976 equivalent. For example, U.S. Bureau of the Census, *Current Population Reports*, series P-60, shows median family income of white male-headed families as ($7,251) in 1965, $7,825 in 1966 and ($14,268) in 1975. This suggested an approximate doubling between the sample period and 1976.

e. These approximations required the additional assumption of heteroscedasticity and the normality of the conditional distribution of $LOGY$ for each specified background rank. The standard error of estimate used (0.1613) was the product of the standardized standard error of estimate $\sqrt{1-R_i^2}$ and 0.209 (the standard deviation of $LOGY$).

f. More than 99.95 percent.

g. Less than 0.05 percent.

is still well above the median. Sons with background ranks 2.5 percent from the top are expected to have incomes at the 10.6 percentile, on the average. The sons from background ranks at the other end of the spectrum are expected to rise correspondingly from the ranks of their parents.

If we represent the top fifth in background rank by the tenth percentile from the top and bottom fifth correspondingly, the expected 1965–66 income of sons of the top group is $12,600, compared to $5,800 for sons from the lowest fifth. This suggests an expected income 117 percent higher for the top group. Even though this figure understates the differential between the top and bottom fifths, it should be compared to the 75 percent differential suggested by Jencks.[54] The differential between sons at the middle of the top and bottom twentieths is considerably higher; the estimates here put their expected incomes at $15,500 and $4,700 respectively.

Since the sample used in the above illustration includes only 120 brothers, the possible sampling error should be considered. The $\bar{R}_i^2$ estimate of 0.404 carries a 0.18–0.59 confidence interval. Confidence intervals for the above predicted values can be estimated by applying the same procedure to these limits. For illustrative purposes the 1965–66 incomes were doubled to approximate 1976 levels. The 1976 prediction of $25,200 for the top fifth in background rank has a 95 percent confidence interval of $22,000–$27,300; the interval for the $11,500 income predicted for the bottom fifth is $10,600–$13,200. In other words, even if the true $\bar{R}_i^2$ were only 0.18, the predicted income for the advantaged son is 67 percent above that for the disadvantaged son. For the comparison of the predictions for the top and bottom 5 percent in background, the intervals are $25,200–$35,100 and $8,300–$11,500 respectively. So, even the weaker intraclass correlation leads to a prediction that the advantaged son has a 120 percent income advantage.[55]

Perhaps more striking than these differentials are those between prob-

---

54. *Inequality*, p. 213. The present estimate is an understatement because the expected income of a son at the tenth percentile is less than the average expected income of all sons ranked in the top background fifth; the estimate for the bottom fifth is, correspondingly, too low. The derivation of the Jencks estimate is not entirely clear from his text, and it is somewhat higher than that implied by his assumed upper limit for R^2, which he puts elsewhere at 0.20 (p. 239, note b).

55. It should be recalled that these figures are based on the more conservative of the two estimates for *LOGY* in table 2-2; the extended sample produced a higher and tighter confidence interval of 0.26–0.58. Under the weaker correlation of 0.26, the son in the top 5 percent is predicted to have 2.6 times the income of his opposite number.

abilities of achieving a given income or higher. Cleveland area sons with backgrounds at the middle of the top fifth are expected to average $25,200 in income, compared to $11,500 for those from the bottom fifth—still the same relative differential. But there is a seemingly sharper contrast between the *probabilities* that the advantaged and disadvantaged sons will achieve a given income. Such a comparison assumes that actual values of *LOGY* are normally distributed around the predicted values; this comparison is thus less reliable than the previous ones, because it requires an additional assumption. However, for moderately high and low incomes the assumption appears plausible.[56] While the expected value of income for the son from the middle of the top fifth is 117 percent higher, his chance of having a family income of $25,000 or more in 1976 is 51 percent, compared to only about 2 percent for the son from the bottom fifth. Their probabilities for incomes of $15,000 or more are 92 percent and 24 percent, respectively.

The predicted 1976 income of a son from the middle of the top twentieth in background is nearly $31,000, compared to $9,300 for a son from the other end of the distribution. Again, however, the contrasting chances of individual sons seem more striking. The indicated chance of receiving an upper-middle-class income of $35,000 or more in 1976 is nearly 37 percent for a son from the top twentieth, whereas those from the lowest ranks have negligible chances of achieving this level or higher. Even a more fortunate son who starts from a background ranked in the middle of the pack has only a 2 or 3 percent chance of achieving the $35,000 level.

These probabilities are, of course, only speculative estimates. However, even the most cautious interpretation rules out the conclusion that individual incomes are determined as though by a gigantic game of chance. Jencks's readers may have acquired the impression that success in life is primarily the outcome of a massive lottery. Since there is indeed a substantial component of chance in the distribution of income, the mechanism does have some characteristics of a lottery, but this one is a rigged lottery. The proprietary "bite" leaves most people losers in a lottery, but if participants from privileged backgrounds were given discounts on purchased tickets they could become perennial winners. And if the most privi-

---

56. This comparison adds the assumption that the conditional distribution of the logarithm of income is normal, given any specified background rank. Constant variance is also assumed. This appears fairly reliable short of the extremes. However, as discussed in chapter 3, the frequencies in the tails appear higher than predicted by the conditional normal distributions.

leged were given the largest discounts, the ordinary lottery would become more like that mysterious one that helps generate the income distribution.[57]

Education, Occupation, Composite Measures, and Transition Matrices

The son's educational attainment is another familiar criterion of achievement; years of education completed, though far from an ideal measure, is at least a practical and concrete concept.[58] Since from an economic point of view, education is appropriately thought of as a means to an end, rather than an indicator of economic status, it will be considered later as a determinant of status. Here it is useful to consider the extent to which educational attainment is itself determined by family background.

Table 2-5 gives estimates of the expected (predicted) educational attainment of sons from various background ranks. The basic sample showed a lower intergenerational correlation and slightly weaker family effects on education than on income. The regression to the mean indicated by the percentile ranks is thus slightly more rapid than in the case of income, but hardly a pell-mell dash toward mediocrity. The educational rank of sons from the top twentieth in background tends toward the 11.4 percentile, on the average; sons with families ranked 10 percent below the top tend to rank at about the twenty-first percentile in educational attainment. Results from the extended sample show substantially closer intergenerational association, with sons from the 2.5 and 10 percentiles tending to regress only to the 8 and 18 percentiles, respectively. Sons from the lower-ranked families are expected to have educational ranks similarly higher than their overall background rank.

According to the basic sample, predicted educational attainment varies substantially with family background rank. Sons emerging from the 2.5 percentile average nearly full completion of college, while their counterparts at the lower end of the scale average only one year of high school. The family effect is considerably stronger in the larger sample, with those from the top rank averaging more than one year of graduate school, compared to the one-half year of high school predicted for those at the same

57. This is not to say that the income-generating process is *merely* a lottery rigged in favor of privileged backgrounds. As will be discussed in chapter 4, there are significant determinants of a son's capacity to make money that are not wholly dependent on his background or initial endowments.

58. The substantial variability in the quality of a year's education weakens this variable as a measure of human capital accumulated, but the sample offers no basis for refining the measure.

Table 2-5. Relation of Predicted Educational Attainment of Sons to Family Background Rank,[a] Cleveland Area Sample, 1965–66

Background rank		Predicted education			
		Basic sample		Extended sample	
Percentile from top[b]	Group represented[c]	Percentile rank[d]	Years attained[d]	Percentile rank[e]	Years attained[e]
2.5	Top twentieth	11.4	15.6	8.2	17.3
5.0	Top tenth	15.4	15.0	12.8	15.9
10.0	Top fifth	21.5	14.5	18.2	15.2
50.0	Median	50.0	12.5	50.0	12.9
90.0	Bottom fifth	78.5	10.4	81.8	10.6
95.0	Bottom tenth	84.6	9.8	87.2	9.9
97.5	Bottom twentieth	88.6	9.3	91.8	8.5

Source: Basic and extended sample data underlying table 2-2.

a. In contrast to table 2-2, no estimates of the probability distributions of expected education are presented because of the presumed clustering of years attained at levels such as 8, 12, and 16. The use of a normal distribution to approximate the frequencies seemed likely to lead to serious error.

b. See table 2-4, note a.

c. See table 2-4, note b.

d. The estimate of the son's expected educational attainment rank from the basic sample may be illustrated by the 2.5 percentile. Assuming normality of the implied background variable, this family ranked 1.96 standard deviations above the mean. The expected value of (ED) (defined in table 2-2, note a) was computed on the basis of $R_i^2 = 0.383$ (table 2-2), indicating a simple correlation (and slope) of 0.619. Assuming validity of the linear relationship, the expected value of (ED) is $(0.619)(1.96) = 1.213$ standard deviations above the mean. Assuming a normal distribution of (ED), this is the 11.4 percentile. From mean (ED) of 4.24 and standard deviation 1.30, the expected value of (ED) is 5.82, implying an educational attainment of 15.6 years.

e. Computation as in note d, except $R_i^2 = 0.502$; mean $(ED) = 4.45$; and standard deviation of (ED) = 1.27.

rank from the bottom. Those from the top rank tend to spend about twice as many years in school as the others.

The educational differentials by family background rank are pronounced enough to be a major factor in the determination of the ultimate economic status of the sons. The three-variable measure of son's economic status (*Croy*) is closely related to the son's education, with a correlation coefficient of 0.625. The effect of educational attainment may be due to various causes, including enhanced productivity and the screening or "sheepskin" effect.[59] On the other hand, the measured effect of education is probably due in part to its association with unmeasured factors such as ability, and thus may exaggerate the potential effects of education policy. Whatever the reasons, it is clear that a substantial part of the influence of family background is conveyed indirectly through its effect on education. Educa-

59. See, for example, Paul Taubman and Terence Wales, *Higher Education and Earnings: College as an Investment and a Screening Device* (McGraw-Hill for National Bureau of Economic Research, 1974), pp. 197–210.

Table 2-6. Relation of Predicted Occupational Rank of Sons to Family Background Rank,[a] Cleveland Area Sample, 1965–66

Percentile from top	Expected occupational class[b]	
	Basic sample	Extended sample
2.5	5.5	6.4
50.0	3.9	4.2
97.5	2.9	2.0

Source: Basic and extended sample data underlying table 2-2.
a. For methodology, see table 2-5.
b. Scale of 1 (low) to 7 (high).

tion also has an independent effect over and above that transmitted from family background; these questions are discussed in chapter 4.

Predicted or expected occupational classes for advantaged and disadvantaged sons are illustrated in an abbreviated fashion in table 2-6. Limiting consideration to sons from the middle of the top and bottom twentieths, and using the same methodology as before, the predicted occupational class for the advantaged son is 5.5 in the basic sample and 6.4 in the extended sample. This suggests a typical occupation class for this son as the second from the top among the seven classes defined in the survey. In the rather vague language of the survey description, this refers to management of a medium-sized enterprise or a "lesser professional" (in contrast with executive or manager of a large enterprise, or a "major professional," as in the top rank).

Sons from the lower background rank are predicted to achieve rank two—semiskilled occupational status—the second class from the bottom. So the prospects for sons from the top and bottom twentieths show a neat symmetry: they are forecast to end up in an occupational rank one notch away from the highest and lowest, respectively, among the seven classes.

Perhaps the most revealing and dramatic illustrations of the effect of background rank on a son's prospects for achieving a given economic status are those available in terms of the composite status indicators. The composite status variables defined in table 2-2 are abstract statistical indexes, but they can easily be infused with practical content, so that the strength of the tendency for status to be inherited is made clearer than ever. For this purpose economic status will be interpreted in terms of typical profiles or configurations embracing several indicators.

Table 2-7 relates illustrative economic status profiles (or combinations of status measures) to background rank. For example, results of a three-variable index (occupation, income, and education) are used to derive

Table 2-7. Observed Economic Status Profiles Approximately Equivalent to Indexes of Status Predicted for Advantaged and Disadvantaged Sons,[a] Cleveland Area Sample, 1965–66

Composite variable (dimensions of status included)	Son's background rank (percentile)	Predicted economic status profiles[b]			
		Occupational class	Income, 1976 equivalent (thousands of dollars)	Education completed	Residence rating[e]
Occupation, income, education, Coye	High (2.5)	2nd highest[d]	14.4–19.2	College graduate	...
		2nd highest[d]	19.2–24.0	College graduate	...
		Highest[e]	14.4–19.2	College graduate	...
	Low (97.5)	Semiskilled	4.8–7.2	High school graduate	...
		Semiskilled	7.2–9.6	Partial high school	...
		Unskilled	9.6–14.4	Partial high school	...
Occupation, income, education, residential quality, Croye	High (2.5)	Highest[e]	14.4–19.2	Graduate school	4
		3rd highest[e]	19.2–24.0	College graduate	6
		2nd highest	24.0–36.0	Graduate school	4
	Low (97.5)	Semiskilled	9.6–14.4	Partial high school	3
		Semiskilled	9.6–14.4	High school graduate	2
		Semiskilled	7.2–9.6	Partial high school	3

Source: Basic sample data underlying table 2-2.

a. The predicted composite economic status indicators were derived as in table 2-4, note c, and table 2-5, note d. For each of the two different composite indicators, three high-status and three low-status sons were chosen (for illustration) with observed composite status indicators close to the predicted values (and averaging even closer to the predicted values).

b. Typical combinations of status indicators.

c. The highest residence rating appearing here is class 6, denoting "second best, sometimes larger older houses in established neighborhoods . . . or smaller new homes in 'best' neighborhoods, but with less grounds than class 1, but large lot size." The lowest quality rank appearing here is class 2, indicating "housing often converted to multiple use in poor condition and crowded together, but not in such disrepair to be substandard. Often in mixed neighborhoods with business and industry."

d. Manager of medium-sized enterprise or "lesser professional."

e. Executive or proprietor of large enterprise or major professional.

predicted values of the index for sons from high and low socioeconomic origins. Since these predicted values have no common-sense meaning, three sons with observed composite indexes approximating the high and low predictions were selected to illustrate combinations of component measures consistent with the predictions.[60]

A remarkably consistent picture emerges. In the case of the three-variable index, the observed values illustrating the predicted status index for advantaged sons all showed occupational status at least second from the top, incomes in the $7,200–$12,000 range (equivalent to about $14,400–$24,000 in 1976), and a completed college education. The illustrative predictions for the disadvantaged sons showed semiskilled and unskilled occupations, incomes below $7,200 (akin to $14,400 in 1976), and high school completion at most. The three sons illustrating the predicted status index for an advantaged son were better off than the lower three on all three criteria. The picture is very much the same when the residence quality variable is added as a component of the status index. The three sons illustrating the predicted index for advantaged sons are still better off than the other three in occupation, income, and education, and the differential is about the same as before. In addition the residence rating for the top sons is also higher in all cases.

Whether or not one is "shocked" by the magnitude of these differentials remains a subjective matter. But these comparisons, based on all available status measures taken together, add a persuasive note to the appraisal of the effects of status inheritance. Sons from advantageous origins can expect to lead on all four counts.

Finally, a general picture of the variation of life chances with family background can be conveyed through a form of "transition matrix." It extends the previous discussion of a few specific results by helping to place in perspective the many intergenerational relationships presented in table 2-2. Table 2-8 relates the probability of a son's achieving a given economic status rank to his background rank. The table is highly abstract be-

60. Since no son's status index exactly equaled the predicted value, three were chosen that were close to the prediction and averaged even closer. Care was taken that the mean of the observed high values differed from the mean low values as predicted. For example, the predicted three-variable index for the advantaged son was +1.17; the observed values chosen for illustration were +1.02, +1.16, and +1.27, averaging to +1.15. The prediction for the disadvantaged son was −1.17, illustrated by sons with observed values of −1.11, −1.22, and −1.27, averaging to −1.20. So the predicted difference in the high and low indexes was 2.34, and the means of the illustrative values differed by 2.35.

Table 2-8. Illustrative Intergenerational Transition Matrices Relating Son's Economic Status to Background Rank, Normal Distributions

Degree of intergenerational association[a]	Background rank		Probability (percent) son's rank is in[d]		
	Percentile from top[b]	Group represented[c]	Top 5 percent	Top 10 percent	Top 15 percent
$\bar{R}_i = 0.40$ $\bar{R}_i^2 = 0.16$	2.5	Top twentieth	17.4	29.5	38.9
	7.5	2nd twentieth	12.2	22.1	30.7
	12.5	3rd twentieth	9.9	18.7	26.4
	50.0	Median	3.7	8.1	12.8
	87.5	18th twentieth	1.1	2.9	5.1
	92.5	19th twentieth	0.8	2.2	3.9
	97.5	Bottom twentieth	0.4	1.2	2.3
$\bar{R}_i = 0.60$ $\bar{R}_i^2 = 0.36$	2.5	Top twentieth	27.8	44.8	56.8
	7.5	2nd twentieth	16.4	30.2	41.3
	12.5	3rd twentieth	11.7	23.0	33.0
	50.0	Median	2.0	5.5	9.7
	87.5	18th twentieth	0.2	0.7	1.5
	92.5	19th twentieth	0.1	0.4	0.9
	97.5	Bottom twentieth	e	0.1	0.3
$\bar{R}_i = 0.80$ $\bar{R}_i^2 = 0.64$	2.5	Top twentieth	44.8	68.4	81.1
	7.5	2nd twentieth	20.6	41.7	57.5
	12.5	3rd twentieth	11.3	27.4	42.1
	50.0	Median	0.3	1.7	4.2
	87.5	18th twentieth	e	e	0.1
	92.5	19th twentieth	e	e	e
	97.5	Bottom twentieth	e	e	e

Sources: Derived from the hypothetical values of R_i^2 in first column, which approximate the range of findings in table 2-2.
a. See table 2-2, note c.
b. See table 2-4, note a.
c. See table 2-4, note b.
d. These probabilities were computed on the assumption of normality of the background variable, and normality and constant variance of the conditional distribution of son's economic status for a given background.
e. Less than 0.05 percent.

cause of its reliance on the assumption of bivariate normality, but even so it is useful for its comparison of the implications of three specified conclusions on the extent to which economic status is inherited.

The first value of the intraclass correlation coefficient $\bar{R}_i^2$ illustrated is 0.16, representing a simple intergenerational economic status correlation of 0.40.[61] Even if the intergenerational correlation were really that weak, a son's chances of achieving a given income would still depend significantly on his starting position. For example, a son from the middle of the top twentieth in background rank would have roughly a 29 percent chance of appearing in the top tenth of the income distribution; his less fortunate opposite number at the bottom has only a 1.2 percent chance. So even this apparently weak intergenerational relationship would imply a rather significant degree of immobility and inherited inequality of opportunity.

The second set of probabilities follows from a simple correlation of 0.60, or $\bar{R}_i^2 = 0.36$, which is typical of the weakest intergenerational relationships found in the present study. Under this degree of economic status inheritance, a son from the top 5 percent has a 45 percent chance of gaining a spot in the top tenth, while the chance of a son from the lowest 5 percent is around one in a thousand. Even a son from the middle rank has only a 5 to 6 percent chance of reaching the top tenth.

The third set of probabilities is based on $\bar{R}_i^2 = 0.64$, which is typical of the closest intergenerational relationships emerging in this study.[62] Under that degree of inheritance, the son from the top twentieth has a 68 percent chance of reaching the top tenth, while the chances of the three tabulated lower ranks are all negligible. Even a son with the median background rank would have only a 1.7 percent chance of climbing to the top tenth.

These hypothetical transition matrices will be supplemented by empirical evidence in chapter 3, but the message there is very much the same, except that table 2-8 tends to understate somewhat the probabilities at the extremes. Even under the weakest relationships (greatest intergenerational economic mobility) appearing in this analysis, the life chances of sons vary enormously with the advantage or disadvantage conferred by their family of origin.

61. This is in the vicinity of the Jencks conclusion with respect to income. There, the "best guess" for $\bar{R}^2$ is 0.15, the upper limit 0.20 (*Inequality,* p. 239, note 36).
62. The closest relationship was for the variable combining occupation, income, and education. The intraclass correlation coefficient was 0.67 for the 124 married brothers in the extended sample. This statistic (not shown in table 2-2) is an impressive one, carrying a 95 percent confidence interval of 0.51–0.79.

Potential Methodological Qualifications

The strong effect of family background on economic status, as indicated by the data for brothers, should be evaluated in light of possible methodological qualifications. A general case has been made for the reliability of intergenerational *relationships* inferred from the Cleveland area sample. More specific limitations of the samples remain to be considered.

How well does the basic sample of interviewed brothers represent all sets of two or more brothers who are sons of the 659 Cuyahoga County decedents? First, what is the evidence of the relative status of those interviewed and those who refused? The one available indication of this is the residence rating specified for both of these categories.[63] The number of brothers included rose from 126 to 231 when residence ratings for nonrespondents were included. As shown in table 2-2, this reduced the mean from 4.20 to 4.04, and implies a mean residence rating of 3.85 for the 105 added to the sample; this is significantly lower than the 4.20 mean for respondents.[64] Inclusion of nonrespondents also reduced the variance explained by family connection ($\bar{R}_i^2$) from 52 percent to 44 percent. Thus it appears that the tendency for men of relatively low status to refuse to cooperate has imparted an upward bias to the family effect as estimated from the basic sample.[65]

A second question concerning the representativeness of the basic sample is raised by the relatively low representation of sons who had left the Cleveland area. For example, if those living elsewhere ("movers") tended to be more successful than their brothers living in the Cleveland area ("stayers"), omission of many of them might understate the variation among brothers; it might also affect the estimates of background effects on

63. Most of these data pertain to the Cleveland metropolitan area, but about 10–20 percent were obtained elsewhere by interviewers sent to a few areas where survivors were concentrated.

64. Although a useful indication, this is not a pure comparison between cooperators and refusers, since some of those added were cooperators who only became part of a set of two or more when refusers were added. In any case, the difference is significant at the 5 percent level, since the standard error of the difference between the two means is about 0.12.

65. This comparison between family effects on respondents and nonrespondents can be made only for the sample of brothers. It cannot be repeated for the later models with explicit background variables, since most of the characteristics of decedents are obtainable only from interviews with the surviving generation.

individual status. An attempt was made to interview only a small fraction of survivors not residing in Cuyahoga County; others were sent a questionnaire. Although the response rate from the questionnaire was rather low, the brothers brought into the sample by the questionnaire had an average occupation status of 5.24, compared to 3.93 in the basic sample, and a mean logarithm of income of 1.023, compared to 0.930 (corresponding to $10,540 and $8,510, respectively). The educational attainment of these men averaged more than two years higher than those in the basic sample. (Residence rating was not included in the questionnaire.)

Fortunately, further scrutiny of the data showed the higher status of questionnaire respondents to be no indication of higher status of nonresidents, since those returning questionnaires had brothers in the Cleveland area with equally high average status. So, given membership in the same family, nonresidents tended to be no better off than residents. It may be tentatively inferred, therefore, that there is no evidence that nonresidents in general tended to have higher status; rather, higher status men were simply more probable respondents. Even so, for other (unknown) reasons, inclusion of the relatively small questionnaire group (extended sample) raised the indicated family effect on all the economic status measures in table 2-2 for which the comparison could be made.[66] This suggests that complete representation of nonresidents would raise the indicated family effect, offsetting to some extent the tendency for inclusion of nonrespondent (primarily) Cleveland area sons to reduce it. In sum, there is no reason to suspect that inheritance estimates from the basic sample are seriously biased due either to incomplete response or the lower representation of nonresidents. This inference (made possible by the data on brothers) is important, since results in chapters 3 and 4 rely solely on the basic sample.

Assuming that results estimated from the basic sample are reliable for inferences about all sons of these Cleveland area decedents, the question remains as to the correct interpretation of a high degree of homogeneity in the status of brothers. The inheritance measures cited here embrace all influences that the sons in a family experience in common as brothers. The effects of explicit family background characteristics will be considered in chapter 3, but it will be useful to note once again potential influences that are not "inherited" in the usual sense. All represent background factors

66. This includes occupation, income, education, and two composites based on them.

beyond the choice or control of the individual son, but they may affect the son's ultimate status independently of parental socioeconomic status or other parental influences. These may be grouped in four categories.

(1) Brothers tend to be brought up in the same location. Regional differences such as urban versus rural origins are determinants of parental status, but these differences may also have an effect on the status of the sons over and above the influence of their parents and account for part of the observed statistical explanatory power of family connection.

(2) It is possible that the influence of brothers on each other also promotes greater homogeneity among brothers than parental influences alone. The data used here do not permit separation of either locational or brother-upon-brother conditioning from parental influences. It will be suggested in the next chapter, however, that explicit parental influences appear sufficient to account for most of the observed homogeneity among brothers.

(3) Brothers tend to be closer in age than living males in general; insofar as male status varies with age, this may account for some of the homogeneity of brothers' status. For example, earned income is assumed to increase with age until retirement is approached. Thus the homogeneity of brothers' status may be due in part to the closeness of their ages. This portion of the indicated family effect does not reflect intergenerational immobility, since it is due to an income-age cycle presumably common to all levels of society, and in no need of remedial policy. As such, its effect must be neutralized in the measurement of inheritance. However, this methodological difficulty did not arise here. The simple correlations of age with residence quality, occupational status, and income were not only insignificant, they were virtually zero. Age and education were significantly correlated, but this age effect was eliminated in a supplementary test of the residuals from the overall regression of education on age. The value of $\bar{R}_i^2$ measuring the fraction of these residuals ("relative education," given age) explained by family effects was higher at 0.42 than the original figure of 0.38 obtained from the basic sample. This absence of spurious association due to age is confirmed in chapter 3 by regressions applied to separate (homogeneous) age groups.

(4) Another potential influence on male status would work in the opposite direction from age, making for greater heterogeneity among brothers and reducing the indicated family effect. The order of birth within a family could affect ultimate status through influences of the primogeniture type, or by other factors stressed by some psychologists. For example, it is sometimes argued that the oldest child tends to be more independent and

successful, or is less afflicted with anxiety.[67] Parents may also invest more resources in the oldest child. If the oldest child generally tends to fare better, this would contribute to greater variation in brothers' status. For example, it would be useful to isolate any advantages accruing to the first child so that compensatory policies could be considered to offset them. Unfortunately, despite the importance of the birth-rank hypothesis in the field of psychology, tests of the effect of birth rank on economic status utilizing the Cleveland sample were inconclusive. This potential effect remains a qualification, however, since evidence of it does exist.[68]

These four propositions, despite the plausible logic behind them, appear to constitute only minor qualifications of the estimates presented in table 2-2. Chapter 3 will show that explicit parental characteristics explain almost as much of the inequality among these men as overall family influences. This suggests that the four factors discussed here are not quantitatively important.

Conclusions

This analysis of a sample of brothers has produced evidence that family background has a powerful effect on economic status. Methodological qualifications of the findings appear to be of secondary importance. If the results presented here are validly interpreted, sheer luck does not play a dominant role in the perpetuation of economic inequality. According to one measure, the inequality of economic status among brothers ranged from 47 to 68 percent of the inequality among families. Depending on the criterion and sample considered, family effects also explained from one-third to two-thirds of the overall variance of economic status. They did so despite exclusion of parental influences such as genetic endowments that may vary among brothers.

These rather abstract statistics can also be strikingly illustrated by the income and education to be expected of Cleveland area sons from varying background ranks. By one estimate, the family income of a son coming from a background rank 5 percent from the top was, on the average,

67. See, for instance, Stanley Schachter, *The Psychology of Affiliation: Experimental Studies of the Sources of Gregariousness* (Stanford University Press, 1959), chaps. 5–6.
68. Lillian Belmont and Francis A. Marolla, "Birth Order, Family Size, and Intelligence," *Science*, vol. 182 (December 14, 1973), pp. 1096–1101.

nearly three times that of a son coming from the lower 10 percent. Adjusting incomes to 1976 levels, the sample results suggest a 63 percent probability that such an advantaged son's own family income is over $25,000, compared to a 1 percent probability for the son with the unfavorable background.

What does the one-third to two-thirds inheritance effect tell us about the causes of overall economic inequality? In concrete terms it means that this fraction of the inequality among the men studied was due to the relative advantage or disadvantage conferred by their family connection, over which, by definition, they have no control. Thus, something on the order of one-half of inequality is caused by the fact that some people start life with substantial head starts and others start from handicapped positions. This statistic is one measure of the freezing effect of inequality of opportunity as a determinant of overall inequality.[69]

The remaining half or so of inequality not explained by family background is itself due in part to factors beyond the control of individuals, such as unmeasured parental influences that differ among brothers, as well as luck and other random factors. But the major role of *inherited* inequality of life chances in perpetuating economic inequality in our society is of greater concern. It is certainly of more immediate and primary importance from the equity and public policy points of view. Inherited inequality of opportunity seems more unfair than random outcomes. Moreover, inequality of economic status due to unequal chances at birth can be directly alleviated by public policy aimed at the institutional barriers against intergenerational mobility.

69. This characterization must, of course, be qualified by recognition that one component of this conception of inequality of opportunity is that stemming from inherited ability or productivity, as distinct from environmental advantage or disadvantage. (For a lucid clarification of these issues, see Okun, *Equality and Efficiency,* especially pp. 75–82.) The data in this sample permit no separation of the effects of inherited ability from environment, but other work on this is considered briefly in chapter 4.

chapter three **Parental Characteristics as Predictors of Son's Economic Status**

The foregoing analysis of brothers examined the extent to which their economic position was determined by *all* background influences—known and unknown, measurable and unmeasurable—that they experienced jointly as brothers. These estimates of family effects understate the degree to which economic status is inherited, because the genetic endowments and environment of brothers are not identical. Even so, the estimated family effects were very strong. It is time to ask if known and measurable background characteristics that are essentially shared by brothers, such as parental education and occupation, can account statistically for an important part of the substantial degree of inheritance of status established in chapter 2. Attention is directed first to the same sample of brothers for comparative purposes, and then larger samples will be utilized for a further evaluation of family effects. This leads to an appraisal of the practical role of specific background characteristics in perpetuating economic inequality and retarding vertical intergenerational mobility. Such an appraisal is necessarily conjectural, since potentially important influences such as parental ability are missing from the analysis.[1]

1. There has been considerable work on the problem of measuring relationships involving unobserved latent variables such as ability. The basic approach uses several indicators of the missing variables, but no such indicators of the ability of either parents or children are available here. For work on unobserved independent variables, see Arnold Zellner, "Estimation of Regression Relationships Containing Unobservable Independent Variables," *International Economic Review,* vol. 11 (October 1970), pp. 441–54; Arthur S. Goldberger and Otis D. Duncan, *Structural Equation Models in the Social Sciences* (Seminar Press, 1973); Gary Chamberlain and Zvi Griliches, "Unobservables with a Variance-Components Structure: Ability, Schooling, and Economic Success of Brothers," *International Economic Review,* vol. 16 (June 1975), pp. 422–49; and J. Behrman and Paul Taubman, "Nature and Nurture in the Determination of Earnings and Occupational Status," forthcoming. Variance components models also treat unobservables. See, for example, Marc Nerlove, "Further Evidence on the Estimation of Dynamic Economic Relations from a Time Series of Cross Sections," *Econometrica,* vol. 39 (March 1971), pp. 359–82.

Some background influences, such as material bequests, are clearly direct, while others operate indirectly, as through parental investment in the son's education. Environmental influences appear to fall in between these extremes and simply "rub off" on the son in unspecified ways. All affect the son's ultimate economic status, but no attempt is made here to distinguish direct and indirect influences. Indeed, it must be kept in mind that even a material bequest that appears to be a predetermined, direct, causal influence may, to some extent, be conveying the indirect influence of latent factors like inherited ability that may affect both generations. For that reason, the background variables are regarded here as statistical predictors of son's status, and such terms as "influence" and "effect" are not intended necessarily to imply causation in a strict ceteris paribus sense. A key point is that the explanatory background variables to be considered here are almost entirely predetermined or given, from the point of view of an attempt to explain the status of the current generation. We can never determine exactly how parental educational and occupational attainment influence the economic status of the sons. Indeed, these background characteristics may be receiving explanatory credit really due to a more fundamental background characteristic such as parental ability. However, we can at least be sure that the overall measured background influence— whatever its underlying causes—is overwhelmingly in the temporally forward direction.[2] To this extent, the son's economic status is determined by factors over which he has no control.

The analysis of brothers in chapter 2 was based on rather small samples, ranging from 115 to 231. These samples were used because samples of brothers have been rare until recently and because a study of brothers covers more family effects than can be estimated from explicit background variables. What is the purpose, then, of going on to consider explicit background characteristics? The samples available for this analysis are larger, ranging from 253 to 430, but they are still smaller than various other samples available for study of the influence of specific parental characteristics.[3] Even so, the present sample has a number of advantages. It covers daughters as well as sons, has three measures of children's economic status

2. The son's status can scarcely affect the education and occupation of his parents. It is true that some of the background variables to be considered may themselves be affected somewhat by the son's status. Help from a wealthy son can augment the ultimate estate of his parent. However, this type of feedback is assumed to be minor. Unfortunately, it remains true that the association of son's status with any particular background factor may be due in part to the influence on both of generation-persistent genetic and environmental factors.
3. The results here will be compared later with those from these larger samples.

in addition to education, and it has parental religion, wealth, and age that have generally been missing from the other samples. The present sample also permits a comparison of the explanatory power of explicit background factors to that of all influences felt by brothers in common as members of the same family. At the same time, it makes possible a breakdown into more homogeneous age groups, as well as a study (in chapter 4) of the marital selection process as a perpetuator of inequality. Finally, presumably owing to the broader background coverage and the combining of several dimensions of son's status, the results from this sample generally show a greater family background effect than found in other samples.

Parental Characteristics: Explicit Influences on Sons' Economic Status

The first step is to set out the available family background characteristics and to specify an explanatory model. The Cleveland area sample of decedents offers an abundant set of indicators of parental economic status. Only those that are essentially predetermined influences on son's status are utilized here. For example, charitable contributions by the decedent is a potential indicator of his or her economic status, but it was sacrificed because of the presumed effect of son's status on the contribution decision.

Before turning to individual explanatory variables, it should be reiterated that they simply represent various dimensions of parental economic status. High occupational status of a father does not "cause" high occupational status of his son; at least, it is not the immediate or direct cause except in the special case in which the father is able to "place" his son or bequeath his own position to him. Much of the association is presumably through intermediate influences. Thus a man with high occupational status will tend to provide an advantageous environment (including education) for his son. His son's occupational status will also tend to be high, but this is a causal relationship in a probabilistic sense rather than a mechanistic one. Though less rigid, the probabilistic relationship is important. Father's occupation is a predetermined influence over which the son has no control. If the corporation president's son has a very high probability of success, this is evidence of inequality of life chances across society, whatever the reasons for the intergenerational relationship.[4]

4. Again, it should be noted that any specific policy implications depend on whether or not the relationship is causal. Although the sons of highly educated parents tend to be economically successful, it does not follow that a policy promoting the education of one generation will necessarily help the next.

Table 3-1. Definition of Parental Characteristics Used as Measures of Decedent's Economic Status

Parental background characteristic	Variable	Definition of status indicator	Mean[a]	Standard deviation[a]
Age and education	AGED	Age of decedent divided by ten	7.094	0.939
	EDD1, 2, 3	Dummies for decedent's education:		
		EDD1 = partial or complete primary school	0.762	0.426
		EDD2 = partial or complete high school	0.159	0.365
		EDD3 = at least partial college	0.079	0.270
	AED2	AGED · EDD2	1.010	2.348
	AED3	AGED · EDD3	0.552	1.898
Occupation	OCDT	For male decedents, occupational rating in seven categories from 1 (low) to 7 (high); for females, mean of occupational rating for males	2.902	1.142
Family size	SIBS	Total number of siblings of each son (one less than decedent parent's number of children)	3.365	1.572
Race	RAC1	White	0.984	0.125
	RAC2	Nonwhite	0.016	0.125
Religion	REL1	Protestant	0.317	0.465
	REL2	Catholic or any other except Protestant and Jewish	0.635	0.481
	REL3	Jewish	0.048	0.213
Wealth	GRST	Common logarithm of gross estate of decedent's parent in thousands of dollars	1.039	0.305
	TES1	Deceased left will (testate)	0.770	0.421
	TES2	Deceased left no will (intestate)	0.230	0.421

Source: See appendix A.

a. The mean and standard deviations were computed for the basic sample of interviewed brothers for whom the residence (RATE) observation was available, although slightly different sets of observations were available for regressions with other status variables. Note that for each of these 126 brothers observations were available for all of these vari-ables. (For description of the sample, see table 2-2, note b.)

A statistical explanation of a son's economic status by a given background variable thus must be interpreted with caution. Furthermore, the extent to which the variables that might be incorporated in the explanatory model are *causal* varies enormously. Methodologically acceptable explanatory variables range from the directly causal through the indirectly causal to the pure proxy variable, and most have multiple roles. For example, a father's material bequest to his son directly and precisely causes an immediate improvement in son's economic status. At the other extreme is the pure proxy variable that has no causal influence at all. In the model to be described a dummy variable distinguishes the parents who left a will from those who did not. This was included as one indicator of family wealth, and its methodological role clearly differs from that of the parent's education. If the family backgrounds of two sons were identical except that one had wealthier parents, the hypothesis would be that the latter would *tend* to achieve a higher economic status, but no such hypothesis would be offered for two sons whose backgrounds differed only in that the father of one left a will.

All of this raises a philosophical question. What is the purpose of a model containing explanatory variables that vary greatly in the type of causal interpretation that can be attached to them, if any? The overall objective of the model is to facilitate interpretation of the previous explicit global estimates of the degree to which economic status is inherited. The closer these explicit, measurable hypothesized parental influences come to achieving the same degree of explanation of status inheritance, the less room there is for extraneous or unknown influences inadvertently picked up by the analysis of brothers, and the more meaningful the findings in chapter 2 become. The more specific, but more cautious, objective is to isolate and evaluate the effect of particular background characteristics.

The predetermined variables are defined and described in table 3-1. The hypotheses underlying them and the ways in which they were built into an explanatory model will be discussed briefly.

Age and Education

Parental education is presumed to influence a son's economic achievement both directly and indirectly. The indirect effect usually stressed is through the effect of parental education in motivating the son's educational attainment (or "marketable" human capital). More recently, attention has been given to the indirect effect of parents' education through its effect on the preschool training of the child.[5] No attempt is made to disentangle these mechanisms in this chapter. What will be measured is simply the *overall* effect of parental education. It is, of course, possible that its measured effect is due in part to association with some unknown excluded (possibly even more fundamental) background characteristics of the parents, such as their genetic endowments. Insofar as the relationship is independent of such factors it is clear that what is being measured is the effect of parental education on son's status, not vice versa. Unfortunately, the data appear to offer no basis for separation of the influence of parental education from any effects due to unobserved factors affecting both parents and children.[6]

Parental age at death can affect the economic status of the son through its relation to the length of time over which the parent has accumulated capital. The decedent's age also requires careful consideration because of its relationship with his or her education. It appeared essential to treat parental age and education together and to allow explicitly for the negative association between the age of the decedent at death in 1964–65 ($AGED$) and his educational attainment (EDD); in the sample of brothers, the correlation was -0.28. The problem posed by this association seems more statistical and pragmatic than theoretical. One hypothesis is that the earlier the birth of the decedent, the more a given increment of education weighs in determining his relative economic status. In other words, one's education *relative* to others of his age is a better predictor of economic success than the absolute number of years of education. "Relative education" in this sense proved to be a very successful explanatory variable.[7] However, an equally effective model portraying explicitly the interaction between age and education is presented here as a preferred approach clarifying the role of both factors explicitly.

Despite the peculiarity of this statistical problem, one of the original

5. See, for instance, work on this subject and a useful summary of the literature in C. Russell Hill and Frank P. Stafford, "Family Background and Lifetime Earnings," in National Bureau of Economic Research, forthcoming volume of the Conference on Research in Income and Wealth. See also Arleen Leibowitz, "Home Investments in Children," *Journal of Political Economy,* vol. 82 (March–April 1964, pt. 2), pp. S111–S131.

6. Potential approaches to the problem of missing variables are referred to in note 1 above.

7. "Relative education" was measured as the residual of actual educational attainment from the regression of education on age.

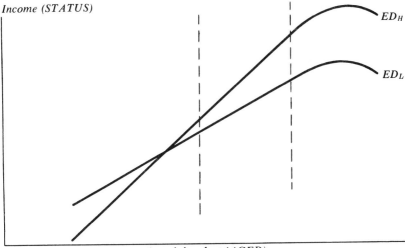

Figure 3-1. **Hypothetical Relationship between Income, Education,**
and Age of Decedents

versions of the human capital model offers some schematic guidance.[8] It can be adapted as shown in figure 3-1.

The curve ED_H (high education) indicates that an individual with high educational attainment tends to start with lower income but be favored by a high income growth rate. Unfortunately the model is not directly applicable to these decedents, for whom the only observation is at an average age of seventy-one. Still, the linear ranges of the model can be defended on historical-institutional grounds as a plausible portrayal of the relationship between a decedent's status, education, and age at death. A case can be made for the validity of both the slopes and heights of the curves in the linear range between the vertical lines.

First, given the decedent's education in years, the older he was at death in 1965–66 (*AGED*), the greater his estimated economic status (*STATUS*). The upward slope is thus rationalized here on grounds of presumed *relative* educational attainment, rather than the accumulation of human capital. On the other hand, the generally higher position of the ED_H curve (for any given age after the very early years) is based on the human capital rationale: the greater the investment in education, the higher one's productivity and income (and overall economic status).

8. See Jacob Mincer, "Investment in Human Capital and Personal Income Distribution," *Journal of Political Economy,* vol. 66 (August 1958), pp. 281–302.

The linear ranges of the diagram then suggest that both the intercept and slope of the relationships between decedent's economic status (*STATUS*) and age (*AGED*) depend on decedent's education (*EDD*). The family of lines is given by:

$$(3\text{-}1) \quad STATUS = (a_1 + a_2\,EDD) + (b_1 + b_2\,EDD)\,AGED$$
$$= a_1 + a_2\,EDD + b_1\,AGED + b_2\,EDD \cdot AGED.$$

These three independent variables were used first to represent the joint contribution of the decedent's age and education to determination of the decedent's status—and, therefore, his son's status. Decedent's education *EDD* was ultimately dropped from the inheritance model because it was very closely correlated to the interaction variable *EDD · AGED*. This amounted to acceptance of a single intercept for the different education lines in the figure.

The specific measurement of the variables was the next methodological question. The relation between income and age is usually found to be non-linear, with low incomes at the early and later stages of life. Dummy variables were therefore used to represent age classes, but no gain in explanatory power was achieved, so the numerical measure of age was retained. Dummy variable representation of the seven educational attainment categories was also tried to allow for nonlinear effects. This improved the fit sufficiently to justify this approach, but the number of categories was collapsed from seven to three. Dummy variables are used throughout to represent (1) partial or complete primary school, (2) partial or complete high school, and (3) at least partial college. The reduction to these three categories can be rationalized by the statistical performance; for example, no difference was found in the measured effects of partial and complete high school. Most of these parents started school around the turn of the century; just 12 percent went to college at all, and only 20 percent were in the partial or complete high school category. If there was any screening effect it appears to have operated with respect to the broad primary, secondary, and higher education categories, rather than diplomas.

Occupation, Family Size, Race, and Religion

These four status-related characteristics were entered as explanatory variables, on the basis of both traditional and more recent rationales. High parental occupational status tends to confer competitive advantages on sons. A large family of origin tends to be disadvantageous. The conventional environmental explanation of this is that family resources for financing education and other aspects of child-rearing are spread thin in large families.[9] Now receiving attention is the additional point that the time available for preschool attention and training varies inversely with the number of children. Both of these considerations are likely to influence the upward mobility of children.[10]

The race and religion of the family of origin can directly influence the son's economic status insofar as there is discrimination in education, employment, and so on, among racial and religious categories. Indirect effects on the son may operate by influencing his motivation and human capital accumulation. It should be emphasized that parental race and usually religion (unlike parental occupation and education) are directly inherited characteristics; as such their causal influence is more clear cut and explicit. The historical differentials in status among these groups are themselves sufficient justification for including these characteristics in an explanatory model.

It was also necessary to choose among alternative measures of these four variables. As a qualitative variable, the decedent's occupational classification was a logical candidate for the dummy variable treatment. However, no explanatory gain was achieved over a single numerical variable representing the occupational ranks from one (low) to seven (high); since the latter was less cumbersome, it is used throughout. However, in the case of women decedents this status indicator was virtually useless, since the great majority were housewives. For that reason, the mean value of the occupation of males was assigned to the variable for female decedents; in some cases, male decedents were studied separately. Family size was also depicted by a single numerical variable, the son's number of siblings

9. See, for example, Peter M. Blau and Otis Dudley Duncan, *The American Occupational Structure* (Wiley, 1967), pp. 295–330. It has also been suggested that "intelligent" persons tend to have fewer children. For one treatment see Anne Anastasi, "Intelligence and Family Size," *Psychological Bulletin,* vol. 53 (May 1956), pp. 187–209.

10. See Hill and Stafford, "Family Background," for a summary of this literature. It should be added that some effects of family size may be conveyed through birth order and the interval between births. For example, the investment of parents in the education of their children may vary with birth order and the interval between births; these differentials seem likely to be greater for large families. However, only the overall effect of family size could be accurately estimated from these data.

(*SIBS*). Dummy variables were used to represent two racial and three religious categories, as defined in table 3-1.[11]

Wealth Indicators

Two measures served as indicators of the material wealth of the decedent. The estate size (whether gross or not) was assumed to be only a fair indicator of his or her lifetime wealth position. Two persons who were equally well off at the height of their careers could leave estates greatly differing in size. For instance, one might consume his capital in later years or make gifts to his children and take advantage of various other measures designed to keep wealth out of the estate for tax purposes. Moreover, the expected positive association between parental wealth and son's status may be obscured by a complex interrelationship. Parental wealth is not a purely predetermined variable. For example, the decisions as to how much capital to consume in later years and the magnitude of gifts to children are undoubtedly influenced by the economic position of the children. The parents of sons who are well-off may tend to use up their savings, tending to produce a negative association between son's economic status and parental wealth. Gifts to children would also reduce parental wealth and increase son's status, also tending to produce a negative association. Thus it is not surprising that estate size was of marginal significance as an explanatory variable, and its role must be carefully qualified.

One proxy was available to supplement estate size as a measure of parental wealth. It was hypothesized that the better off the decedent, the greater the probability that he left a will. A dummy variable representing testacy of the decedent was therefore included and defined as indicated in table 3-1. This variable is not interpreted as a causal influence in any sense, and it is not being asserted that a man can improve his son's life chances simply by drawing up a will! Testacy is interpreted as just one more on a long list of imperfect indicators of the economic status of the decedent. It is included in the model in the same spirit of pragmatism that the French income tax form includes a question as to whether the taxpayer plays golf. Golf playing, like will writing, is interpreted as one "outward

11. More elaborate treatment of categorical variables is being discussed in a growing literature. See, for instance, Yvonne M. Bishop, Stephen E. Fienberg, and Paul W. Holland, *Discrete Multivariate Analysis* (M.I.T. Press, 1975), and Marc Nerlove and S. James Press, *Univariate and Multivariate Log-Linear and Logistic Models,* R-1306–EDA/NIH (Rand Corporation, 1973).

sign of wealth."[12] From the point of view of the tax collector, use of this "indication" makes perfectly good sense—even though he might hesitate to recommend taking up golf as a road to riches.

Unsuccessful Hypotheses

Statistical tests of all the hypotheses discussed above proved rather consistently successful or significant in explaining the composite economic status indicators, but less so in explaining residence quality, occupation, income, and education individually. Variables used in unsuccessful hypothesis tests were dropped from the model, but they deserve brief mention here. (1) It was thought there might be different relationships for male and female decedents.[13] For example, women in wealthy families who died before their husbands might not have much wealth in their own names. However, there were not many such cases; the gross estates of women averaged about the same as those of men, and tests showed no difference in relationships. (2) It was hypothesized that decedents born in regions considerably poorer than the United States might tend to be disadvantaged and transfer this disadvantage to their children. The birthplace categories available showed no such relationship when tested with various combinations of dummy variables. (3) A third hypothesis was that a son's birth rank in his family and its timing might affect his economic success. For example, an older son might be given greater opportunities or might tend to develop a productive independence. Various dummy variable constrictions unearthed no such relationships, but the feasible tests were inadequate and by no means conclusive.[14] So birth order and rank remain as potential background influences on sons that are not included in the present estimates of the inheritance of economic status. (4) Finally, it was thought that large inheritances would affect the economic status of the sons. Undoubtedly these inheritances do affect significantly the material

12. Peter Kalischer of Columbia Broadcasting System News, as reported in *TV Guide*, February 8, 1975, p. 14.

13. This refers to relationships in addition to those involving the useless female-occupation category discussed earlier.

14. The ages of nonrespondent sons were not available, so assignment to a category such as oldest child could not be made with confidence. Strong birth order effects have been found by others: see, for example, Lillian Belmont and Francis A. Marolla, "Birth Order, Family Size, and Intelligence," *Science*, vol. 182 (December 14, 1973), pp. 1096–1101. However, most such studies have also had the benefit of very large samples.

wealth of the son, but it is not surprising that the four available economic status indicators—occupation, income, residence, and education—were found to be unaffected by the size of the bequest. Very few of the decedents were wealthy, and the inheritance had just been received, if at all, at the time of the survey. Even over the longer run, material inheritance seems likely to have much less impact on these dimensions of economic status than inherited human capital. Most sons received little or no inheritance, especially when there was a surviving spouse; moreover, the income in an across-the-board sample like this is primarily from wages and salaries. Of course, this reasoning does not cast any doubt whatever on the hypothesis that material inheritance would be an extremely important determinant of the material wealth of the very wealthy.

The Basic Model

All these considerations led to a single basic model for the explanation of individual economic status. As indicated in table 3-1, six types of family background (or parental) characteristics are utilized: the specified age-education construct, occupation, family size, race, religion, and wealth. The age-education formulation in equation 3-1 was modified as previously discussed. As indicated in table 3-1, the model reduces to the following linear relation with ten independent variables and error term u:

$$(3\text{-}2) \quad STATUS = a + (b_1\ AGED + b_2\ AED2 + b_3\ AED3) \\ + (b_4\ OCDT) + (b_5\ SIBS) + (b_6\ RAC2) + (b_7\ REL2 \\ + b_8\ REL3) + (b_9\ GRST + b_{10}\ TES2) + u.$$

The variables within each of the six sets of parentheses represent the six family background characteristics just listed. This relation is designated the "basic model" for the reasons mentioned. It will be applied repeatedly to various samples to explain various status measures. Some variations of this model performed somewhat better or worse in some contexts (as will be mentioned below). However, this basic form is presented repeatedly for the reasons mentioned, for brevity, and to facilitate comparisons.

Regression Results for Brothers

Regression results for the sample of brothers analyzed in chapter 2 are presented in table 3-2. The preliminary restriction of the analysis to the sample of brothers has a special purpose. The question explored in chapter 2 was what fraction of variation among all these men ($\overline{R}_i^2$) could be explained by family effects—that is, by all factors, known and unknown, that the brothers have in common as members of the same family; each $\overline{R}_i^2$ may be interpreted as the upper limit for the fraction of variance explainable by the *explicit* background variables introduced in this chapter. It is a global yardstick against which to measure the success of the explicit explanatory model.

There are several reasons for comparing the results from explicit explanatory variables to the overall or gross explanations in chapter 2. First, the comparison permits evaluation of the adequacy and completeness of the explanatory model and the available set of variables. The present results are mixed in this respect. For some of the status measures in table 3-2, the regressions with explicit variables produced $\overline{R}^2$s impressively high in relation to the $\overline{R}_i^2$ measuring the gross family effect. For the composite indicator *Croy,* the 44 percent explanation by the explicit background variables is nearly four-fifths of the 57 percent gross figure. This is a quite remarkable performance, since the set of background variables pertains primarily to the decedent parent only and is clearly incomplete (without income information, for example), the wealth variable is defective, and some of the data are based primarily on the questionable recollections by children of the socioeconomic characteristics of their parents.[15]

On the other hand, the explicit explanatory model for family income explains less than one-third as much of its variance as did the brother analysis, and family size emerges as the only significant variable. The education regression does not fit much better. The weak relationship between income and the family background measures in this sample of brothers makes a surprising contrast with the 44 percent explanation of the three-variable status indicator which *includes* income.

A second implication of the comparison between the $\overline{R}^2$ value and the $\overline{R}_i^2$ of table 2-2 is that a large discrepancy between them could be due to nonbackground influences captured by the brother analysis. The low $\overline{R}^2$ values for income and education, for example, could very well be caused

15. The latter does not appear to be a very serious problem. For example, conflicts between responses of siblings seemed slight (in such cases responses were averaged). As an objective check, $\overline{R}_i^2$ were computed for brothers' responses on parental education and occupation; the results of 0.931 and 0.906, respectively, indicated fairly close agreement, suggesting only a modest downward bias in the size of the coefficients.

Table 3-2. Regression Coefficients Relating the Economic Status of Brothers to Explicit Parental Characteristics, Cleveland Area Basic Sample,[a] 1965–66

Parental background characteristic[b]	Variable or statistic	Measure of son's economic status[c]					
		RATE	OCC	LOGY	Croy	(Croye)	(ED)
Age and education	AGED	0.06	0.14	0.011	0.12	0.08	-0.14
		(0.69)	(0.82)	(0.45)	(1.41)	(0.92)	(1.04)
	AED2	-0.02	-0.05	0.005	0.01	-0.01	-0.06
		(0.57)	(0.87)	(0.61)	(0.22)	(0.46)	(1.11)
	AED3	0.02	0.06	0.014	0.08*	0.10*	0.10
		(0.48)	(0.73)	(0.90)	(1.71)	(2.05)	(1.28)
Occupation	OCDT	0.15	0.24	0.008	0.09	0.09	0.15
		(1.51)	(1.47)	(0.30)	(1.03)	(1.05)	(1.03)
Family size	SIBS	-0.10*	0.09	-0.024*	-0.09*	-0.09*	-0.08
		(2.08)	(1.07)	(1.87)	(2.26)	(2.24)	(1.05)
Race	RAC2	-2.11*	-1.69	-0.151	-1.37*	-1.08*	-0.76
		(3.17)	(1.57)	(0.91)	(2.64)	(2.11)	(0.78)
Religion	REL2	-0.41*	-0.97*	-0.076	-0.39*	-0.35*	-0.52
		(2.01)	(2.80)	(1.52)	(2.32)	(2.12)	(1.75)
	REL3	0.11	0.06	0.041	0.11	0.13	-0.10
		(0.30)	(0.10)	(0.38)	(0.36)	(0.41)	(0.19)
Wealth	GRST	0.14	0.64	0.082	0.30	0.39*	0.63
		(0.48)	(1.37)	(1.12)	(1.32)	(1.73)	(1.46)
	TES2	0.38*	-0.45	-0.042	-0.35*	-0.31*	-0.21
		(1.98)	(1.45)	(0.81)	(2.24)	(2.01)	(0.75)
	$\bar{R}^2$	0.281	0.288	0.120	0.442	0.440	0.164
	$\bar{R}^2_d$	0.525	0.342	0.404	0.573	0.556	0.383
	Mean status	4.20	3.83	0.930	0.00	0.00	4.21
	Standard deviation of status	0.92	1.58	0.209	0.78	0.77	1.28

Source: See appendix A.

* Regression coefficient significant at the 5 percent level on the one-tail test.

a. The basic sample is defined in table 2-2, note b.

b. These indicators of parental status are defined in table 3-1: where responses by siblings conflicted, these responses were averaged.

c. Measures of economic status are defined in table 2-2, note a, except that composite *Croye* adds son's education to *Croy*. The numbers in parentheses are *t*-ratios.

d. This is the intraclass correlation coefficient—the estimated fraction of the status variance explained by family affiliation; see table 2-2, note c.

by irregularities in the status measures or important omissions from the list of background characteristics. But it is also possible that the brother analysis has picked up the influence of factors other than family background characteristics, such as location of upbringing, age homogeneity, and brothers' influence on each other.[16] The age effect will be minimized by later tests, but the other two possibilities remain. However, it is again important to emphasize that when the three variables are combined into composite indicators, the explicit background influences show up almost as strongly as suggested by the brother analysis. That would tend to indicate that the weak explanation of income and education levels in table 3-2 may be due to erratic variations in their relationship to the background variables, such as those caused by transitory income effects. This hypothesis is supported by the fact that combining them appears to have averaged out these irregularities, revealing an impressive performance by the model. In any case, these composite indicators are more complete measures of overall economic position. On that criterion, the evidence of family effects—the inheritance of economic status—remains unequivocally strong.

Discussion of the performance of equation 3-2 in explaining the economic status within the sample of brothers has been confined to its goodness-of-fit. Even in the case of the three-variable status index *Croy,* only half of the variables are significant. In any case, the more speculative consideration of the indicated effects of specific background factors and their practical implications will be reserved for the better fits and more accurate estimates for the larger samples.

Results for Larger Samples

The basic sample of all sons is more than double the size of that for brothers. Subsamples of married sons and sons of male decedents were also considered. The sample of married sons of male decedents yielded the highest $\bar{R}^2$ at 0.45. However, results from these various samples differed little, and only the married sons will be discussed here.[17]

---

16. Any effects of birth order (discussed earlier) would decrease, not increase, the relative explanatory power of the brothers model.

17. For a comparison of the samples and reasons for the choice of married sons, see appendix C.

The Sample of Married Sons

Table 3-3 presents results for the basic explanatory equation 3-2 applied to married sons in the basic sample. The sample size is roughly twice that for brothers. The $\bar{R}^2$ values for the larger sample are not markedly different except in the case of income and education. For income the variance explained increased from 12 percent to 24 percent, and for education the increase was from about 16 percent to 28 percent. These results alleviate somewhat the concern that the brother analysis may have picked up the effects of substantial influences other than parental characteristics. Not many of the regression coefficients were significant in the regressions for brothers in table 3-2. Here many more coefficients are significant at the 5 percent level and in *all* such cases they carry the expected sign. Table 3-3, based on samples of 231 to 248 married sons, establishes sturdier credentials for the explanatory background variables.

Sons from large families are shown to have significantly lower residential quality ratings than those from small families. Residential rating is also linked adversely (and significantly) to nonwhite race, to religious heritage other than Protestant or Jewish; a low residence rating also tends to be found with a small parental estate and the absence of a will.[18] Given the way the model is specified, only a college-level parental education (multiplied by the parent's age) had a significantly favorable effect on residence quality.

The parental age-education component of this background model shows much stronger influence on occupation and income. All three variables designed to portray the joint impact of parental age and education show significant positive effects on occupation, and two were significant predictors of income.[19] Turning to the composite variables, the pattern becomes completely and consistently clear. The residence-occupation-income status index is significantly related to all the nine background variables except estate size. When son's education is included to form the four-variable index *Croye,* all ten variables are significant at the 5 percent level or better in the expected direction. The family background model explains more

18. It is, of course, implied conversely that a son's housing quality is positively related to smallness of family of origin, white race, Protestant or Jewish heritage, and wealth of the decedent parent.

19. An interpretation of the effects of joint variations in age and education of the decedent will be suggested below.

than 44 percent of the variance in this comprehensive status index for married sons.

Comparison to Estimates from National Samples

Results from the basic family background model 3-2 in explaining logarithm of income may be compared to those from other models applied to four national samples. The samples chosen are from the Current Population Survey, 1961, Parnes's, 1966, and the Survey Research Center surveys of 1964 and 1971.[20] All cover over 1,000 noninstitutionalized male individuals of working age. The standard deviation of the common logarithm of *earnings* varied from 0.307 to 0.384; the 1961 sample covered the logarithm of *income,* and the standard deviation was 0.357. The most comparable sample in this study is that of all sons in the basic sample— 263 in number.[21] The standard deviation of $LOGY$ for the Cleveland area men was in the same vicinity at 0.319, though this seems slightly low, given that the income variant in this sample includes property income. Among the national samples, only the 1961 Current Population Survey used this broader income variant, rather than earnings, and its standard deviation was 0.357.[22]

The $\bar{R}^2$ values for models explaining either earnings or income in the four national samples range from 0.123 to 0.191. The Cleveland result for model 3-2 was at the upper end of this range at 0.199.[23] The Cleveland regressions concurred with the national results for explanatory variables common to both. Thus it was consistently advantageous to be the son of well-educated, white parents with high occupational status and relatively few children. However, the Cleveland analysis also derived explanatory power from parental age, religion, and wealth.

The explanatory variables available in these samples varied considerably. For example, the 0.191 $\bar{R}^2$ obtained for the Survey Research Center

20. These surveys, the available background variables, and the associated estimates are reported in Mary Corcoran, Christopher Jencks, and Michael Olneck, "The Effects of Family Background on Earnings," *American Economic Review,* vol. 66 (May 1976, *Papers and Proceedings, 1975*), pp. 430–35.

21. See appendix C, table C-1.

22. Measured variation in the Cleveland area sample is biased downward, since the observations are grouped in classes, and all within-class variation is suppressed.

23. As shown in table C-1, the $\bar{R}^2$ values were higher for all other status measures in the Cleveland area sample.

Table 3-3. Regression Coefficients Relating Economic Status of Married Sons to Explicit Family Background Variables, Cleveland Area Basic Sample,[a] 1965–66

Parental background characteristic[b]	Variable or statistic	Measure of son's economic status[c]					
		RATE	OCC	LOGY	Croy	(Croye)	(ED)
...	Constant	4.074[d] (8.18)	1.53[e] (1.83)	0.843[d] (7.25)	−1.12[f] (2.76)	−0.95[f] (2.46)	4.34[d] (6.09)
Age and education	AGED	0.05 (0.78)	0.29[f] (2.90)	0.017 (1.24)	0.13[f] (2.80)	0.09[e] (2.01)	−0.12 (1.46)
	AED2	−0.01 (0.25)	0.06[e] (1.77)	0.012[e] (2.28)	0.03[e] (2.03)	0.04[f] (2.52)	0.08[f] (2.46)
	AED3	0.05[e] (1.83)	0.17[d] (3.81)	0.033[d] (4.97)	0.11[d] (4.98)	0.12[d] (5.85)	0.20[d] (4.89)
Occupation	OCDT	0.07 (1.39)	0.18[e] (2.14)	0.003 (0.21)	0.08[e] (1.99)	0.08[e] (2.03)	0.08 (1.13)
Family size	SIBS	−0.12[d] (3.81)	−0.06 (1.26)	−0.015[e] (2.10)	−0.07[f] (3.06)	−0.07[f] (3.08)	−0.10[e] (2.17)
Race	RAC2	−1.27[d] (3.36)	−1.34[e] (2.19)	−0.244[f] (2.77)	−1.12[d] (3.86)	−0.94[d] (3.41)	−0.62 (1.13)

		(1)	(2)	(3)	(4)	(5)	(6)
Religion	REL2	-0.33[f]	-0.34[e]	-0.042	-0.25[f]	-0.20[e]	-0.12
		(2.72)	(1.72)	(1.43)	(2.53)	(2.12)	(0.70)
	REL3	0.32	0.78[e]	0.114[e]	0.46[f]	0.45[f]	0.44
		(1.35)	(2.03)	(1.99)	(2.46)	(2.50)	(1.28)
Wealth	GRST	0.24[e]	0.26	0.017	0.15	0.21[e]	0.59[e]
		(1.71)	(1.11)	(0.49)	(1.25)	(1.92)	(2.90)
	TES2	-0.22[e]	-0.40[e]	-0.051	-0.24[f]	-0.21[e]	-0.15
		(1.70)	(1.90)	(1.63)	(2.33)	(2.11)	(0.77)
	Number of sons	248	241	239	231	231	247
	$\bar{R}^2$	0.257	0.278	0.239	0.417	0.442	0.280
	Mean	4.375	4.220	0.957	0.000	0.000	4.300
	Standard deviation	0.942	1.542	0.217	0.795	0.774	1.379
	Standard error of estimate[g]	0.812	1.311	0.189	0.621	0.591	1.171

Source: See appendix A.
a. The basic sample is defined in table 2-2, note b.
b. These indicators of parental status are defined in table 3-1: where responses by siblings conflicted, these responses were averaged.
c. Measures of economic status are defined in table 2-2, note a, except that composite *Croye* adds son's education to *Croy*. The numbers in parentheses are *t*-ratios.
d. Significant at the 0.1 percent level.
e. Significant at the 5.0 percent level.
f. Significant at the 1.0 percent level.
g. Standard error of estimate, adjusted for degrees of freedom.

sample of 1,188 men in 1964 used six background characteristics: race, birthplace and education of father, number of siblings, birthplace of son, and whether or not the son was raised on a farm. Geographical variables showed little explanatory power in the Cleveland area sample, although some tests tended to support the surprising result in three of the national samples that sons of foreign-born fathers earn somewhat more than sons of native-born fathers. As in those cases, however, inclusion of other variables eliminated this differential, so the geographical variables were dropped from the present model.

These comparisons suggest that the Cleveland results are not inconsistent with the national findings. The $\bar{R}^2$ value here of 0.199 does not seem especially high, given the effective additional explanatory power of parental age, religion, and wealth that were not available in the national sample. Although missing the latter factors, the Current Population Survey of 1961 had better occupation variables and more geographical information, plus the presence or absence of father when the son was fifteen; its $\bar{R}^2$ was 0.166. While these various findings are not entirely comparable, it seems reasonable to conclude that the strength of the family background effect on income found in the Cleveland area sample is fairly typical.

The effects of family background on education and occupation have also been estimated from national samples. For example, one much less comprehensive model showed the greatest effects of background on education, less on occupation, and least of all on income.[24] The present findings show equal effects on education and occupation and concur that income is less well explained. Given the narrower scope of the earlier model, the present education and occupation estimates are not called into question; in fact, the background effect on education found here seems conservative in comparison with the other, and that for occupation is consistent.

Practical Implications of Regression Results

The meaning of the results in table 3-3 may be approached on two levels. First, as in chapter 2, the predicted economic success of sons from a *generally* favorable economic background can be compared to the prospects for disadvantaged sons. Second, the indicated predictive power of

24. Otis D. Duncan, David L. Featherman, and Beverly Duncan, *Socioeconomic Background and Achievement* (Seminar Press, 1972), p. 43.

Table 3-4. Illustrative Family Background Profiles among 231 Married Sons Representing Families of High and Low Economic Status, Cleveland Area Basic Sample, 1965–66

Parental background characteristic[a]	Variable	Hypothetical[b]		Actual extremes[c]	
		High	Low	High	Low
Age and education	AGED	87	55	80	77
	AED2⎱ AED3⎰	Some college	Primary only	Graduate school	Under 8 years
Occupation[d]	OCDT	5.3	1.2	7	1
Family size	SIBS	0.4	5.5	1	6
Race	RAC2	White	Nonwhite	White	White
Religion	REL2⎱ REL3⎰	Jewish	Catholic	Protestant	Catholic
Wealth	GRST	$63,000	$2,300	$55,000	$6,000
	TES2	Testate	Intestate	Testate	Intestate

Source: Developed from regression results in table 3-3.

a. These indicators of parental status are defined in table 3-1; where responses by siblings conflicted, these responses were averaged.

b. The high and low categories for the quantitatively measured variables represent ranks 5 percent from the top and bottom, respectively, on the assumption of normality.

c. These extremes represent the highest and lowest family background rankings among the 231 sons with data available for *Croy* and *Croye* economic status indexes, ranked by first principal component of ten background variables (see table 2-2, note f). In the computations, redefinitions of some variables were required. For example *SIBS* was made negative to relate it positively to status.

d. For male decedents, this is an occupational rating in seven categories ranging from 1 (low) to 7 (high).

specific background characteristics can be considered on the assumption that other variables in the model are held constant.

Predicted Economic Success of Advantaged and Disadvantaged Sons

One way to gauge the effect of contrasting family backgrounds on a man's chances of economic success is to profile extreme cases. These are specified in table 3-4. The hypothetical high and low cases are extreme in that the advantaged son is assumed to have a decedent parent who ranked high on all six counts.[25] His parents went to college even though he (or she) was born early—in approximately 1877. His occupational class was high—two notches above the average of fathers in the sample.[26] The decedent parent had no other children to support. He was white, Jewish, and

25. Note that the quantitative variables are set at the estimated midpoints of the top and bottom tenths. The categorical variables are assigned values in accordance with the regression results in table 3-3.

26. The average occupational rank of the fathers was one lower than that of the sons.

died testate leaving an estate of $63,000. This was an altogether favorable background from which the hypothetical advantaged son emerged. His opposite number in the illustration survived a parent who did not attend high school, even though born much later—about 1909. He was an unskilled worker supporting six other children, and belonging to disadvantaged racial and religious groups. This parent died intestate leaving only about $2,300.

Table 3-5 presents the predicted levels of success achieved by these hypothetical sons. The expected residence quality ratings are just one away from the extremes among the seven classes. Since the standard deviation is only 0.9, this four-rank difference in residential class is quite substantial. The model went out of bounds in its prediction of occupational rank of the advantaged son, and the figure is rounded down here to the defined maximum of seven.[27] His opposite number is expected to be an unskilled worker.

It is important to recognize that the potential estimating error in these predictions is very high. This is best illustrated for the quantitative variable, income. The son with the very favorable background is predicted to have a 1976 family income of nearly $55,000, or about nine times the family income of the other son; these figures are about three times the median and one-third, respectively. The predictions are themselves subject to substantial sampling error, but the variation of individual incomes around them iş even greater. Rough 95 percent prediction intervals may be constructed on the basis of the standard error of estimate of *LOGY* shown in table 3-3. For the hypothetical advantaged son, this prediction interval is very wide, at $23,000 to $128,000; for the disadvantaged son it is $2,700 to $15,000. According to these rough estimates, very wide variations in income can be expected among both advantaged and disadvantaged sons. Even so, for these extreme cases the prediction intervals do not overlap, and it appears that any son with a head start of this magnitude will rarely have a lower income than the extremely disadvantaged son in the illustration.

The meaning of the contrasting composite economic status indexes (*Croy*) can be illustrated by actual values of that index for sons in the sample. The extreme observed values fell slightly short of the predicted

---

27. This out-of-bounds prediction reflects, in part, a general problem in the treatment of qualitative variables: the regression analysis using ranks is not entirely appropriate. The problem could be alleviated by the use of more elaborate log-linear and logistic models. See Nerlove and Press, *Univariate and Multivariate Models*.

Table 3-5. Predicted Economic Status Levels for Illustrative Sons Profiled in Table 3–4, Cleveland Area Basic Sample, 1965–66

Parental economic status[a] or statistic	*Predicted measure of son's economic status*[b]				
	RATE (scale, 1–7)	OCC (scale, 1–7)	Income (1976 equivalent dollars)[c]	Croy[d]	Education (years)
Hypothetical					
High	6.0	7.0[e]	54,600	2.11	17.6
Low	2.0	1.0	6,400	−2.23	9.4
Actual extremes					
High	6.3	6.9	38,200	1.11	16.6
Low	3.2	2.8	12,400	−0.97	9.3
Mean	4.4	4.2	18,100	0.00	12.6
Standard deviation	0.9	1.5	66[f]	0.80	2.8
Standard error of estimate	0.8	1.3	54[f]	0.62	2.3

Source: Regression results using family background profiles developed in table 3-4.
a. See table 3-4 for the characteristics that contribute to the level of economic status.
b. Predicted on basis of table 3-3. For definition of measures of economic status, see table 2-2, note a.
c. Predicted LOG Y transformed to 1965–66 dollars and doubled to approximate the 1976 equivalent (see table 2-4, note d).
d. Composite economic status index combining residence rating, occupational status, and income (mean of the index = 0).
e. This predicted occupational class was rounded down from 7.7, since the latter figure exceeds the defined maximum of 7.
f. Expressed as a percentage.

values for these hypothetical sons, but they still offer useful illustrations. The most successful son, on this criterion, had a *Croy* index of 2.06. This represented a top residence rating of 7, an occupational classification next to the top at 6, and an income in the top class—about equivalent to $36,000 or over in 1976. The lowest observed economic status index was −1.95, representing a residence rating next to the lowest, a semiskilled occupation, and the lowest observed income—equivalent to the $4,800–$7,200 range in 1976. Finally, the advantaged son is expected to be aided in achieving his relative success by an eight-year educational advantage through completing a year or two of graduate school. His opposite number is expected to complete only a year or two of high school.

These predictions from model 3-2 indicate that the six family-background characteristics taken together are very effective predictors of a son's chances for economic success. However, these hypothetical advantaged and disadvantaged sons represent rather extreme cases since they are contrasted on all six characteristics. It is perhaps more realistic to look at actual cases of contrasting backgrounds. Thus table 3-5 adds a profile of the two families with the highest and lowest composite background indexes among the 175 families from which the 231 sons came.[28]

These two families differ just about as sharply as the hypothetical families in all respects except race and religion. Both observed families of origin were white, and there was less contrast between their two religions with respect to prediction of each son's economic status. The *effective* contrast in education levels was also less because of the lesser difference in age. The net result is that the predicted economic success levels for the observed families differ considerably less than for the hypothetical advantaged and disadvantaged sons. Even so, the predicted residence ratings differ by three notches, occupation by four, and education by seven years. And the predicted income of the advantaged son is more than three times as high as that of the disadvantaged.

The expected high and low composite measures of success are $+1.11$ and -0.97, representing well over one standard deviation in each case. The meaning of these can be illustrated with observed values of $Croy$. The success measure for a number of sons was 1.13; this represents a residence rating of 5, occupation rank at the top 7, and income in the 1976 equivalent of the \$24,000–\$36,000 class. On the other hand, the four sons with an index of -0.97 had residence and occupation ratings of 3 and equivalent 1976 income in the \$9,600–\$14,400 class. While these contrasts in expected economic success are considerably less than between the two hypothetical sons, they still show a sharp differential associated with the five background characteristics on which they differ.

These are such extreme contrasts in life chances that it seems appropriate to consider also some less sharp contrasts in background. This will be done systematically in the next section in terms of intergenerational "transition matrices." In the meantime it is safe to conclude from the Cleveland area sample that the six general family background characteristics, *taken collectively,* are very impressive predictors of a son's chances of economic success.

The Measured Relation of Economic Success to Parental Education

The regression coefficients in table 3-3 and earlier purport to measure the effect of each background variable while the others are held constant. However, such attempts to isolate the effects of particular variables are

28. The first principal component was used to derive these indexes, as described in table 2-2, note f.

necessarily less reliable than their collective predicted effect discussed above. Not only are many background variables still missing, but the closer the correlation among the background variables, the less confidence can be placed in the estimated effects of particular variables. Fortunately, the collinearity of the ten background variables is much less severe than might be expected. Table 3-6 presents the matrix of first-order correlations. Although the sample contains 248 observations, only one-third of these coefficients are significant at the 5 percent level. However, for both the occupation and estate-size variables, five out of nine of the correlations are significant. The marginal performance of these explanatory variables in the regression analysis has been a puzzle, but these correlations help to explain it. On the other hand, race and testacy were correlated with only one other variable in each case, helping to explain their surprisingly effective explanatory performance. Some background variables were inevitably rather strongly correlated, such as testacy and estate size, Catholic religion and family size, and occupation and education. However, in only two cases did one variable account for more than 10 percent of the variance of another. It is not surprising, then, that collinearity seems a minor problem for this model, which explains more than 40 percent of some variants of success.

More serious than multicollinearity is the fact that some of the available background variables are correlated with missing background variables that may be of causal significance. Examples of this are parental ability, home environment, family income, and characteristics of the second parent. Thus, some of the available variables may be given explanatory credit when they are merely fronting for more fundamental causal influences. (Of course a proxy variable such as testacy makes no pretense of being causal.) In particular, the results for parental education to be discussed next almost certainly overstate the effect of a change in this factor alone.

The discussion here is confined to the decedent parent's education, which is the most interesting and consistently strong among the explanatory variables. (The roles of other individual background factors are discussed in appendix D.) As discussed above, the influence of age and education on the economic status or success of the sons under study is treated jointly in models 3-1 and 3-2. The formulation in the model implies this hypothesis: the older the decedent at death, the greater the effect of his given level of education on his own economic status and, indirectly, on that of his son. However, the decedent's age was introduced into the model

Table 3-6. Correlation Matrix for Ten Family Background Variables, Sample of 248 Married Sons,[a] Cleveland Area, 1965–66

	Variable									
Variable	AGED	AED2	AED3	OCDT	SIBS	RAC2	REL2	REL3	GRST	TES2
AGED	1.000	−0.251[b]	0.049	−0.084	0.100	0.084	−0.087	−0.095	0.089	−0.083
AED2	...	1.000	−0.169[b]	0.073	−0.115	0.077	−0.129	0.245[b]	0.124	0.090
AED3	...	...	1.000	0.454[b]	−0.117	−0.050	−0.205[b]	−0.088	0.243[b]	−0.027
OCDT	...	...	...	1.000	−0.205[b]	−0.036	−0.328[b]	0.152[b]	0.298[b]	−0.106
SIBS	...	...	...	...	1.000	0.015	0.290[b]	−0.094	−0.095	0.039
RAC2	...	...	...	...	...	1.000	−0.103	−0.036	−0.165[b]	−0.112
REL2	...	...	...	...	...	...	1.000	−0.284[b]	−0.033	−0.086
REL3	...	...	...	...	...	...	...	1.000	0.130[b]	0.010
GRST	...	...	...	...	...	...	...	...	1.000	−0.359[b]
TES2	...	...	...	...	...	...	...	...	...	1.000

Source: See appendix A.

a. These simple correlation coefficients were computed for the 248 sons in the basic sample for whom the residence rating variable was available. Slightly smaller numbers of observations are available for other success measures. The variables are defined in table 3-1.

b. Significant at the 5 percent level on the two-tail test.

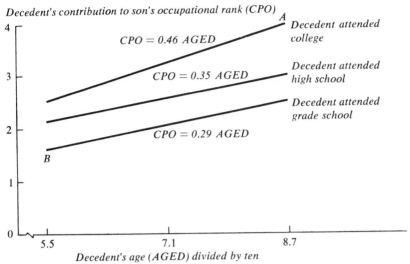

Figure 3-2. Relation between "Contribution" to Son's Predicted Occupational Rank
and Decedent's Age and Education, Cleveland Area Basic Sample, 1965–66
Source: Based on table 3-3.

solely to allow for the changing effect of a given education level over time.
No hypothesis is implied concerning any independent effect of decedent's
age on son's economic status, either directly or indirectly through correlation with son's age. In fact, there was virtually no relation between son's
success and his parent's age at death.[29]

The interpretation of the relation between son's success and decedent's
age and education is clarified in figure 3-2, which is based on the regression explaining son's occupation in table 3-3.[30] The family of lines represents three alternative educational levels attained by the decedents. For
example, at the mean decedent age of seventy-one, the contribution of

29. The simple correlations between the six measures of son's economic status in
table 3-3 and the decedent's age were 0.07, 0.16, 0.07, 0.16, 0.11, and −0.10. The
0.16 values are barely significant, but these coefficients represent a mere 2.5 percent
explanation of the variation of economic status. The success measures are not correlated at all with son's own age, except for the *intermediate* variable—son's education.
These six correlation coefficients are 0.04, 0.04, 0.06, 0.09, 0.00, and −0.28. The last
coefficient (relating son's age and education) indicates no depressing effect of age
on economic status; it merely reflects the trend over time toward more education—
the older the son in 1965–66, the lower his education tended to be.

30. Son's occupation was chosen for the illustration because all three coefficients
in the age-education construct are significant. (See table 3-4 for explanation of age
levels specified.)

college attendance to predicted occupational rank is 3.3, compared to 2.1 for a son who did not attend high school. For that age group, the son of a parent who went to college is expected to average 1.2 occupational ranks higher, assuming the background of the two sons is identical in all other characteristics covered by the model. This relation of occupation to parent's education for a given age group supports the human capital hypothesis. Note also that the vertical distance between the lines increases with decedent's age. This empirical finding supports the hypothesis that a given educational differential has a greater effect on son's occupational rank the earlier the birth date of the decedent.

Figure 3-2 also shows the expected upward slope in the relationship between son's occupational rank and decedent's age for any given educational attainment by the decedent. This supports the hypothesis that the older the decedent at death, the greater the advantage given him by a particular level of education, and, as a consequence, the greater the predicted occupational rank of his son. Further support for this conclusion was derived from an alternative regression that excluded decedent's age from the model and substituted "relative education" for the three age-education variables. Since relative education was represented by the residuals from a regression of decedent's education on his age, the variable was, by definition, uncorrelated with decedent's age. The fact that this adjusted education variable performed as well as the other three was further evidence that there is no independent effect of decedent's age.[31]

For all the above reasons, the entire pattern of effects on son's occupation depicted in figure 3-2 (and the effects on other success measures) will be attributed to the decedent's educational attainment: that is, the entire vertical distance between points A and B in the figure is attributed to parent's education. The predicted difference in occupational rank is 2.4 between the son of an eighty-seven-year-old who attended college and the son of a fifty-five-year-old who did not attend high school.

Table 3-7 makes both of these types of comparisons with various success measures. The first number in each pair is the predicted differential for sons of decedents of the same age; the second number allows for the greater influence of a given level of education on the son of the older decedent by comparing the prediction for the specified birth date with that for the younger father born in 1909. The purpose of the table is to pro-

31. The three-variable formulation was retained because of its explicit portrayal of the age-education relationship.

Table 3-7. Contribution to Son's Economic Success of Parent's Educational Attainment, Cleveland Area Basic Sample, 1965–66[a]

Decedent's educational attainment and birth date of parent	Measure of son's economic success[b]				
	RATE	OCC	INCOME (percent)	Croy	(ED) (years)
Partial or complete primary					
1909[c]	0.0	0.0	0.0	0.0	0.0
	0.0	0.0	0.0	0.0	0.0
1893[d]	0.0	0.0	0.0	0.0	0.0
	*	0.5	*	0.2	*
1877[e]	0.0	0.0	0.0	0.0	0.0
	*	0.9	*	0.4	*
Partial or complete high school					
1909[c]	*	0.3	16	0.2	0.9
	*	0.3	16	0.2	0.9
1893[d]	*	0.4	22	0.2	1.1
	*	0.9	29	0.3	0.8
1877[e]	*	0.5	27	0.3	1.4
	1.4	44	0.5	0.7	
At least some college					
1909[c]	0.3	0.9	52	0.7	2.2
	0.3	0.9	52	0.7	2.2
1893[d]	0.3	1.2	71	0.9	2.8
	0.4	1.7	82	1.0	2.4
1877[e]	0.4	1.5	94	1.0	3.5
	0.6	2.4	119	1.4	2.8
Standard deviation	0.9	1.5	65	0.8	2.8

Source: Based on table 3-3.

a. For each success measure and birth date two differentials are given. The first compares predicted success measures for the birth date specified. The second compares the prediction for the birth date specified with that for the 1909 birth date.

b. For definitions, see table 2-2, note a. The percentage differential for INCOME is derived from the differential in LOG Y.

c. Estimated median year of birth among youngest tenth.

d. Mean year of birth of all decedents.

e. Estimated median year of birth among oldest tenth.

* Not significant at 5 percent level.

vide estimates of the effect on predicted son's status of a differential in age-adjusted education, with all other characteristics in the model held constant.

Among the son's economic status indicators least affected by parental education is the residence rating: a son of a college-educated parent of average age is predicted to live in a home only one-third of a grade higher than a man of the same age from the low educational background, but with otherwise identical parental characteristics. Even the comparison of sons whose decedent parents also differ in age by thirty-two years show a predicted differential of only six-tenths of a grade. Since the standard deviation of this success measure is only 0.9, this differential is modest, even though the coefficient of the college education is significant. A convenient interpretation is available on the assumption of normality. Suppose the son of the least educated parent in this illustration is predicted to achieve median residential status—the fiftieth percentile from the top—and that the son with the most favorable parental education has the same background in all respects except age-education. The latter son is forecast to have a residence rating at the twenty-fifth percentile from the top—not a very impressive differential.[32]

The indicated effect of education on occupational rank is much stronger. The average-age comparison shows a 1.2 notch advantage for the son of the college-educated parent, and the largest differential illustrated is 2.4 notches on the one-to-seven scale; this amounts to 1.6 standard deviations. If the son with the low parental education is predicted to have the median occupation, the son with an advantage in parental education only is expected to come out 5 percent from the top in occupational ranking—or next to the top among the seven categories.

We can also compare very roughly their probabilities of achieving other occupational ranks.[33] Suppose the background of a son with the most educationally disadvantaged parents in table 3-7 (fifty-five-year-old decedent without any high school) is such that the model predicts he will achieve the middle of the occupation grade two—semiskilled worker. It would then be predicted that another son, with the illustrated background advantage in parental education only, would achieve an occupational rank 2.4 notches higher, or 4.4. The latter has roughly a 20 percent chance of ending up in one of the two administrative or professional grades at the top—on the order of twenty times the remote chance of the first son.[34] Furthermore, the advantaged son would have a less than 10 percent

32. Although residence, occupation, and education are limited to seven discrete categories, these percentile comparisons will be made as though the measures were continuous. The twenty-fifth percentile is the rank of a son 0.6/0.9 standard deviations above the median in a normal distribution.

33. These comparisons utilize the standard errors of estimate in table 3-3 and assume normality of the conditional distribution of success measures at each predicted success level.

34. This illustration assumes that an estimated occupational rank of 5.5 or better would put a man in one of the top two occupational classes.

chance of being an unskilled or semiskilled worker, as forecast for the other son. Again, it should be remembered that these estimates are extremely speculative: they are based on point estimates from an incomplete model, and they also assume normality and deal in simplistic fashion with the discrete occupation categories.

The income comparison is also striking. The comparison of sons of decedents of average age predicts a 71 percent higher income for the most advantaged son, even though he is advantaged with respect to parental education only. The son of an eighty-seven-year-old decedent with college experience is predicted to have a family income 119 percent higher than the son of a fifty-five-year-old decedent without high school attendance. If the latter's background warrants the prediction that he will be at the median income, the expected income rank of the former is 6 percent from the top.[35] In terms of annual incomes, if the first son is expected to receive the median family income of married couples (1976 equivalent) of about $18,100, the son with a more advantageous background in parental education only is predicted to receive an income of nearly $40,000.

Again, it is revealing to compare probabilities of achieving different income levels, assuming that the expected values are correct. This is done in table 3-8 for sons with the same contrast in parental education—a parent who did not go to high school (born in 1909) versus a parent with college experience (born in 1877). The illustrative pairs of sons are presumed to be alike in all other measured respects. The chances of achieving a family income over $25,000 in 1976 offer clear-cut contrasts. In the case where the relatively disadvantaged son is expected to have a median income, his chances do not seem very low compared to the other son. However, if his predicted income is at the lower quartile, at about $13,000, he has only a 7 percent chance of making $25,000 or more, compared to a 62 percent chance for the son with the more educated parent. And if the disadvantaged son is forecast to have a $9,600 income (the bottom decile), he has about one chance in seventy of having family earnings of $25,000 and up, compared to the one-in-three probability of the son who differs from him only in parental education (as adjusted for age).

These estimated differentials in the expected incomes of two hypothetical sons seem remarkable when it is remembered that the two men are

---

35. This comparison utilizes the raw results in terms of *LOGY*, rather than the percentage differentials in table 3-7.

The Inheritance of Economic Status

Table 3-8. Predicted Incomes and Probability Distribution (1976 Equivalent)
of Disadvantaged Son (Parent without High School Education, Born in 1909) and
Advantaged Son (Parent with College Education, Born in 1877) Who Differ Only
with Respect to Parental Education, as Adjusted for Age, Cleveland Area Basic Sample,
1965–66

Predicted incomes (dollars)[a]		Probability (percent) of income over					
Dis-advantaged[b] son (D)	Advantaged[c] son (A)	$15,000		$25,000		$50,000	
		D	A	D	A	D	A
18,100[d]	39,700	67	99	23	86	1.0	30
13,000[e]	28,500	37	93	7	62	0.1	10
9,600[f]	21,000	15	78	1+	34	[g]	2+

Source: Based on tables 3-3 and 3-7. Probabilities depend on standard errors of estimate and assume normality and constant variance of the conditional distribution of LOG Y for each specified predicted value of LOG Y.
a. As implied by the predicted logarithms.
b. The three illustrative "predicted" incomes for the disadvantaged sons are the starting points. It is assumed that they have been predicted by some configuration of background factors, including a parent without high school diploma who was born in 1909.
c. Derived by applying the 119 percent differential reported in table 3-7.
d. Estimated median income approximated from mean LOG Y.
e. Estimated income ranked 25 percent from the bottom (median of bottom half).
f. Estimated income ranked 10 percent from bottom (median of bottom fifth).
g. About one-hundredth of 1 percent.

assumed alike in all measured respects except age-adjusted education. Neither has any measured advantage over the other in parental occupation, family size, race, religion, or wealth. Insofar as the estimates are accurate, the differences in predicted incomes are due entirely to an education differential pertaining to only one parent of each son.

Some of these predicted economic status differentials due to contrasting parental education alone are so large as to be suspect. It is tempting to suggest that they point to parental education as a stimulus to the son's achievement. However, it is highly likely that parental education is to some extent a proxy for missing variables such as genetic endowments and family income.[36] In any case, it may be noted that the coefficients on

36. It might also be supposed that the parental education coefficients are exaggerated due to weak competition from the occupation variable for which females were represented by the mean for males. The regressions for married sons of male decedents were examined for evidence of this, and no bias was revealed. The coefficients for the college-graduate variable were virtually identical, although the t-ratios were smaller in this sample with 40 percent fewer observations. For example, the coefficients in the regression explaining the composite status index Croy were identical at 0.11, while the t-ratios were 4.98 for the large sample and 3.84 for the sample of male decedents only.

the college-level variable run from four to six times their standard errors except in the case of residence rating. Even if inclusion of relevant missing variables cut the coefficients in half, the evidence of a strong influence from parental education would remain impressive.[37] Insofar as this relationship is a causal one, it is encouraging, since this intergenerational influence is subject to public policy initiatives, at least in the long run. Much has been made of the indicated weakness of stimulation of educational attainment as an antipoverty device. But this evidence suggests that even if it does not do much for the current generation, it may do more for the next.

Differentials in predicted economic status associated with the five other available background characteristics covered in table 3-3 are of less direct policy relevance, even if causality could be established. However, some of the relationships are persistently strong, as summarized in appendix D.

A More General Picture of Intergenerational Economic Mobility

The foregoing regression analysis offered predictions of the economic success levels of individuals from varying backgrounds and their chances of achieving specified goals. The relationship of these predictions and probabilities to family background was interpreted as an indication of the extent to which economic status or success is inherited.

As an alternative to regression analysis, the intergenerational economic relationship can be pictured in "transition matrices" linking the economic status of sons and parents. This device has the disadvantage that no attention is paid to particular background influences and it is necessary to rely on single indexes of background rank and the economic success of sons. But the approach has at least two advantages over regression. First, it is possible to present systematically a whole array of intergenerational moves from rank to rank. Second, each son is represented individually in a cell of the array; that is, a detailed picture of the actual intergenerational changes is developed, not dependent on theoretical probability distributions based on summary statistics, such as those underlying tables 2-4 through 2-8.

37. Some hints as to potential bias in the parental education coefficients are provided in chapter 4, where biases in the estimates of the effect of son's own education are considered.

The Index of Parental Economic Status

Various dimensions of a son's economic success and background have been defined. For this analysis it was necessary to derive single indexes of the economic status of the successive generations. Once again reliance was placed on the first principal component adopted previously for comprehensive measures of a son's success. Other methods of ranking the two generations were also tested, but the findings proved virtually independent of this methodological choice.[38]

The credentials of these background indexes can be appraised briefly. It has already been noted that the ten independent variables used to explain economic status fall somewhat short of the hypothetical goal set by the analysis of overall family effects in chapter 2. However, as shown in table 3-2, these ten variables did reach about 77 percent and 79 percent, respectively, of the way toward that objective for the success indexes *Croy* and *Croye*. It was to be expected that falling back on a single background index combining the same ten background variables would result in a further attrition of intergenerational explanatory power. Table 3-9 illustrates this for a few variations. The original regression model explained 39.4 percent of the variance of residence-occupation-income measure *Croy* for all sons. The two background indexes fall about 15 percent short of this goal. The explanation of the broader economic status index for sons falls only about 10 percent short of the goal set by the regression, a highly satisfactory performance by a single variable in relation to that accomplished collectively by its separate components.

The two variants of the background index described in the table gave essentially the same answers; thus results for only the first will be pre-

38. For the definition of the first principal component, see table 2-2, note f. The background index was derived from the six general background characteristics and ten variables used in table 3-2 and later. However, in computing the first principal component, some variables were redefined by changing their signs. For example, the sign of family size was changed to relate it positively with economic status. Also used, as an alternative background index to the first principal component, were the predicted values of son's economic status derived from the regression on the ten background variables. This measure was more closely related to each measure of son's status, but it is open to the methodological objection that it was derived with the aid of the variable that it is attempting to explain. So it seemed appropriate to settle for the less striking results based on the first principal component. Equal weighting was also used for an alternative index of son's economic status, but this variation was dropped because it made little difference.

Parental Characteristics as Predictors   107

Table 3-9. $\bar{R}^2$ **Values for Regressions of Son's and Son-in Law's Economic Status on Background Indexes (*BI*) and Background Variables (*BV*), Cleveland Area Sample, 1965–66**

	Economic status measure[a]					
	Croy			Croye		
Variant of basic sample	BI_1[b]	BI_2[c]	BV[d]	BI_1[b]	BI_2[c]	BV[d]
All 253 sons	0.337	0.335	0.394	0.381	0.384	0.424
231 married sons plus 199 sons-in-law	0.327	...	0.386	0.373	...	0.417

Source: Derived from the six background characteristics and ten variables in table 3-2.
a. For definitions see table 2-2, note a. *Croye* adds son's education to *Croy*.
b. Background index 1: the first principal component of ten background variables in table 3-2. (See table 2-2, note f.) In this variant of the computation, the background characteristic was included for each child.
c. Background index 2: as in note b, except that the background characteristic of a decedent parent was used in the computation once only. Note that this variation had virtually no effect.
d. Regression results for all sons are those in appendix table C-1; for married sons and sons-in-law combined, a dummy is added to each variable to distinguish sons-in-law (discussed in chapter 4).

sented. The results for the combined sample of married sons and sons-in-law did not differ appreciably from those for all sons. However, in addition to the sample of sons, the larger sample will be retained because its greater size adds detail to the transition matrix.

The purpose of the comparisons in table 3-9 is to qualify the results to be presented next in the transition matrixes. The need to rely on single indexes for each generation in constructing the matrixes weakens the demonstrated intergenerational link. It has already been shown in table 3-9 that these explicit background variables have about 21 to 23 percent less success in explaining the *Croy* and *Croye* indexes than the brother analysis of overall family effects. Now a further 10 to 15 percent of the degree of intergenerational association must be sacrificed in order to acquire a single background index. Taken together, these two erosions of the degree of association have given up about 35 and 30 percent of the explanation of *Croy* and *Croye,* respectively. Even so, the transition matrices to be presented still reveal a very high degree of inheritance of economic status. The point to be emphasized here is that if the background indexes had the same explanatory power indicated by the analysis of brothers, the demonstrated effect of inheritance would be a great deal stronger than shown here.[39]

39. The transition matrices reported here are descriptive devices that offer a detailed picture of the upward and downward mobility of sons and daughters from varying backgrounds. More elaborate statistical methodology is called for in future research. For example, log-linear probability models have been applied to transition

Method and Findings

To construct tables 3-10 and 3-11, decedent parents and sons were ranked in approximate tenths according to the indexes discussed above.[40] Table 3-10 gives results for the residence-occupation-income index of son's economic status (*Croy*). The numbers in a given row represent the total number of cases from the parental rank indicated for that row. The distribution of these cases among the ten columns representing the economic status of the sons is thus a conditional frequency distribution of son's economic status, *given* the parental rank of that row. The results from the narrowest and broadest samples of sons are given in the two halves of the table. The findings for married sons of male decedents are presented separately for the reasons discussed in appendix C. Elimination of female decedents and unmarried sons avoids methodological problems and yields a somewhat closer intergenerational relationship at the expense of reducing the sample size. However, this sample of only 144 reveals a strong intergenerational relationship.

Seven of the 14 sons who emerged from the top tenth in background were themselves found to be among the top tenth of the 144 sons; none fell farther than the fourth tenth. There is no need for chi-square procedures or any other tests of statistical significance to appraise the patterns shown; the intergenerational relationship has already been shown to be highly significant. The purpose of these transition matrices is to convey a more general impression of the relationship. Even so, it is interesting to note that if 14 sons were chosen at random from the 144, the probability that all would achieve the top 40 percent rank in economic status rank is just over two in a million.[41]

---

matrices; for a basic article, see Leo A. Goodman, "Ransacking Social Mobility Tables," *American Sociological Review*, vol. 75 (July 1969), pp. 1–40. In the present case, the transition probabilities could be allowed to depend on background variables, including smoothing of the data and estimating probabilities for empty cells. See Nerlove and Press, *Univariate and Multivariate Models*, sec. 5.

40. Since the tenths of frequencies did not oblige by emerging as whole numbers, the table deals with whole number approximations; the "minority" whole number was assigned to the center of the distribution. For example, in the first sample of 144, the four cells with fifteen cases were assigned to tenths numbers 4 through 7. The row totals based on background ranks conform to these a priori assignments; this was achieved by randomizing the sons to be included when background ranks were tied. Column totals vary slightly from row totals because sons' composite success ranks were used as is, with no randomization for tied ranks.

41. The tenths were unequal in number; the first four tenths were assigned 14, 14, 14, and 15 cases, respectively. So this probability actually refers to the chance that none of the 14 sons would fall below the 57th rank out of 144.

Table 3-10. Transition Matrices Relating the Economic Status Ranks, in Tenths, of Successive Generations, for Son's Status Measure *Croy*,[a] Cleveland Area Sample, 1965–66

Rank of decedent parent[b]	Rank of sons										Mean rank of son[c]
	1 (top)	2	3	4	5	6	7	8	9	10	
Sample of 144 married sons of male decedents (rs = 0.600)[d]											
1	7	4	2	1	...	...	...	...	...	...	11.4
2	1	3	4	4	1	1	...	...	...	...	27.1
3	...	2	5	1	2	1	2	1	...	...	32.9
4	2	1	2	1	...	4	1	1	1	2	49.7
5	...	4	...	...	1	3	2	2	2	1	54.3
6	...	...	1	3	3	1	3	3	1	...	55.0
7	1	1	1	1	3	1	1	1	3	2	57.0
8	1	...	...	1	2	2	2	1	3	2	63.6
9	...	1	...	2	3	...	1	2	1	4	64.3
10	...	...	...	...	...	2	1	3	2	6	80.7
Sample of all 253 sons (rs = 0.518)[d]											
1	14	2	4	5	...	...	...	...	...	...	15.0
2	4	2	7	3	2	3	3	...	1	...	35.8
3	1	8	1	2	3	3	2	1	3	1	43.0
4	3	3	4	1	...	3	3	3	2	3	49.4
5	1	4	...	3	6	3	3	4	2	...	48.8
6	...	2	3	4	1	4	7	3	1	1	52.7
7	...	1	2	3	4	3	2	6	1	4	60.0
8	2	...	1	1	4	3	...	3	2	9	66.6
9	1	1	...	4	3	2	4	5	1	4	60.6
10	1	...	...	1	3	1	3	5	5	6	71.8

Source: Derived by ranking parents in tenths according to index of parental economic status described in text, and distributing sons according to their rank by the *Croy* index.
a. The economic status measure *Croy* is defined in table 2-2, note a.
b. Decedents are ranked by the first principal component of the background variables in table 3-2. For the definition of the first principal component, see table 2-2, note f. This is variant 1 of the background index, as defined in table 3-9, note b.
c. Percentile from top estimated from midpoints of tenths.
d. Spearman coefficient of rank correlation.

Only 6 sons from the lowest background were consigned to that rank themselves, but not one of the 14 sons reached the top half of the economic ladder. It should be added that there was not a single case of overlap in the success measures of the 14 sons from the top tenth and the 14 from the bottom tenth; every one of the former was better off than every one of the latter. It is this *contrast* between the life chances of sons from upper and lower background ranks that is the most powerful message of these transition tables.

What emerges here is a picture of a handicapped race and an idea of the magnitude of that handicap. It is realistic to view the most advantaged

14 sons as starting the race for success in life with a position in the first 10 percent, while the other 14 started with a handicap that placed them at the end of the pack of 144 starters. As children, their economic status was essentially that of their family. Furthermore, the ten variables used here to rank their family backgrounds, except the (generally insignificant) gross estate, were already fixed when the sons were children, and therefore the same then as when measured in this sample. Moreover, the matrix in table 3-10 reveals the magnitude and consequence of that starting handicap. Not one son starting from behind caught up with even the slowest son with the head start. It is as though there were two separate fields in the race.

Since this sample is rather small, it is useful to look also at the economic status ranks attained by sons from the top and bottom fifths. Among the 28 sons who started life in the front-running fifth, 15 were still in that rank when surveyed at an average age of about 42; only one son who started from among the most handicapped fifth achieved that rank. Among the 28 sons from the bottom rank, 12 remained there, while no advantaged son was in that position.

It might be objected that since the average age of the sons is only forty-two—about midcareer—their race for success in life is not over. Some handicapped starters who were gaining might pass a few of the slower sons among those who had a head start. The economic success index based on residence rating, occupational rank, and income undoubtedly varies somewhat with age. However, occupation is virtually fixed by age forty-two, and it seems likely that a man's *relative* residence and income position is fairly well determined by that time (even though everyone's real income tends to rise for some years after that). Educational attainment is essentially determined by midcareer, so its inclusion in the index in table 3-11 makes for an even more nearly final result as of midcareer. So, a snapshot of the race taken at this time should give a good forecast of the outcome. Of course, the sons of these sons will start with a lesser handicap—a matter for consideration later.

The intergenerational association is somewhat weaker for *all* sons, as indicated in table 3-10 by the rank correlation of only 0.52, compared to 0.60 in the smaller sample. However, 14 out of the 25 sons starting in the top tenth held that position themselves, compared to one who rose from below; basing the comparison on the extreme fifths, the figures are 22 and 3, respectively.

Results for the broader economic status index for sons, including edu-

Table 3-11. Transition Matrices Relating the Economic Status Ranks, in Tenths, of Successive Generations, for Son's Status Measure Croye,[a] Cleveland Area Sample, 1965–66

Rank of decedent parent[b]	Rank of sons										Mean rank of son[c]
	1 (top)	2	3	4	5	6	7	8	9	10	
Sample of 144 married sons of male decedents ($r_s = 0.605$)[d]											
1	9	3	2	...	...	...	...	...	...	...	10.0
2	1	3	5	2	2	1	...	...	...	...	33.6
3	...	4	3	1	2	2	1	...	1	...	37.1
4	2	...	1	2	1	3	2	3	...	1	51.0
5	1	3	...	1	...	3	2	...	4	1	54.3
6	...	...	1	2	2	3	3	2	2	...	57.6
7	...	1	1	2	2	1	3	3	...	2	57.6
8	1	...	...	2	2	1	1	1	4	2	63.6
9	...	...	1	3	2	...	1	2	2	3	63.6
10	...	...	...	...	2	1	2	2	1	6	77.1
Sample of all 253 sons ($r_s = 0.548$)[d]											
1	13	5	6	1	...	...	...	...	...	...	13.0
2	3	4	6	3	5	3	...	...	1	...	32.2
3	2	6	3	...	2	5	2	3	2	...	42.6
4	4	1	3	3	...	4	3	1	5	1	49.0
5	1	4	2	1	4	4	3	4	3	...	51.2
6	...	3	1	6	1	1	6	6	1	1	53.8
7	...	...	3	3	3	5	3	3	2	4	60.0
8	1	1	...	2	3	3	3	2	2	8	66.6
9	1	...	1	4	6	...	3	3	5	2	59.0
10	...	1	...	1	3	2	3	3	4	8	72.6

Source: Derived by ranking parents in tenths according to index of parental economic status described in text, and distributing sons according to their rank by the *Croye* index.
a. The economic status measure *Croye* adds son's education to *Croy*, which is defined in table 2-2, note a.
b. Decedents are ranked by the first principal component of the background variables in table 3-2. For the definition of the first principal component, see table 2-2, note f. This is variant 1 of the background index, as defined in table 3-9, note b.
c. Percentile from top, estimated from midpoints of tenths.
d. Spearman coefficient of rank correlation.

cation (table 3-11), are similar. Of the 28 sons starting in the top fifth in the smaller sample, 16 achieved this rank themselves, compared to *none* of the 28 with the most disadvantaged starting position. In the larger sample, 25 starting in the leading fifth remained there, versus just two sons who caught up with that rank after starting in the lowest fifth.

In a quest for greater detail, sons were combined with sons-in-law to construct table 3-12. (As will be shown in chapter 4, the relation of the son-in-law's economic status to his wife's background is nearly as close as the link to son's own parents.) It is important to recognize that in this

Table 3-12. Transition Matrix Relating the Economic Status Ranks, in Twentieths, of Successive Generations for Combined Sons and Sons-in-Law, Status Measure Croye,[a] Cleveland Area Sample, 1965–66

Rank of decedent[b]	Rank of sons and sons-in-law in combined sample of 430 ($r_s = 0.518$)[c]																			
	1 (top)	2	3	4	5	6	7	8	9	10	11	12	13	14	15	16	17	18	19	20
1	13	2	3	2	···	1	···	···	···	1	···	···	···	···	···	···	···	···	···	···
2	2	4	2	6	3	2	1	···	1	1	···	···	···	···	···	···	···	···	···	···
3	3	3	2	2	4	1	2	2	1	···	···	···	···	···	···	1	···	···	···	···
4	2	3	3	3	···	1	1	3	2	2	1	···	···	2	1	1	···	···	···	···
5	···	1	3	···	2	1	1	2	1	1	···	···	···	0	···	2	1	3	···	···
6	2	2	1	1	1	···	3	···	1	3	2	2	1	3	2	···	1	···	2	1
7	2	···	1	1	1	2	1	···	···	1	1	4	1	1	···	2	1	1	···	1
8	1	···	2	1	2	1	4	1	1	1	1	···	···	3	···	2	2	1	1	1
9	···	1	2	···	···	···	···	1	1	1	2	···	2	1	1	2	2	1	···	···
10	···	···	1	···	···	···	1	1	···	1	1	···	···	1	1	4	2	1	2	···
11	···	···	···	1	2	3	1	···	···	1	2	6	2	1	1	1	2	1	2	2
12	···	···	···	2	2	1	···	···	2	3	···	2	4	2	···	···	3	2	1	1
13	···	1	1	···	···	···	2	1	···	1	4	1	2	1	1	2	1	···	1	···
14	···	···	···	···	2	4	2	1	···	1	2	1	2	4	1	1	2	2	1	···
15	···	1	···	···	2	1	2	2	2	2	2	1	···	···	···	1	2	2	···	···
16	···	···	···	1	···	1	···	2	1	1	1	1	1	1	1	4	3	2	4	2
17	···	···	1	1	1	1	1	···	1	1	···	3	2	3	1	3	2	2	···	2
18	···	···	···	···	1	1	···	2	1	···	1	3	2	1	1	3	1	1	2	3
19	1	1	1	···	1	1	1	1	1	···	2	3	3	3	···	···	2	1	2	3
20	···	···	···	···	1	···	···	1	1	2	···	3	1	1	···	···	2	1	4	5

Source: Derived by ranking parents in twentieths according to index of parental economic status described in text, and distributing sons and sons-in-law according to their rank by the Croye index.

a. The economic status measure Croye adds son's education to Croy, which is defined in table 2-2, note a.

b. Decedents (parents of sons or daughters) are ranked by the first principal component of the background variables in table 3-2. For the definition of the first principal component, see table 2-2, note f. This is variant 1 of the background index, as defined in table 3-9, note b. The economic status of daughter is defined as that of her husband.

c. Spearman coefficient of rank correlation.

matrix the family background and starting point in life is that of the married daughter, rather than the son-in-law. Since there was no satisfactory independent measure of the economic success of the daughter on her own, the pragmatic choice was to identify her economic success with that of her husband.[42] So this analysis pools sons and daughters to rank their background or starting positions in the economic success race. Although the table is based on the son-in-law's economic success, it is best seen here as relating the daughter's success (measured by her husband's) to *her own* starting position.

With 430 in the sample, it was appropriate to rank the two generations in twentieths.[43] Of the 21 most advantaged sons and daughters, 13 ended up in the top twentieth themselves and 20 were in the top fifth. Among the 22 most disadvantaged, none reached the top fifth and only five achieved the top half. Just one of the 22 sons and daughters from the most handicapped background succeeded in overtaking one of the 21 who had the greatest head start among the 430 in this race for economic success. Put more conventionally, the two conditional distributions of economic success—one for the 21 with the best head start and one for the 22 most handicapped—just barely overlap at their extreme values.

Of the 43 in the tenth that led at the start, 21 achieved that slot, compared to one son or daughter who started among the 43 most disadvantaged. Among the 86 starting from a background in the top fifth, 53 stayed there, while only 4 sons and daughters achieved this rank from a start in the lowest fifth. None of the 86 from the top fifth fell to the bottom fifth, but 31 who started there remained there.

All five matrices exhibit an important contrast between observed upward and downward intergenerational economic mobility. Sons with a good head start were less likely to fall behind than handicapped sons were likely to overcome their disadvantage. In the samples of sons as well as the combined sample of sons and daughters, from one-half to two-thirds who started in the first tenth managed to hold their rank, while usually less than one-third who started in the last tenth remained in that position. This pattern appears consistent in terms of other ranks also. For example, in

42. It should be repeated that this is an entirely pragmatic device, and emphasized that the son-in-law's economic success index may be molded in part by the daughter; she may have contributed to family income, the attainment of the residence, and even to her husband's occupational rank.

43. Consecutive twentieths were assigned alternating numbers of cases, starting with 21 at the top—21, 22, 21, 22 . . . —so that each tenth would contain the same number (43).

the largest sample (table 3-12), 53 out of 86 sons and daughters held their places in the top fifth, while only 31 were still in the bottom fifth where they started.[44]

The greater upward than downward mobility from the extreme fifths was, of course, offset by a reshuffling in the center of the distribution. For example, 83 sons and daughters who were in the third, fourth, and fifth tenths lost ground by at least one decile, while only 67 of their opposite number moved up at least one decile. It is interesting to ask at whose expense the substantial exodus from the bottom fifth occurred. No son or daughter from the top fifth replaced any of the 55 who moved up from the bottom; their places were taken by 13 from the second fifth, 19 from the third, and 23 from the fourth. Compared to the top fifth, the second fifth fared especially poorly. Although only 33 sons and daughters fell from the top (and none of these to the lowest fifth), 45 dropped from the second fifth, including the 13 who went all the way to the bottom fifth. In short, there was a substantial degree of upward economic mobility out of the low fifth at the expense of the fourth, third, and even second, but not the first.

This lack of symmetry in upward and downward economic mobility is consistent with the hypothesis that gains by the disadvantaged tend to be achieved primarily at the expense of the broad middle range of the population. This pattern is somewhat more evident in the combined son and daughter sample than in the case of sons alone, suggesting that it may be in part related to marital selection patterns, as discussed in chapter 4. However, the pattern is still convincing, even in the case of sons. This is most clearly seen in terms of average ranks. For example, the first sample in table 3-10 shows sons from the top tenth having an average rank 11 percent from the top, while their opposite numbers achieved an average rank 19 percent from the bottom. Even clearer is the contrast in the sample of all sons (table 3-11), using the same success index as the table on sons and daughters. The sons from the top tenth were themselves 13 percent below the top, on average; their disadvantaged counterparts made their way up to an average rank 27 percent above the lowest.

The findings from these matrices are especially persuasive because their interpretation depends on no specified regression model and no assump-

44. This sample difference between the fractions who stayed in the top and bottom fifths is highly significant, representing more than three standard errors.

tions about the nature of the distribution of the variables. The decedents and their sons were ranked independently by a standard technique, and the transition matrix follows directly from these rankings. The Spearman coefficient of rank correlation (r_s) is also listed in each table and is based on the underlying data; it too requires no assumption about the nature of the distribution (such as normality) for its interpretation. The observed values of r_s in the 0.5–0.6 range are unusually high for the results from a cross-section.

Importance of the Economic Mobility Patterns

What is to be made of these effects of the head starts and handicaps assigned to people at the start of their economic careers? The consensus of tables 3-10 and 3-11, for example, is that about one-half of the sons born in the top fifth end up there; for the combined son and daughter sample, 62 percent held on to their initial ranks in the top fifth. Does this represent a serious qualification of the American ideal of equality of opportunity?

Several points should be made in evaluating results such as these. First, the transition matrices necessarily rely on a single indicator of family background, which, as shown in table 3-9, explains only about 34 to 39 percent of the variation in son's economic status, as measured by *Croy*. It has already been noted that falling back on this single background index causes a loss in explanatory power in two stages. The analysis of brothers suggests that a truly comprehensive index would explain 55 percent or more of the variation in son's status. Although the present estimates based on these matrices have special value in that no assumption of normality was required, they are obviously very conservative.

The second point concerns one's reaction to the conservative estimate that 50-plus percent of sons born in the top fifth stay there. It may seem that any interpretation of these estimates is like deciding whether a glass is half empty or half full, but certain supplemental figures can help put them in perspective. For example, one could say that "only" 62 percent of the sons and daughters persisted in the top fifth; but who would put it that way if told that 5 percent reached that level from a handicapped start in the bottom fifth? Put another way, there is indeed a "regression toward the mean" in this intergenerational relationship, but it is far less pronounced than those found by Galton for other characteristics. Sons who start at the top have nowhere to go except down, but how far down do they go? For example, the 28 married sons in the top fifth in table 3-10 started out with an average rank about 10 percent below the top. When their own economic success was rated, they were found to have slipped to an average rank 19 percent below the top—but still a long way up the ladder from the median.

Third, it should be remembered, on the other hand, that the effect of family background rank on a son embodies an unknown degree of inherited ability and productivity. As discussed in chapter 1, inequality of outcomes due to this type of inheritance seems less unfair than that due to pure privilege. Indeed, some may feel that inherited productivity differentials do not constitute inequality of opportunity in any meaningful sense.

Finally, it may be suggested that the problem of the inheritance of economic status is less serious than it appears, since the regression to the mean continues rapidly with each passing generation; as, for example, a grandson's economic status is obviously less closely related to his grandfather's than his father's was. But this is not necessarily true of the multiple relation between the son and *both* sets of grandparents. In any case, the problem at hand is the tendency of family affiliation to generate inequality of opportunity among the current generation. If the influence of the first generation on the well-being of the second is unjustifiable, this is hardly mitigated by the knowledge that the third generation is less closely related to the first. A son who is poor mainly because his father was poor is not likely to be consoled by the knowledge that his grandfather's economic status has less effect on him.

Even though the regression to the mean visible in these transition matrices may seem rather leisurely, the long-run results may seem perplexing. Why is economic inequality so stable over time? If the intergenerational relationship, though strong between adjacent generations, attenuates over time, why does this process not steadily reduce inequality? The answer is that inequality is measured at a single point in time. In a given year a man's economic status may be weakly related to that of his paternal great-grandfather, but it will be more strongly related to the collective status of all his great-grandparents. The relationship to grandparents will be closer still, and the influence of his immediate forebears even greater. So the weaker link between more distant generations appears irrelevant for appraising the inheritance of economic status as a perpetuator of inequality.

Qualifications and Conclusions

A brief appraisal of the detailed findings of this chapter may be in order.

The Age Effect in Perspective

It might be suggested that the correlation between son's age and decedent's age could be partly responsible for the goodness-of-fit of these regression models. One possibility is that the son's economic status (particularly the income dimension) might be positively related to his age and, therefore, to the age of his parents. Such a relationship would contribute to $\overline{R}^2$ and the indicated degree of explanation of inequality by family background, but it would be irrelevant to an analysis of inequality of opportunity, and it would be desirable to remove any such effect from the estimates of $\overline{R}^2$. It was noted above that there was no evidence of any age-status association in this sample, but, as a precaution, one additional effort was made to abstract from any possible age effects.

The object was to hold the son's age as nearly constant as possible in order to minimize any irrelevant age effect. The married son sample analyzed in table 3-13 was separated into age groups. Fortuitously, the 35–44 and 45–54 age classes each included about 80 observations, accounting for about two-thirds of the total between them. These subsamples were large enough for estimation and yet homogeneous enough virtually to eliminate any potential age effect. (The standard deviation of son's age was 2.7 years in the 35–44 group and 2.9 years in the 45–54 class, compared to 10.4 years in the sample as a whole.)

Table 3-13 gives salient features of these regressions by age class. As was to be expected from the lack of correlation of son's economic status with age, there is no substantial difference between the mean residence, occupation, or income measures of the two age groups.[45] The regression equation fitted is the same as in table 3-3, the basic model 3-2. The results are mixed. The fit for the 35–44 age group is closer than for the other group in all cases; more important, it is closer than for the entire sample

---

45. The slight differences that do appear show the older group lower on all three counts. In the case of income, at least, this is the opposite of the usual hypothesis. The substantially lower average education of the older group, on the other hand, was as expected.

Table 3-13. Regression Statistics Relating Economic Status of Married Sons, by Age Class, to Explicit Family Background Variables, Cleveland Area Sample, 1965–66[a]

Statistic and son's age class	Measure of son's economic status[b]					
	RATE	OCC	LOGY	Croy	(Croye)	(ED)
Sample size						
All	248	241	239	231	231	247
35–44	82	82	80	80	80	82
45–54	81	81	79	79	79	80
Mean						
All	4.38	4.22	0.957	0.000	0.000	4.30
35–44	4.50	4.34	0.962	0.000	0.000	4.49
45–54	4.33	4.25	0.951	0.000	0.000	4.11
$\bar{R}^2$						
All	0.257	0.278	0.239	0.417	0.442	0.280
35–44	0.236	0.318	0.259	0.435	0.485	0.344
45–54	0.231	0.282	0.148	0.307	0.347	0.236
Variables significant at the 5 percent level[c]						
All	GRST SIBS AED3 REL2 RAC2 TES2	All except GRST SIBS	SIBS AED2 AED3 REL3 RAC2	All except GRST	All	GRST SIBS AED2 AED3
35–44	SIBS REL2	GRST SIBS AGED AED3	AED2 AED3	GRST SIBS AGED AED3 REL2	GRST SIBS AGED AED3 AED2	GRST AED3
45–54	AED3 RAC2 TES2	GRST[d] AGED AED3 OCDT	AED3	AED2 AED3 REL3 RAC2	AED2 AED3 REL3 RAC2	SIBS AGED AED3

Sources: All ages, table 3-3; ages 35–44, regression results from same model used in table 3-3, but applied to the age groups separately.

a. The basic sample is defined in table 2-2, note b.

b. The measures of economic status are defined in table 2-2, note a, except *Croye*, which adds son's education to *Croy*.

c. The variables are defined in table 3-1.

d. Sign opposite from that hypothesized.

on all criteria except the residence rating. So, for this very homogeneous age group the family effect appears even more strongly than before, thus indicating no misleading role of age in the previous results. On the other hand, the family effect in the older group appears weaker than that for the entire sample except in the prediction of occupation. On average, the separate fits are closer for occupation than the global result, but less so for residence and income. For the composite status measures, on balance the overall fit is somewhat closer than for the homogeneous age groups.[46] So there is evidence of only a very slight previous exaggeration of the intergenerational relationship.

The regression coefficients themselves do not dispute this conclusion. Table 3-13 shows that cutting the sample size by two-thirds left fewer significant coefficients. But the 40 that were significant in the subsamples all supported the original hypotheses except the gross estate variable in the occupation equation. This factor has been generally insignificant throughout, and its significance here at the 5 percent level can be dismissed as a chance occurrence.[47]

Finally, the same test was repeated for the married daughter (son-in-law) sample with virtually identical results; in fact, there was even less evidence of any misleading age effect. In short, these exercises controlling for age leave no concern that any spurious age effect has been exaggerating the importance of the inheritance of economic success.

Other Qualifications and Comparisons

The results above for age groups may be checked for plausibility against those in the Duncan study, based on a huge 1962 sample.[48] Their background variables were father's educational attainment and occupational status and the son's number of siblings. For non-Negro men in 1962, these variables explained 20 percent of the variance in occupation in the 35–44 age group and 17 percent in the 45–54 age group. The results for the different sample and broader model used here were 32 percent and 28 percent, respectively. Duncan and colleagues explained 9 percent and 10 percent of the variance of income for these two age groups, while here the results for the *logarithm* of income were 26 percent and 15 percent. For the intermediate variable, education, the Duncan $\bar{R}^2$ values were 27 percent and 26 percent; the present broader model did little better, with $\bar{R}^2$ values of 34 percent and 24 percent.

Do these comparisons cast any doubt on the present results? The greater

46. For example, the overall explanation of *Croye* is 44.2 percent, compared to an average of 41.6 percent in the age-controlled groups.
47. On the other hand, gross estate was more influential in the younger group than in the whole sample, but it is difficult to develop a rationale for this.
48. Duncan, Featherman, and Duncan, *Socioeconomic Background*, p. 43.

background effect on occupation and income found here seems entirely in line with what would be expected from the more detailed information available.[49] The fact that the present explanation of income is very much more complete could be due in part to the logarithmic transformation.[50] The Duncan results also cast no doubt on the even higher $\bar{R}^2$ values found elsewhere in this study. One gain was achieved by combining son's economic status measures, thereby reducing the noise in the data. Furthermore, a more complete explanation of son's status was accomplished by the analysis of brothers, which in effect utilized all background factors, known and unknown, that affected them jointly as members of the same family.

Possible qualifications of the present analysis were discussed in chapter 2 with respect to the study of brothers; they were judged to be largely offsetting and minor in net effect. The same seems true in the present context, a conclusion reenforced by the dismissal of the age difficulty above.[51] All in all, the various qualifications discussed throughout probably suggest that on balance the inheritance effect is underestimated, if anything. At least four features point in that direction. First, measurement error reduces the degree of explanation. Second, if more measures of son's status were available to combine, there would be a less erratic status measure and probably a higher degree of explanation. Third, chapter 2 showed that if the sample questionnaire results could have been included, the regressions would have been more successful. Fourth, if data were available on the second parent (and other forebears), the explanation would be even more complete. Finally, it may be added that the transition matrices presented here can be interpreted without the usual parametric assumptions. They present individual cases and may be judged for exactly what they are.

The gist of the broad conclusions of this chapter can be stated briefly. The explicit regression models rival the analysis of brothers in chapter 2, at least in explaining the composite indexes of son's economic success. This

49. The inclusion of nonwhites in the present study made for somewhat higher variance, but the effect on $\bar{R}^2$ was probably small because of their small number.
50. That the present model did not improve much on Duncan's explanation of education is a mystery, but it is of less interest in the present context where the main interest is in the ultimate economic status of the sons.
51. One additional technical check was run for the explicit regressions in this chapter. A generalized least-squares analysis was applied to find whether the within-family correlations seriously biased downward the standard errors. The analysis produced only slightly higher standard errors.

suggests that most of the background factors have been covered, either directly or by proxy. Still, the effects of specific background influences must be presented with caution. They show a startling net independent influence of parental education on the success of the son that is encouraging from the point of view of practical policy, at least in the long run. The results from a very small sample of nonwhites support the findings of others on the net effect of race, even when nonwhite sons are compared to white sons who are alike in the other measured respects. This too, like the less severe religious differentials and the family size factor, has practical policy implications, subject to the qualifications emphasized.

The magnitude of the predicted differentials in economic success attributable to different family backgrounds seems very large. Moreover, as shown by the equations and transition matrices, a son's chances of achieving specified economic goals vary enormously with the extent to which his family background gives him a head start or handicaps him in his career. This general conclusion is, of course, on firmer ground than the measured influence of any simple explicit background factor such as parental education.

chapter four **The Role of Education and Marital Selection in the Intergenerational Transmission of Economic Status**

In chapters 2 and 3 the inheritance of economic status has been shown to be a major force perpetuating economic inequality. What can be said of the working mechanism through which economic status is transmitted across generations? This is much more difficult to pin down than the process of transmission of *material* wealth; wealthy parents can influence the wealth of their sons clearly and directly through gifts and bequests. The concept of inheritance of economic status used here, however, refers to parental influence on a son's occupational achievement, income, and residence quality. When interviewed at an average of about forty-two, most of the sons in this across-the-board sample had only recently received a bequest, if they had at all; in virtually no case could a bequest have substantially affected these dimensions of a son's economic status. But parents rarely dictate by any other direct means the standing of their sons on these three criteria. Why then is there such a strong tendency for economic status to be inherited?

Chapter 2 assessed the overall closeness of the intergenerational economic relationship, and chapter 3 attempted to account for it statistically in terms of specific family background influences, a more difficult and speculative venture. Even more problematical is the present objective—to show *how* economic status tends to be transferred from parents to children. It is one thing to say that children start life with the same economic status as their parents, and thus some have head starts while others have handicaps. It is quite another to show why these childhood head starts and handicaps persist so strongly through life that their influence tends to be reflected in the son's own economic position as an adult.

The intergenerational statistical relationships portrayed here are very

122

clear, but the process underlying them is in deep shadow; at the very least, any conclusions must be carefully qualified. The chronic difficulty of interpreting some observed statistical relationships found in economics has been colorfully pictured by Robin Marris: "Imagine a man facing a closed box, into which he cannot see but out of which project through holes a large number of moveable pistons. He believes these pistons to be connected together inside the box by a complicated mechanism of cogs and levers."[1] We might think of one set of these visible pistons as representing the socioeconomic status characteristics of the present sample of parents, and another set the economic success measures for their sons. We have observed that when the parental pistons are depressed, those of the son usually are also. But what we want is a description of the invisible internal mechanism itself.

We can only speculate concerning the role of unmeasured factors such as ability and motivation represented by cogs and levers inside Marris's black box. Unfortunately, in economics (unlike the natural sciences) it is rarely possible to experiment, as one could by planned manipulation of these pistons. As Marris points out in terms of his analogy, the social sciences have special problems: there is a great deal of "play" in the mechanism; the basic linkages in the system are not in fact unchanging; and the investigator is not able to manipulate the pistons. "In short, the box is literally alive with gremlins."[2]

In the present case, interpretation of the observed statistical relationships is especially treacherous and is limited by the paucity of information on the intermediate factors responsible for the relationships. Having thus emphasized the speculative nature of any such interpretations, it remains to shed as much light as possible on the role of the intermediate processes. The logical starting point is the educational attainment of the son himself, the only clue available here as to the amount of human capital he has accumulated.

Education is an indicator of earning power. Insofar as it is inherited, it constitutes a part of the process through which economic status is transferred. Unlike a material inheritance, however, the inheritance of education remains in part a statistical concept—no more than a tendency. While many parents provide higher education directly and outright to their children, others do so only indirectly as taxpayers or through general encouragement. Even so, it seems safe to say that the parental influence

1. Robin Marris, *Economic Arithmetic* (Macmillan, 1958), p. 149.
2. Ibid., p. 151.

on the son's formal educational attainment is the most direct and concrete aspect of the process of economic status transmission.[3] It will be seen, however, that this available measure of son's human capital accumulation falls far short of explaining the observed degree of status inheritance. This inevitably encourages speculation as to other factors involved in the status transfer process. Part of the explanatory gap is undoubtedly due to the inadequate measurement of the son's human capital. Also involved are the inheritance of ability, ambition, and other unmeasured characteristics like speech and dress that may affect earning power both directly, and indirectly through their effect on education. It is tempting at least to speculate on these aspects of the inheritance process because the policy implications of any observed degree of inheritance depend in part on which processes underlie it.

Having concentrated so far (for methodological reasons) on *son's* inheritance of economic success, it is also time to ask to what extent parents tend to transfer their economic status to their daughters. At the time of the present survey, most of the daughters were housewives; the economic status of married daughters with respect to the three status criteria was therefore identified with that of their husbands. This amounts to interpreting the inheritance of economic success by the daughters as a matter of marital selection.

How did the economic head starts and handicaps of the daughters influence their economic status as adults through marriage? It will be shown that daughters tend to select husbands whose economic status is almost as closely related to that of their parents-in-law as is the relationship between sons and their own parents. Marital selection thus tends to perpetuate inequality. At the same time, it is interesting to note in passing that daughters in this sample tended to marry men of lower economic status than their own brothers.

The Role of Son's Education and Other Intermediate Factors in the Intergenerational Transmission of Economic Status

Horace Mann proclaimed education to be "the great equalizer." For years it was assumed that equalizing educational opportunity would go a

3. Of course, this influence is conveyed in various ways. Also, the emphasis on formal education is not intended to downgrade the importance of parental influence on the preschool educational environment that affects later attitudes, attainments, and utilization of education.

long way toward equalizing individual chances of economic success. This assumption was behind the great emphasis on education and training in the "war against poverty" declared in the sixties by the U.S. government. Studies of the determinants of earnings gave early support to this assumption and to the human-capital explanation of inequality by indicating a substantial return to each additional year of schooling.[4] To many this suggested that raising the educational levels of the lower economic strata would promote equality. Skeptics replied that educational attainment is very strongly influenced by socioeconomic origins. In this context the efficacy of education policy as an economic equalizer gained additional support from work dealing explicitly with the effects of socioeconomic origins, such as that of Blau and Duncan in 1967.[5] These studies found a relatively weak effect of family background on educational attainment. More important, they found a man's educational attainment to have a substantial effect on his chances of success, *independently* of his socioeconomic origins. However, as disillusion with the war against poverty (in practice) began to set in, studies appeared challenging the power of education to alleviate poverty.[6]

Educational attainment of sons plays two separable roles in the determination of economic inequality, one inherited and one independent. The first objective here is to estimate the extent to which the observed inheritance of economic status is accomplished through the intermediate inheritance of educational attainment. This involves decomposition of the intergenerational correlation into what have been conventionally called the direct effect of family background, and its indirect effect through its influence on son's education (which, in turn, affects his success).

The second role of educational attainment is its own estimated direct effect independent of family background and any other factors such as

4. See, for example, Giora Hanoch, "An Economic Analysis of Earnings and Schooling," *Journal of Human Resources,* vol. 2 (Summer 1967), pp. 310–29. These studies of earnings functions tended to confirm the human-capital hypothesis as presented, for example, in Jacob Mincer, "Investment in Human Capital and Personal Income Distribution," *Journal of Political Economy,* vol. 66 (August 1958), pp. 281–302.

5. Peter M. Blau and Otis Dudley Duncan, *The American Occupational Structure* (Wiley, 1967).

6. See, for example, W. Lee Hansen, Burton A. Weisbrod, and William J. Scanlon, "Schooling and Earnings of Low Achievers," *American Economic Review,* vol. 60 (June 1970), pp. 409–18. For a downgrading of the effects of *both* family background and schooling, see Christopher Jencks and others, *Inequality: A Reassessment of The Effect of Family and Schooling in America* (Basic Books, 1972).

ability that may precede and influence it. So the objective here is to measure the extent to which son's education explains the residual degree of inequality after all prior influences have been allowed to explain whatever they can. Insofar as these prior influences have been adequately represented in the model, the estimated independent effect of son's education would be of obvious relevance to the formulation of public policy.

Educational Attainment as a Conveyor of Economic Status across Generations

This effort to disentangle the direct effects of family background from its indirect effects via son's educational attainment is supported by the plausibility of an assumed "recursive" chain of causation. In its simplest form, the model assumes the following causal order: family background (socioeconomic status) to son's educational attainment to son's economic status. Each variable is assumed to depend on the variables before it, and not vice versa.[7] The a priori plausibility of this unambiguous causal ordering is about the only bright spot in an otherwise bleak methodological scene. It alleviates the usual problems faced in dealing with simultaneous relationships, but it does not eliminate them. It may be difficult to establish that the relationship is causal, but if it is, at least we know which way it goes. For example, we can define model I as consisting of two approximate linear relations among two endogenous variables and the predetermined variable, family background.[8]

(4-1) $$ED = a_1 + b_1\,FB \qquad\quad +u_1$$
(4-2) $$LOGY = a_2 + b_2\,FB + c_2\,ED + u_2.$$

Education is viewed here as an intermediate variable serving to mediate the transmission of economic status from parent to son. The first equation portrays the tendency for education to be inherited in the sense that a son's educational attainment is dependent on parental economic status.

7. As mentioned earlier, some dimensions of family background, such as wealth, may be influenced by the son's economic status, but these feedbacks are assumed to be of second-order importance.

8. Parental economic status is denoted by FB, the son's educational attainment by ED, and the logarithm of his family income by $LOGY$. (The us are assumed to be random deviations from the relationship.) Other variants of model I appear later, in which other economic status variables such as the composite indicator $Croy$ are substituted for $LOGY;$ also the son's age and number employed in the family are entered into the recursive chain.

The coefficient b_1 is the estimate of the total effect of FB on ED, including the direct effects of FB and its indirect effects through ability and other excluded mediating factors. The second relation recognizes that son's income depends not only on family background but is also subject to the independent influence of the son's own education.

Chapters 2 and 3 were concerned with the overall relationship between economic status and family background, without consideration of the intermediate role of son's education. For example, chapter 3 included estimates of the reduced-form equation derivable from model I:

(4-3) $LOGY = (a_2 + a_1c_2) + (b_2 + b_1c_2) FB + (u_2 + c_2u_1).$

A single estimate of the coefficient $(b_2 + b_1c_2)$ was taken as a measure of the extent to which $LOGY$ was inherited—that is, the total effect of FB on $LOGY$. Estimation of the two equations in model I offers a decomposition of this total into a direct and indirect effect of FB on $LOGY$. The direct effect of FB on $LOGY$, with ED held constant, is given by b_2. But an indirect effect through the influence of FB on son's ED is also recognized by the model. A unit advantage in FB is reflected in an estimated inheritance of b_1 extra units of education; then relation 2 indicates that this inherited educational advantage leads to an estimated b_1c_2 extra units of $LOGY$.

It is useful to check this decomposition via model I against the reduced-form estimate of total effect by equation 4-3. For that reason table 4-1 gives two or three equations explaining each economic status variable. In model I, for example, the first equation for $LOGY$ gives the estimated total effect; the second yields the decomposition and sum of the components. Insofar as this type of decomposition is accurately estimated, it is useful for its implications as to the effect of altering by public policy the degree to which education is inherited.

Even though the variables in model I operate in a convenient causal sequence, a potential bias remains in the estimation of education effects. Insofar as unmeasured factors such as genetic endowments persist across generations, affecting both the son's education and his status, and are not controlled by the available background variables, the coefficient for education will have an upward bias. Some of the indicated explanatory power would actually be due to the missing ability factor, and the effect of changing education by policy would thus be exaggerated. For example, some parents may have significantly greater ability than predictable from their known characteristics. If this ability also exerts a positive influence

Table 4-1. Recursive Models Decomposing Effects of Family Background and Son's Education on Son's Economic Status: Beta Coefficients, Cleveland Area Basic Sample of All Sons,[a] 1965–66

Intermediate variable	Dependent variable[b]	Predetermined variable			Effect of FB[d] via		Total effect of FB	$\bar{R}^2$
		FB[c]	AGE	ED	AGE	ED		
Model I:								
Son's education (ED)	ED	0.501 (0.052)	...	...	...	...	0.501	0.246
	LOGY	0.424 (0.056)	...	...	...	...	0.424	0.174
	LOGY	0.305 (0.064)	...	0.231 (0.064)	...	0.116	0.421	0.210
	Croy	0.573 (0.052)	...	...	...	...	0.573	0.323
	Croy	0.364 (0.056)	...	0.396 (0.056)	...	0.198	0.562	0.435
Model II:								
Son's age (AGE) and education (ED)	AGE	-0.073[e] (0.060)	...	...	...	...	-0.073	-0.002
	ED	0.501 (0.052)	...	...	...	...	0.501	0.246
	ED	0.484 (0.050)	-0.260 (0.050)	...	0.019	...	0.503	0.311
	LOGY	0.424 (0.056)	...	...	...	...	0.424	0.174
	LOGY	0.431 (0.056)	0.122 (0.056)	...	-0.009	...	0.422	0.186

Model III:
Product of age and education (AGE·ED)

			AGE·ED		AGE·ED		
LOGY	0.277 (0.063)	0.206 (0.057)	0.307 (0.066)	−0.015	0.154	0.416	0.246
Croy	0.573 (0.052)	...	...	...	...	0.573	0.323
Croy	0.578 (0.051)	0.109 (0.051)	...	−0.008	...	0.570	0.332
Croy	0.346 (0.054)	0.198 (0.047)	0.450 (0.055)	−0.014	0.225	0.557	0.470
A·E	0.424 (0.054)		...		...	0.424	0.174
LOGY	0.424 (0.056)		...		...	0.424	0.174
LOGY	0.257 (0.059)		0.370 (0.059)		0.157	0.414	0.280
Croy	0.573 (0.052)		...		...	0.573	0.323
Croy	0.386 (0.052)		0.418 (0.052)		0.177	0.563	0.462

Source: See appendix A.

a. For a description of the sample, see table 2-2, note b. The beta coefficients are "standardized" by estimating them after transformation of the variables to standard deviation units measured from the mean. Reduced forms are included for comparison. Figures in parentheses are standard errors.

b. For definitions, see table 2-2, note a.

c. FB denotes parental economic status. It is the "first principal component" of the ten family background variables in table 3-2. For explanation of first principal component, see table 2-2, note f.

d. These effects can be estimated by the formulas of path analysis. See, for example, Otis D. Duncan, "Path Analysis: Sociological Examples," American Journal of Sociology, vol. 72 (July 1966), pp. 1–16. Or they can be estimated intuitively by multiplication. For example, in the first of the three recursive models, the indirect effect of FB on LOGY through ED is (0.501) (0.231) = 0.116. In the second model the indirect effect of FB on LOGY through AGE is (−0.073) (0.206) = −0.015, and through ED is (0.501) (0.307) = 0.154. The sum of direct and indirect effects differs from the original total effect in each case, because of the slight difference in the observations available for regressions at different stages in the system. (The effect of FB through ED includes the indirect effect of FB on ED [through AGE].)

e. Not significant at the 5 percent level.

on both son's education and ultimate economic status, the error terms in model I will be correlated, causing a bias in the education coefficient.[9]

For simplicity, table 4-1 uses the single composite measure of family background FB, even though this index explains much less of the variation of son's economic status than was accomplished by the earlier analysis of brothers. The coefficients of the predetermined variables in the table are significant at the 5 percent level or better except where indicated. The regression of $LOGY$ on FB yields a coefficient of 0.424 as a measure of the total effect of family background on income.[10] However, family background also explains about one-quarter of the variation in the intermediate variable—son's education. Thus when education is added as an explanatory variable the direct effect of family background is found to be only 0.305. The indirect effect of FB through ED is $(0.501)(0.231) = 0.116$.[11] This breakdown of direct and indirect effects totals 0.421, agreeing closely with the 0.424 estimate of the total effect of FB on $LOGY$. The standard errors of the coefficients are small, and this decomposition appears quite accurate. So this model suggests that about one-quarter of the effect of family background on income is conveyed through its causally prior effect on son's education.

The message of the regressions involving the composite index of son's economic status $Croy$ is similar. The total effect of family background is 0.573, but more than one-third of this effect is conveyed indirectly through the effect of family background on the son's education, which in turn promotes his economic success. These results must all be qualified, of course, by the recognition that the son's education may be getting some credit here for other intermediate influences with which it is correlated, such as son's ability.

One intermediate variable that is available and clearly correlated with son's education is his age: the older the son, the less his predicted educa-

9. For recent work using a recursive model, see Gary Chamberlain and Zvi Griliches, "Unobservables with a Variance-Components Structure: Ability, Schooling, and the Economic Success of Brothers," *International Economic Review*, vol. 16 (June 1975), pp. 428ff.

10. The beta coefficient recorded there is identical to the simple correlation coefficient.

11. The indirect effect may be illustrated by a family background one standard deviation above the mean. The predicted value of ED is 0.501 standard deviations above the mean. Since an education one standard deviation above the mean yields a predicted $LOGY$ 0.231 above, this indirect effect of FB through ED is the product of the two coefficients, or 0.116.

tion. Model II in table 4-1 inserts *AGE* in the recursive chain between *FB* and *ED*. The family background measure *FB* has no significant effect on son's age, but the latter plays an important role in the rest of the recursive system. It contributes significantly to the explanation of *LOGY* and *Croy,* but (as concluded in chapter 3) its contribution should be regarded as that of a control variable that, in effect, sharpens the meaning of the measure of education in years. Its coefficient is positive when included with *ED* in the explanation of son's economic status because, given education in years, the older the son, the greater his competitive educational standing.[12]

So the inclusion of *AGE* is simply a methodological device. It brings out more strongly the role of education as an intermediate variable conveying the effects of family background. Model II shows the indirect effect of *FB* on *LOGY* via education to be 0.154/0.424, or about 36 percent of the total background effect. In the case of the composite index *Croy,* son's education conveys about 39 percent of the background influence on son's success. Note also the trivial (insignificant) role of *AGE* as an intermediate variable. The presence of son's age in the model served only to sharpen the education measure by, in effect, placing it on a relative basis. The result was a substantial and plausible increase in the role of education as a conductor of economic status, compared to the findings in model I.[13]

If the insignificant indirect effects through age are due to its association with education and attributed entirely to the latter, the estimated role of education is diminished very slightly. The purpose of including age explicitly was simply to show its insignificant independent role as a conveyor of background effects. As a simplification then, the entire difference between the total effect and direct effect in this model will be attributed to education. For example, the indirect effect of *FB* on *LOGY* via *ED* will be put at $0.424 - 0.277 = 0.147$, or nearly 35 percent. For the composite

12. It may also be true that son's age proxies for experience and on-the-job training as determinants of earnings. See Mincer, "Investment in Human Capital." However, no effect of age on economic status, independent of education, was revealed in this sample. This may be due in part to the fact that the sons in the sample are rather homogeneous in age, and that most may be on the relatively level portion of the age-income profile.

13. It is apparent that the breakdown of direct and indirect effects in these models conflicts appreciably with the original estimate of total effects, primarily owing to the use of all available observations at each stage in the recursive model. For example, there were more observations available for son's education than for son's income.

index, the estimate of the indirect effect of family background mediated by education is 0.227, or about 40 percent. This estimate is reasonably accurate; the standard error of the 0.277 estimate for *Croy* is about 0.075. However, it must be remembered that an important part of this statistical role of education may itself be mediated by prior factors such as ability.

Since the indirect effects via *AGE* itself proved trivial, the interaction term *AGE·ED* was tested in model III to portray the net effects of education in a single variable.[14] This approach shows inherited age-adjusted education conveying nearly 40 percent of the effect of family background on *LOGY*, but its estimated indirect effect on *Croy* is cut to about 30 percent. The 35 percent figure for the indirect effect of education on *LOGY* in model II appears to be the most typical, and it seems appropriate to use it for illustration of the practical meaning and significance of the concept of the inheritance of education.

What may be concluded from this evidence on the extent to which family background effects are channeled through their influence on son's education? The results offer a basis for estimating the *maximum* effect of a hypothetical neutralization of the influence of family background on educational attainment.[15] The reason that the available estimates should probably be viewed as the maximum is that son's education is undoubtedly proxying in part for excluded intermediate influences such as image, ability, and motivation, which are presumably also correlated with family background. Thus, reducing the educational advantage of a privileged son would have less net effect than indicated. However, working in the opposite direction is our inability to allow for variations in the quality of education. This means that the effect of education will be exaggerated less than it might appear.

Suppose the total family effect on education were eliminated, as, for example, by such a crude policy as randomization of educational attainment. The coefficient representing the total effect of *FB* on *ED* in model II would be reduced from 0.501 to zero, as would the indirect effects of family background via education. How would this affect the predicted economic status of advantaged and disadvantaged sons? For example, in the case of income, the original estimate of total background effect pre-

14. The correlation of *AGE·ED* with its components was so close that inclusion of the latter made accurate estimation impossible.

15. This does not necessarily refer to complete equalization of education, but only to the neutralization of parental influence on it. Educational attainment could continue to be allocated unequally even if the criteria were not correlated with family economic status.

dicts that a son 5 percent from the top in socioeconomic background rank will have an income $(1.645)(0.424) = 0.697$ standard deviations, or 38 percent, above the median.[16] If the indirect advantage via education were erased, the remaining direct effect of his favorable background would yield a forecast of an income only 23 percent above the median.[17] If, on the other hand, the indirect background effect through education is present, a son from a family 5 percent from the bottom rank is predicted to have an income 28 percent below the median, but only 19 percent below if the educational disadvantage is eliminated. Put another way, the total family background advantage yields a prediction that the son from the high-ranking family will have an income 92 percent higher than the man from the poor family. Eliminating the indirect family effect through education would reduce the predicted income differential to 52 percent.

These predicted income differentials due to the inheritance of education are smaller than would be obtained from the comprehensive family background analysis in chapter 2 based on brothers. There the total effect of background on $LOGY$ was estimated at 0.636;[18] in that case the predicted value of income for the advantaged son in the last example would be 174 percent higher than for the disadvantaged son. A typical result in table 4-1 is that the inheritance of education accounts for about 35 percent of the total family effect. If this indirect effect were eliminated, the expected income advantage of the favored son would be cut to 92 percent.

As stressed earlier, these reductions in predicted differentials are rough upper limits that assume the estimated indirect effect of family background in table 4-1 to be conveyed entirely through its influence on son's education—a variable subject to control through public policy. Almost certainly this assumption exaggerates the effect of simply breaking the link between son's educational attainment and family background.

Education as a Transmitter of Specific Background Influences

Table 4-2 displays recursive models relating son's economic status to intermediate factors and to the ten basic measures of six explicit parental influences—education, occupation, number of children, race, religion,

16. This prediction assumes normality of the implied economic background index as well as normality of $LOGY$. It uses the standard deviation of $LOGY$ for all sons.
17. The entire difference between 0.424 and 0.277 is attributed to education. The prediction is $(1.645)(0.277)$ standard deviations above the median, or 23 percent.
18. This is the square root of $\bar{R}_i^2$ in table 2-2.

Table 4-2. Total Effect of Specific Family Background Variables and Their (Implied) Indirect Effect via Intermediate Variables: Beta Coefficients, Cleveland Area Basic Sample of All Sons, 1965–66

| Dependent variable[a] | Family background variables[b] | | | | | | | | | | Other predetermined variables | | | $\bar{R}^2$ |
	AGED	AED2	AED3	OCDT	SIBS	RAC2	REL2	REL3	GRST	TES2	ED[a]	AGE·ED	EMPL[c]	
ED[d]	−0.087*	0.157	0.350	0.082*	−0.116	−0.080*	−0.024*	0.090*	0.142	−0.077*	...	...	...	0.267
LOGY	0.108	0.156	0.292	0.035*	−0.147	−0.120	−0.074*	0.083*	0.061*	−0.071*	...	...	...	0.199
LOGY	0.126	0.123	0.218	0.017*	−0.123	−0.103	−0.069*	0.064*	0.031*	−0.055*	0.211	...	...	0.228
LOGY	−0.054*	0.125	0.170	0.013*	−0.097	−0.109	−0.042*	0.046*	0.030*	−0.040*	...	0.382	...	0.287
LOGY	−0.056*	0.124	0.213	−0.001*	−0.138	−0.105	−0.022*	0.066*	0.047*	−0.047*	...	0.343	0.288	0.367
ED[e]	−0.040*	0.144	0.349	0.094*	−0.128	−0.077*	−0.020*	0.092*	0.156	−0.060*	...	...	...	0.291
Croy	0.160	0.131	0.283	0.154	−0.184	−0.195	−0.117	0.111	0.076*	−0.120	...	...	...	0.394
Croy	0.175	0.076*	0.150	0.118	−0.135	−0.165	−0.110	0.076*	0.017*	−0.096	0.382	...	...	0.495
Croy	−0.030*	0.101	0.155	0.125	−0.130	−0.185	−0.085*	0.070*	0.041*	−0.094	...	0.414	...	0.494
Croy	−0.034*	0.102	0.172	0.116	−0.147	−0.183	−0.079*	0.078*	0.051*	−0.095	...	0.402	0.112	0.504

Source: See appendix A.
a. For definitions, see table 2-2, note a.
b. For definitions, see table 3-1.
c. Number employed in son's family.
d. Regression run on observations for which LOGY was available.
e. Regression run on observations for which Croy was available.
* Not significant at the 5 percent level.

and wealth.[19] The table shows first that the ten-variable background model explains about 27 percent of the variance of son's educational attainment. The significant measured influences were found to be parental education, number of children, race, and estate size.

The indirect effect of these specific characteristics on income through son's education may be estimated as the product of their coefficients and the 0.211 coefficient for *ED* (when the latter is added to the background model explaining *LOGY*). The indirect background effects of *AED2*, *AED3*, *SIBS*, and *GRST* are 0.033, 0.074, −0.024, and 0.030, respectively.[20] These indicate that for the four significant background variables the percentage of their influence on *LOGY* accounted for by son's inherited education is 21, 25, 16, and 49, respectively. These fractions seem rather low, except for the transmitted effect of estate size, and the total effect of the latter on income was not significant in the first place. In the case of the other four background measures that significantly affected both son's education and ultimate economic status, the first impression is that the role of education as a conductor of background influences on income seems minor.

One reason for the seemingly ineffective role of inherited education as an intermediate variable is the crudity of the education measure in the absence of an age adjustment. The third equation for *LOGY* shows the effect of substituting the interaction variable *AGE·ED* for unadjusted son's education. The effect of this interaction variable is again attributed entirely to the son's relative educational position. With this refined portrayal of son's education, $\bar{R}^2$ rises from 23 to 29 percent, and the coefficient of the variable representing son's education increases substantially. Its indicated intermediate role is markedly enhanced in the case of two of the significant parental variables, *AED3* and *SIBS*. Inherited education is now estimated to account for 42 percent of the influence of parental college education and 34 percent of the effect of family size.

The only other available intermediate factor besides education that was

19. See equations 3-1 and 3-2 for derivation of the basic background model. The decedent's age is not listed among these parental influences, since its use in the model has been interpreted purely as a methodological device for revealing more clearly the role of parental education.

20. These estimated indirect effects are identical to the difference between the coefficients in the first two equations for *LOGY*. This alternative estimate of the indirect effect of each background characteristic is the residual between total and direct effects. It agrees with the first in this case because the two equations explaining *LOGY* used the same observations as the one explaining ED.

found to affect son's economic status consistently was the number employed in the family, *EMPL* (the number of earners in the family when headed by sons at an average age of forty-two). It can be assumed, therefore, that *EMPL* comes after education in the causal chain.[21] The addition of number employed to the model raises $\bar{R}^2$ again from 29 percent to 37 percent, and the coefficient is highly significant with a *t*-ratio near six. However, this cuts the indicated effect of *AGE·ED* in the prior equation by only 10 percent. Thus, this second substantial improvement of the model diminishes only slightly the overall role of son's education in transmitting the effect of family background on son's income. Even so, this small decline in the estimated role of education is clearly responsible in part for the greater apparent direct effect of a parent's college education and number of children on *LOGY*. The combined mediation of *AGE·ED* and *EMPL* accounts for only 27 percent and 6 percent, respectively, of the total effect of these two background factors.[22]

All models continue to show about 20 percent of the effects of parental high school attendance on income and only 10 to 15 percent of the effects of race to be indirect via education.[23] The results for race are interesting, although weak since there are only five nonwhites in the sample. The third equation suggests that only about one-tenth of the effect of nonwhite race can be attributed to the inheritance of less education, as measured in years. This is basically consistent with the tentative conclusion reached

21. The relation of this variable to income is less clear. The primary direction of causation is undoubtedly from the number employed to income: the more family members who work, the more they tend to bring home. However, a possible reverse causation must be recognized as a minor qualification: the higher the family income, the less need for more than one person to work. Still, the strong positive relationship actually observed indicates such a feedback to be of second-order importance at most. This question is discussed in Jacob Mincer, *Schooling, Experience, and Earnings* (Columbia University Press for the National Bureau of Economic Research, 1974).

22. The magnitude of the coefficients of *AED3* and *SIBS* rose substantially and inexplicably with the insertion of *EMPL* in the recursive model. This implies that *EMPL* is transmitting a negative indirect effect of *AED3* on *LOGY* and a positive indirect effect of *SIBS* owing to a negative coefficient on *AED3* and a positive coefficient on *SIBS* in the background model explaining *EMPL*. These coefficients are significant and difficult to rationalize, but it might at least be suggested that the more siblings a son has, the less advantaged he is, and the more likely a second earner is to be needed in the family.

23. Some of the insignificant effects of background factors on *LOGY* are also reduced in magnitude. For example, the weak coefficient for occupation was wiped out by the addition of the two intermediate variables, indicating any effect to be indirect. The indicated total effect of each wealth variable was also seen to have an appreciable indirect component.

in chapter 3, where nonwhite race was found to depress income substantially even though the race factor did not significantly reduce the years of education completed by the sample of married sons. Here, in the sample of all sons, the depressing effect of race on the son's years of education is of at least marginal significance, but the principal conclusion is the same; the effect of race on income is not due in any major degree to the intermediate effect of race on education. The explanation must still be sought elsewhere in discriminatory practices, the quality of education, and other unmeasured causes.[24]

Next to be considered is the three-variable indicator of son's economic status *Croy*. This criterion indicates a stronger role played by education in transmitting the effects of family background, revealed first in the indirect effects of parental characteristics implied by a comparison of the first two *Croy* equations in table 4-2. Again, *AED2, AED3, SIBS,* and *GRST* are the background factors significantly affecting the son's education. However, according to this model, the inheritance of education is responsible for 42, 47, 27, and 78 percent, respectively, of the effects of these background influences. This suggests that nearly half of the favorable effects of parental high school and college attendance and a quarter of the effect of family size are transmitted through their intermediate effects on the son's educational attainment. Although gross estate had no significant effect on ultimate economic status, its substantial impact on education accounted for nearly all of the observed effect on *Croy*. All background factors except gross estate size showed significant influence on the index of son's economic status. Although religion and testacy did not have a significant impact on education, the intermediary role of education was appreciable in these cases. One-third of the advantage of a Jewish heritage was conveyed through its influence on the son's education; one-fifth of the wealth disadvantage indicated by the proxy intestacy was transmitted through son's education.[25]

The enhanced role of education in the determination of the son's composite economic status index (compared to its effect on income) is due to

24. For recent evidence on the quality of black education, see Finis Welch, "Measurement of the Quality of Schooling," *American Economic Review,* vol. 56 (May 1966, *Papers and Proceedings, 1965*), pp. 379–92; and idem, "Black-White Differences in Returns to Schooling" (National Bureau of Economic Research, 1972; processed).

25. The variable *AGED* is shown to have had an insignificant negative impact on son's education, leading to minor negative indirect effects of *AGED* on both *LOGY* and *Croy*. This negative relation between decedent's age and son's education is plausible, but can be dismissed as being far short of statistical significance. The variable *AGED* continues to have only a methodological role.

Table 4-3. Breakdown of Effects of Family Background and Son's Education on Two Criteria of Son's Economic Status, Cleveland Area Basic Sample of Brothers,[a] 1965–66

Economic status measure[b]	Beta coefficients[c] of predetermined variables		Indirect effect of FB via (ED)[e]	$\bar{R}^2$
	FB[d]	ED		
ED	.636	...	...	.405
OCC	.603	...	...	.364
OCC	(.152)	.709	.452	.663
Croy	.752	...	...	.566
Croy	(.471)	.441	.281	.671

Source: See appendix A.

a. For a description of the sample, see table 2-2, note b.

b. For definitions, see table 2-2, note a.

c. From the regression on family dummy variables, except as noted.

d. FB is the hypothetical family background index that would yield the same $\bar{R}^2$ as the regression on family dummy variables. The coefficient in the cases with one independent variable—the total effect of FB—is the square root of $\bar{R}^2$. The coefficient in parentheses is the estimated direct effect of FB derived as the difference between the total effect of family background (first coefficient) and the indirect effect through son's education (see note e).

e. This is the product of (1) the coefficient of the regression of ED on FB and (2) the coefficient on ED in the multiple regression. Thus, for OCC, the indirect effect of FB via ED is (0.709)(0.637) = 0.452.

the much larger independent effect of education on this index. The beta coefficient is 0.382 (compared to 0.211 for income) and carries a t-ratio greater than seven. This is due in turn to the strong correlation of the son's occupation (included in the economic status index) with his educational attainment. This is also the strongest intermediary role of educational attainment found in this study. To illustrate and confirm it, an aggregate analysis of family background effects based on the original sample of brothers is shown in table 4-3. The set of family dummies represents a more inclusive portrayal of the effects of family background and achieves a greater degree of explanation of economic status. Yet it explains only 36 percent of son's occupational classification. Despite the extreme roughness of the latter measure, addition of son's educational attainment to the model raises the $\bar{R}^2$ to a striking 66 percent.[26] More germane to the decomposition of family influences is the estimated 0.452 indirect effect of family background on occupation transmitted through education. This indicates that about three-quarters of the family effect on occupational status in this sample of brothers is transmitted via the inheritance of educational attainment.[27]

26. The ability of education to explain this crude occupation index is attested to by a simple correlation of 0.767; this is a 59 percent explanation of the variance in occupation. Of course, as will be shown, much of this represents indirect background effects.

27. It should be repeated that part of this measured influence of son's education probably reflects its correlation with unobserved genetic and environmental factors.

The strong intermediary role of education in the occupation model shown in table 4-3 helps explain its importance in determination of the economic status index *Croy*, which comprises occupational as well as residence and income.[28] The estimated 37 percent indirect overall effect of background on this index through education is reasonably consistent with the strong indirect effects of specific parental characteristics in table 4-2. It also agrees closely with the estimated intermediary role of education in table 4-1. The purpose of table 4-3 here, however, is to highlight the very important role of the correlation between occupation and education in the process of transmitting overall economic status from parent to son.

Table 4-2 shows that taking account of son's age and the number employed in the family has less importance for the explanation of the composite index than of income. However, the age-adjusted education measure restores parental high school education to a significant role and reduces the estimated fraction mediated by son's education from 42 percent to 23 percent. Similarly, the fraction of racial effects attributable to the son's educational disadvantage is cut to a mere 5 percent. Finally, the relatively low educational attainment of Catholic sons accounts for about 27 percent of the indicated effect of that religious origin on economic status. The direct effect of Catholic origins on the composite status index is thus no longer significant when the intermediate role of education is taken into account.

In sum, the relationships in table 4-2, though mixed, are generally consistent with the aggregative analysis in table 4-1. Inherited levels of educational attainment account for up to 45 percent of the effect of parental education and family size. The most pronounced intermediary role is in the case of the parent who attended college. Also, the intermediate role of son's education is clearly stronger in the case of the economic status index *Croy*, because son's occupation is more strongly influenced by his education than is his income. On the other hand, some background influences,

28. The strong relationship between occupation and education also invites a variation of the recursive model explaining *Croy* to insert occupation itself in the causal chain between education and ultimate economic status. This was tried with the composite index stripped to include only residence rating and income. However, the available sample was not large enough to overcome the explosive effects of this strong collinearity of education and occupation. For a more successful application of this type of model, see Hansen and others, "Schooling and Earnings." It is also likely that a components of variance analysis would make more efficient use of the data than the dummy variable approach which consumes many degrees of freedom. (See Marc Nerlove, "Further Evidence on the Estimation of Dynamic Economic Relations from a Time Series of Cross Sections," *Econometrica*, vol. 39 (March 1971), pp. 359–82.

especially race, show much less evidence of being conveyed through son's education. On balance, the role of education in transmitting specific parental influences appears sufficient to account for the results of the aggregative analysis in table 4-1.

Independent Effects of Educational Attainment

Until now, the analysis has focused on the fraction of family effects on ultimate economic status that can be accounted for by inherited educational attainment. The next question is the *independent* effect of son's education over and above its role as a conduit for measured background influences. In terms of the simple model I (equations 4-1 and 4-2), the first task entailed breaking down the total effect of family background on *LOGY* into a direct effect b_2 and an indirect effect estimated as b_1c_2—the portion of background effect accounted for by inherited education. Now the interest is in c_2 itself—a measure of the effect of education with family background held constant (through its inclusion in the same equation). Once again the analysis must be qualified by the fact that a portion of the estimated independent effects of education are themselves not truly independent, since they inevitably transmit the effects of *excluded* prior variables that affect education, such as ability. It is also true that measurement error in the *included* background variables can lead to exaggeration of the independent role of education. (These qualifications are considered in detail later.)

Various estimates of the independent effect of education have already appeared in table 4-1, which is based on a single composite background index. The beta coefficients for education range from 0.231 in the sample explaining *LOGY* to 0.450 in the determination of the composite economic status index. Model II allows for variations of the son's education with his age, and the composite measure of success includes the occupational grade which is more closely correlated with education than is income.

Since the accuracy of the measurement of family background affects estimation of the independent effect of education, results are given in table 4-4 for two more reliable background constructs. The first is based on the individual background characteristics underlying the single background index used in table 4-1; the second is based on the analysis of brothers, which implicitly includes all known and unknown factors

Table 4-4. Independent Effect of Son's Education on Son's Economic Status, Cleveland Area Basic Sample,[a] 1965–66

Status measure for sons[b]	Sample and background variables[c]	Beta coefficients of independent variables			$\bar{R}^2$
		ED^d	$AGE \cdot ED^d$	$EMPL^e$	
LOG Y	All sons, ten basic variables	.211 (.065)	...	...	.228
	($\bar{R}^2 = .199$)	...	.382 (.067)	...	.287
		...	.343 (.064)	.288 (.050)	.367
	Brothers, family dummies	.129 (.127)	...	...	.393
	($\bar{R}^2 = .392$)	...	.278 (.140)	...	.426
		...	.292 (.129)	.346 (.095)	.514
Croy	All sons, ten basic variables	.382 (.054)	...	...	.495
	($\bar{R}^2 = .394$)	...	.414 (.059)	...	.494
		...	.402 (.059)	.112 (.046)	.504
	Brothers, family dummies	.441 (.095)	...	...	.671
	($\bar{R}^2 = .566$)	...	.485 (.114)	...	.660
		...	.491 (.112)	.132 (.079)	.669

Source: See appendix A.
a. For a description of the sample, see table 2-2, note b. Figures in parentheses are standard errors.
b. For definitions, see table 2-2, note a.
c. Values of R^2 in parentheses are results when these background variables are the only independent variables included.
d. Son's education.
e. Number employed in son's family.

brothers have in common as members of the same family.[29] The model using the ten individual background variables produces coefficients and

29. This second approach avoids measuring background characteristics and offers a more complete treatment of them; however, the sample is smaller, and the use of family dummies sacrifices nearly half of the available degrees of freedom in the sample of brothers. As previously pointed out, a components-of-variance analysis may be a more efficient approach.

standard errors for *ED* and *AGE·ED* roughly the same as those for the composite background variable in table 4-1. The ten-variable background model is slightly preferred on a priori grounds, however, for its fuller use of the information. Its low standard errors make it preferable also to the brother analysis for an appraisal of education effects, despite the higher $\bar{R}^2$ values in the model for brothers. The analysis of brothers is presented here only to show that even with an allowance for family background effects more complete than provided by the explicit variables, the son's own education has a powerful independent effect.[30] The brother analysis produces the most erratic results in table 4-4. For example, it shows a lower effect of education on income, but a stronger effect on the composite economic status index. However, on balance, this more comprehensive family background treatment shows no less impact from education than the more accurate estimates based on explicit parental characteristics. The beta coefficient of 0.491 for *AGE·ED* in the last equation explaining the composite index for sons is the highest listed and carries a *t*-ratio of 4.4. It is impressive to find that, with family background (and the number of earners) held constant, a man's educational advantage of two standard deviations is predicted to yield an advantage of about one standard deviation in his ultimate economic status.[31] In more practical terms, a man who is average in all respects covered in the model, except that he ranks 5 percent from the top in education, would have a 30 percent chance of ending up among the top 10 percent in economic states. However, a second man, identical to the first except that he ranks 5 percent from the bottom in education, would find the odds 120–1 against his achieving that economic status.[32] Part of this measured effect of education may be due, of course, to unobserved background influences. However, given the degree to which background has been controlled, this is rather persuasive evidence that on

---

30. The results for brothers, of course, do not control completely for background effects. It has been argued that inadequate control for background influences in some studies has exaggerated the estimated effect of education on success. See, for instance, Samuel Bowles, "Schooling and Inequality from Generation to Generation," *Journal of Political Economy*, vol. 80 (May–June 1972, pt. 2), pp. S219–S251. This problem is considered in the next section.

31. The *AGE·ED* variable is again interpreted as measuring educational effects only. As shown in table 4-1, the coefficient for son's education is not markedly different when his age is included separately in the model.

32. This is the implication of the 0.491 coefficient on the assumptions of normality and heteroscedasticity.

Table 4-5. **Indexes of Son's Expected Family Income for Various Age-Education Combinations, with Background Variables and Number of Earners Held Constant, Cleveland Area Basic Sample, 1965–66**
Index = 100 for high school graduate, without college, born in 1925[a]

Son's educational attainment			Year of birth (and age in 1965)		
		Years	1915	1925	1935
Category[b]	Description	(approxi-mate)	(50)	(40)	(30)
2	Finished elementary school	8	85	81	76
3	Some high school	10	98	90	83
4	High school graduate	12	112	100	90
5	Some college	14	128	112	98
6	College graduate	16	146	124	106
7	Some graduate school	18	167	138	115
Income advantage of an additional year of education (percent)[c]			7.0	5.3	4.1

Source: Based on the equation yielding the beta coefficient of 0.343 for $AGE \cdot ED$ in table 4-4. Expected contributions of $AGE \cdot ED$ to the determination of $LOG\,Y$ were computed from the raw coefficient and each product of the educational attainment category and age in years. The indexes of expected incomes were then derived from the predicted differentials between $LOG\,Y$ for each $AGE \cdot ED$ combination and the base combination. The t-ratio for this coefficient for $AGE \cdot ED$ was 5.4; the 95 percent confidence interval for the coefficient in this model is therefore about 0.22–0.47. This suggests that the estimates are probably reasonably accurate, assuming the model is presenting a valid picture.
a. This is close to the sample average.
b. This is the actual variable used in the regression. Category one is omitted, because there were no observations in the sample.
c. The percentage tabulated for each age is the estimated percentage income differential associated with an extra year of education (approximated by one-half an education category).

top of the strong influence of family background, there is also a strong independent effect of educational attainment.

Although this independent effect appears somewhat less strong, it is more relevant to the formulation of public policy. Table 4-5 is based on the equation yielding the 0.343 coefficient for the age-education variable in table 4-4.[33] For comparison of the net effects of the son's education, this table fixes the family background and the number of earners in the son's family. It portrays the effects of variations in the son's age and years of education on his predicted income. These predicted incomes are stated relative to a base of 100, which is the ceteris paribus prediction for a high school graduate born in 1925. These two benchmarks are close to the means in the sample.

33. This coefficient is a compromise estimate, between the results for models II and III in table 4-1, and intermediate in table 4-4. It is also more than five times its standard error.

Consider first the effects of net (independent) educational attainment for a given age cohort. For the group born in 1925, the expected income of the elementary school graduate was 19 percent below that of the high school graduate. Sons with some graduate school are predicted to have a 38 percent higher family income than the latter. According to the model, the difference between a college diploma and a high school diploma was worth 24 percent for sons with identical backgrounds (and number of earners in the family). The income differential due to a single extra year of education is estimated at 5.3 percent. The most extreme predicted income differential is between that of the elementary school graduate and the son who had been to graduate school.[34] The expected value of the latter's income is 70 percent higher than that of the son who did not go beyond elementary school.

As hypothesized, a year of education counted for even more for sons born earlier. A marginal year was estimated to be worth 7 percent in extra income for a man born ten years earlier (in 1915). A man who had done some graduate work could expect nearly double the income of the most educationally disadvantaged son, and the college graduate is predicted to have a 30 percent income advantage over the high school graduate. Correspondingly, an extra year of education meant much less for a man born much later (in 1935). The estimated income differential for him is only 4 percent per year of education, and the advantage of college completion over high school is a more modest 18 percent.[35]

Even the lower independent effects of education cited above for younger men seem impressive in light of the detailed efforts to abstract from the effects of differential family economic status (and the number of earners in the family). The estimates also appear to be accurate insofar as the model is valid. All are based on a net regression coefficient more than five times its standard error, carrying a 95 percent confidence interval of 0.22–0.47. The 95 percent confidence intervals for the predicted income indexes have about the same relative breadth.[36] These figures reveal highly significant differences in the income expectations of the men

34. Lower educational attainments are omitted from the table because they were out of the range of observation.

35. These interpretations again assume that the function of age in this model is simply to allow for the changing importance of a given level of education over time. Since income and age were not correlated in this relatively homogeneous sample, there was no evidence of a return to experience or on-the-job training.

36. This refers to the confidence intervals for *predicted* values, not for the incomes of individual sons.

of low and high education, even when their family backgrounds and the number of earners in their families are identical.

The above illustrations have focused on the variations of predicted incomes by educational level. Another practical interpretation may be offered in terms of the varying chances of individual men. Table 4-6 presents estimates of the differential chances of having a family income double that predicted for the base son (a high school graduate born in 1915). Suppose, for example, that the predicted income for the base son was the sample median—about $9,000 in 1965–66 and about $18,000 on a 1976 basis. Table 4-6 gives the probability that men who differ from him only in age and education will achieve double the base predicted income.

The probability that the base son will achieve double his predicted level is 4 percent. The probability for a grade school graduate of the same age is only 1.2 percent, compared to an 18 percent probability for a man with some graduate training. In other words, if the base prediction is $18,000 (in 1976 terms), the man with graduate work has about a fifteen times greater chance of having a family income of $36,000 than the least educated man. Similarly, the probability that a college graduate will achieve that upper-middle-class income status is about three times that for a man who did not go beyond high school. These again are striking differentials in prospects for men who differ only in educational attainment.

The differentials in chances are again more extreme for older men, for whom a year of education means more. The man born in 1915 with the highest education in the table has about a twenty times greater chance of achieving upper-middle-income status than the man who stopped with grade school, even though both are about average in other respects. On the other hand, for men born in 1935, the ratio of their respective chances is about ten to one. Even though the advantage conferred by a given number of years of extra education declines over time, these results are at odds with the conclusion of some writers that education has little effect on one's prospects for economic success.[37]

37. This conclusion may be due in part to the fact that some of these studies tried to control explicitly for IQ in estimating the effect of education. See, for example, Jencks and others, *Inequality*, chap. 1; and Bowles, "Schooling and Inequality." Although the results for brothers presented here did not control completely for ability, it is not certain that the ability measures used in these other studies were more successful in doing so.

Table 4-6. Probability That an Individual Son's Income Index Exceeds 200
Percent

	Year of birth (and age in 1965)		
Son's education	1915 (50)	1925 (40)	1935 (30)
Finished elementary school	1.7	1.2	0.8
Some high school	4.0	2.4	1.5
High school graduate	7.0	4.0	2.4
Some college	14.0	7.0	4.0
College graduate	22.0	12.0	6.0
Some graduate school	33.0	18.0	8.0

Source: Based on indexes of expected incomes in table 4-5 and the standard error of estimate of $LOG Y$ in the underlying regression (0.175). For example, the fifty-year-old son with only an elementary education would need to achieve 200/85, or 2.35 times his predicted income index. In terms of $LOG Y$, this is 0.371/0.175, or 2.12 standard errors of estimate above his predicted index. Assuming normality of the conditional distribution of $LOG Y$, the probability of achieving this level is 1.7 percent.

Qualifications of Findings on the Role of Education

The evidence put forward here suggests that educational attainment has two important roles in the perpetuation of individual inequality. First, it is influenced to a substantial extent by family background, and apparently conveys and indirectly accounts for some 35 to 40 percent of the effect of family background on ultimate economic success. Second, education exercises a powerful independent effect on a man's economic status over and above its role as a conduit for background influences. Both of these findings are subject to two fundamental methodological criticisms. First, both the mediating and independent roles of educational attainment per se will be exaggerated to the extent that education is picking up explanatory credit that should really be allotted to prior causal factors omitted from the analysis. Second, inaccurate measurement of the prior factors in the causal chain will lead similarly to an exaggeration of the two roles of education as a determinant of economic status.

Consider first the problem of omitted variables. Although family background is included throughout in the present analysis, it may be useful to consider first what would have been found if it were not. Early studies showing a strong relation between earnings and schooling were criticized on the ground that the schooling coefficient was probably getting credit for the explanatory power of the underlying background influences on schooling itself. If valid, this criticism implied that policies aimed at stimulating educational attainment would accomplish less than suggested by the schooling coefficient. There have been varying opinions on the

Table 4-7. Effect of Educational Attainment with and without Allowing for Prior Influences of Family Background: Beta Coefficients, Cleveland Area Basic Sample,[a] 1965–66

Economic status[a]	Family background	AGE[c]	ED[a]	$\bar{R}^2$
RATE	Dummies	0.061 (0.179)	0.280 (0.115)	0.548
	Excluded	0.143 (0.083)	0.455 (0.083)	0.178
OCC	Dummies	−0.115 (0.144)	0.675 (0.098)	0.661
	Excluded	0.135 (0.057)	0.792 (0.057)	0.596
LOGY	Dummies	0.449 (0.210)	0.265 (0.139)	0.423
	Basic ten[d]	0.287 (0.091)	0.283 (0.068)	0.254
	Excluded	0.216 (0.087)	0.413 (0.087)	0.148
Croy	Dummies	0.196 (0.151)	0.500 (0.105)	0.674
	Basic ten[d]	0.127 (0.075)	0.407 (0.056)	0.499
	Excluded	0.245 (0.071)	0.671 (0.071)	0.434

Source: See appendix A.
a. For definitions, see table 2-2, note a.
b. The figures in parentheses are standard errors.
c. AGE = son's age.
d. Family background was represented here by the ten basic variables included in table 4-2 and subsequent tables.

extent of this bias due to omission of background factors, but it certainly appears substantial on the basis of the sample used in this study.[38]

Table 4-7 illustrates the effect on the educational attainment coefficients of ignoring family effects. Estimates with and without family variables are given for four measures of son's economic status. The coefficient for son's education is lower in all cases when family background is included (greatly improving the explanation of son's status). Only for occupation does the bias seem minor.[39] The other three education coefficients are

38. For a view that the specification bias is minor, see Zvi Griliches, "Notes on the Role of Education in Production Functions and Growth Accounting," in W. Lee Hansen, ed., *Education, Income, and Human Capital* (Columbia University Press for the National Bureau of Economic Research, 1970), pp. 71–115.

39. This is not surprising in view of the extremely strong correlation between occupation and income and the relatively small improvement in explanation that can be achieved by adding background.

overstated by an estimated 34 to 62 percent. Since the standard errors in the dummy variable models are high, additional estimates for income and the composite index are included in the table based on explicit background measures (and more degrees of freedom). The estimates of the influence of education with background held constant in this way have lower standard errors than in the brother analysis and continue to be much lower than suggested by the model that ignores parental characteristics.[40]

The most glaring omission from the present models is the son's ability.[41] This shortcoming, like the omission of family background, could affect the indicated role of education both as a medium of status transmission and as an independent force. No measure of ability was available for the Cleveland area sample, nor does any set of indicators of this unobserved quantity exist.

Many attempts to isolate the ceteris paribus effect of educational attainment on economic status have been criticized for their small or unrepresentative samples, poor measures of education and ability, or improper analysis.[42] Some recent research appears less vulnerable, however; for instance, studies based on a sample of World War II veterans for whom scores on the Armed Forces Qualifying Test (AFQT) are available. These were concerned with the upward bias in the education coefficient when ability is excluded from models explaining income but the quality of education is also considered.

Griliches and Mason find a strong influence of schooling on income independent of the ability and background measures.[43] They also found a rather weak independent effect of ability, as measured by the AFQT. Holding various background measures and this test score constant, a year of extra education was worth 4.6 percent in extra income—a finding close

40. The son's age was also included in the model and was positive as expected, reflecting the fact that the older the son, the greater the effect of a given level of education. The indicated bias is less clear cut in this coefficient, but estimates taking background into account are again smaller in all cases except son's income. (The assumption, based on the evidence, continues to be that age differentials do not predict a return to experience for this sample of sons.)

41. This inadequacy is less serious elsewhere because the more homogeneous brothers are with respect to ability, the more ability tends to be correlated with measured background characteristics.

42. For a bibliography of studies so criticized, see Paul Taubman and Terence Wales, *Higher Education and Earnings* (McGraw-Hill, 1974), p. 2n.

43. Zvi Griliches and William M. Mason, "Education, Income, and Ability," *Journal of Political Economy*, vol. 80 (May–June 1972, pt. 2), pp. S74–S103.

to those in table 4-5 above, where ability was excluded—and a 10 percent increment to the test score added only about 1 percent to income. The bias in the education coefficient due to omission of ability was put at 10 to 15 percent.[44] J. C. Hause, however, estimates many interaction effects.[45] He concludes that ability and schooling have a complementary effect on earnings, and also that the effect of ability has grown over time.

Taubman and Wales, who consider additional samples, find a greater role for ability.[46] They argue that mathematical ability, rather than IQ, is the chief competitor against educational attainment as an influence on earnings. The biases in the education coefficient when mathematical ability is omitted range from 8 to 25 percent, depending on the education level. These are viewed as lower bounds, and the estimated upper bounds average about 50 percent higher.[47]

The findings of Griliches and Mason on the one hand and Taubman and Wales on the other appear to typify the range of recent sophisticated disagreement on the importance of the bias in the education coefficient in models that omit ability.[48] The impression created by this controversy is that the ability bias is neither trivial nor very large. Certainly the indicated independent effect of educational attainment on earnings (whether due to productivity or merely screening) has not been undermined by these

44. Paul Taubman has criticized the IQ measure used in this study and suggested that more attention should have been given to interaction among the explanatory variables. "Comment," *Journal of Political Economy*, vol. 80 (May–June 1972, pt. 2), pp. S104–S107.

45. "Earnings Profile: Ability and Schooling," ibid., pp. S108–S138.

46. *Higher Education and Earnings*. They also treat the role of education as a screening or signaling device, suggesting that education may benefit individuals but have a low social payoff.

47. Ibid., p. 91.

48. For further development of their research, see Gary Chamberlain and Zvi Griliches, "Unobservables with a Variance-Components Structure: Ability, Schooling, and the Economic Success of Brothers," *International Economic Review*, vol. 16 (June 1975), pp. 422–49; Gary Chamberlain, "Education, Income, and Ability Revisited," Discussion Paper no. 392 (Harvard Institute of Economic Research, 1974; processed); J. R. Behrman and P. Taubman, "Nature and Nurture in the Determination of Earnings and Occupational Status," forthcoming. The first two papers continue to find a relatively minor "ability bias." Behrman and Taubman suggest a merging of the variance components model and recent analysis of missing variables. They add that the ability bias may be greater when dealing with brothers than with unrelated individuals. The recent book by William H. Sewell, Robert M. Hauser, and others, *Education, Occupation, and Earnings: Achievement in the Early Career* (Academic Press, 1975), also deals extensively with ability as a determinant of earnings.

studies. It should also be repeated that the measured effect of parental education was very strong. The tentative view here is that the role of educational attainment is significantly but not greatly exaggerated by omission of the ability factor.[49] However, it remains possible that a full representation of *all* missing variables, including genetic endowments, birth order, upbringing, and other missing environmental factors, would show a serious bias in the education coefficients.

Samuel Bowles argues that the influence of education is overstated for a different reason.[50] The relatively weak influence of family background found in some studies and the strong effect of education with background held constant could be due to incomplete representation and inaccurate measurement of family background. This point is a less troublesome one in the present context, because the analysis of brothers (and the use of family dummy variables) allows more fully for the effect of background characteristics and influences, without even the need to measure them. Estimates such as those in table 4-4 show a very strong independent effect of years of schooling, even when family background is more fully allowed for in this way.

Nothing in the literature explored here suggests that a full representation of intermediate factors in the models would decimate the indicated independent effect of education. Nor does it seem likely that indirect effects through these intermediate variables could come close to accounting for the strong total effect of family background on ultimate economic success. For example, even when Sewell and Hauser added teachers' and parents' encouragement, high school performance, "significant others," and educational and occupational aspirations to a complicated model, "socioeconomic origins continue to influence directly one's chances for higher education."[51] Their use of nine intermediate variables also fails to shake the indicated direct effect of parental income on son's earnings.

This persistence of direct background effects not accounted for by education, IQ, and so forth, raises another question. How is that part of the influence of family background not accounted for by intermediate factors

49. For a remarkably concise and informative articulation of the continuing controversy over the role of education in economic success, see Zvi Griliches, "The Changing Economics of Education," Discussion Paper no. 426 (Harvard Institute of Economic Research, 1975; processed).

50. "Schooling and Inequality."

51. William H. Sewell and Robert M. Hauser, "Causes and Consequences of Higher Education: Models of the Status Attainment Process," *American Journal of Agricultural Economics*, vol. 54 (December 1972), p. 857.

actually transmitted to the next generation? Since the explanation has not been found in measurable factors, there is much room for speculation.

Kohn has put forward a psychological hypothesis concerning the tendency of parents to prepare their children for a life in the same social class: "Whether consciously or not, parents tend to impart to their children lessons derived from the conditions of life of their own social class— and thus help prepare their children for a similar class position. . . . Class differences in parental values and child rearing practices influence the development of the capacities that children someday will need. . . . The family, then, functions as a mechanism for perpetuating inequality."[52] Bowles and Gintis add to this the view that effects of the "hierarchical division of labor" are reflected in family life. "Families in turn reproduce the forms of consciousness required for the integration of a new generation into the economic system. Such differential patterns of child-rearing affect more than the worker's personality as is exemplified in Kohn's study. They also pattern self-concepts, personal aspirations, styles of self-presentation, class loyalties, and modes of speech, dress, and interpersonal behavior. While such traits are by no means fixed into adulthood and must be reinforced at the workplace, their stability over the life cycle appears sufficient to account for a major portion of the observed degree of inter-generational status transmission."[53]

These are interesting conjectures, but it is not at all clear why parents should so obligingly frustrate economic mobility by modeling their children in their own image. Neither interpretation asserted that this molding is primarily conscious. Even so, the parents are credited with determining many characteristics of their children, whether consciously or not. There is no reason to doubt the existence of such parental influences, but they seem almost superfluous as a cause of vertical immobility. The realities of life in the contrasting socioeconomic strata seem entirely sufficient to account for a large part of the observed intergenerational economic immobility.

We have recognized that the rich are favored over the poor in educational opportunity and that this accounts for a substantial part of the inheritance of economic status. But it is not surprising that such measurable advantages do not come close to telling the whole story. The fact that a

52. Melvin L. Kohn, *Class and Conformity: A Study in Values* (Dorsey Press, 1969), p. 200.
53. Samuel Bowles and Herbert Gintis, *Schooling in Capitalist America: Educational Reform and the Contradictions of Economic Life* (Basic Books, 1976), p. 147.

child from a poor family tends to go less far in school is only a part of the problem. His relatively poor diet, health, speech, dress, degree of parental attention, and many other characteristics are also disadvantageous without any need for parental molding or even a "culture of poverty" to make them operative. In other words, poverty tends to reproduce itself automatically, despite any efforts of educational policy. Some encouraging evidence on the effects of education has emerged here, but the size of the component of the inheritance of economic status not explicitly accounted for should not surprise anyone.

The Role of Marital Selection in Perpetuating Inequality

A very much neglected element in the maintenance of economic inequality is the tendency for individuals to marry others of similar socioeconomic background.[54] The evidence already presented showed a strong influence of parental socioeconomic status (as well as son's education) on the economic success of sons in the sample. Suppose that daughters tended to choose husbands randomly, or at least independently of their own socioeconomic background and education. Assume also that the daughter's economic status is defined as that of her husband. In this situation, the fraction of the variation in economic status of sons and daughters combined explained by background would be only about one-half that found for sons only. Such a random marital selection process would presumably mitigate substantially the force of socioeconomic background in the perpetuation of inequality.

The ultimate effect of this hypothetical random mating on overall inequality is not immediately obvious. The economic status of the men these daughters marry would still be heavily influenced by their *own* socioeconomic background. Since we have defined the economic status of a couple as that of the husband, this might suggest that random mating would not make any difference. However, in practice, the effects would undoubtedly be substantial. We have shown that a son of a poor man is very likely to be poor, but he would be less likely to end up in that state if his chances of marrying an educated woman from a rich family were the same as his probability of marrying an uneducated woman from a

54. For theoretical treatment of the marital selection process, see Gary S. Becker, "A Theory of Marriage: Part I," *Journal of Political Economy,* vol. 81 (July–August 1973), pp. 813ff.; "Part II," vol. 82 (March–April 1974), pp. S11–S26.

poor family. At least it does not seem rash to assume that the depressing influence of the man's own background would tend to be mitigated by an economically fortuitous marriage. At the very least, the prospects of his own children would be markedly improved.

The analysis below shows that mating is decidedly not random, however. More surprisingly, it shows that the relationship of the economic status of sons-in-law to the socioeconomic background of their wives is not only very strong; it is almost as strong as the relationship between sons and their own parents. Put another way, we would not be able to explain the economic success of these sons-in-law very much better if we had information on their own parents—not even if we knew them to be identical to the wives' parents. For that reason the role of marital selection in perpetuating inequality is almost as strong as it would be if the daughters married their brothers.[55]

Sons-in-Law and Parents-in-Law: The Overall Relationship

The socioeconomic background of daughters is represented first by the composite index based on parental education, occupation, family size, religion, race, and wealth. Table 4-8 is based on the combined sample of 231 sons and 199 sons-in-law; their economic success indicator (based on residence, occupation, and income) is related to the composite background index estimated from the pooled sample of 430 married sons and daughters. The first equation shows 33 percent of the economic status of the two sets of men explained by this background index, even though the background of sons-in-law is represented by that of their wives. The regression coefficient is highly significant, nearly fifteen times its standard error.

A dummy variable is added in equation 2 to distinguish sons-in-law (*SIL*). It is perplexing to find this variable significantly negative, since it

---

55. Some minor qualifications may be mentioned. The sample contained few divorced, widowed, or single women, so the study was confined to currently married women. In any case, the exclusion of the former appears to pose no problem, since we are comparing the transmission of economic status to married women and married men, respectively. The age of the sons-in-law was not available, but it seems likely that their ages played only the same minor role as found for married sons in table 3-13. Similarly, no difference in measurement error for the background variables is to be expected; daughters furnished in-law background just as sons furnished their own. It will be suggested later that daughters may tend to underestimate their own family incomes, but there is no reason to suspect less accuracy in recall of background.

Table 4-8. Models Explaining Composite Success Index $Croy$[a] for Combined
Sample of Married Sons and Sons-in-Law: Beta Coefficients,
Cleveland Area Basic Sample, 1965–66

Equation	Dependent variable[a]	Independent variable[b]					$\bar{R}^2$
		BGC[c]	SIL[d]	$SIL \cdot BGC$	ED[e]	$AGE \cdot ED$[e]	
1	$Croy$	0.575 (0.040)	...	...	...	...	0.329
2	$Croy$	0.563 (0.040)	−0.080 (0.040)	...	...	...	0.333
3	$Croy$	0.586 (0.051)	−0.081 (0.040)	−0.038 (0.051)	...	...	0.333
4	$Croy$	0.419 (0.055)	−0.081) (0.038)	0.001 (0.059)	0.186 (0.046)	...	0.392
5	$Croy$	0.428 (0.052)	−0.070 (0.037)	0.003 (0.043)	...	0.325 (0.041)	0.418

Source: See appendix A.
a. Index of the economic status of sons and sons-in-law computed from the combined samples. For definitions, see table 2-2, notes a and f.
b. The figures in parentheses are standard errors.
c. Index of socioeconomic background of married daughters based on ten variables. See table 2-2, note f, and chapter 3, note 38.
d. Dummy variable for son-in-law. This may also be regarded as a dummy variable designating the daughter whose economic status is defined as that of her husband.
e. For definition, see table 4-1.

implies that daughters from a given background rank tend to marry men of lower economic status than the sons from the same rank;[56] this puzzling result persisted throughout the analysis and will be considered briefly later. The original purpose of the dummy variable SIL was to multiply it by the background composite BGC to test the hypothesis that slopes in the relationship were the same. This dummy was added in equation 3, and it falls far short of significance. It indicates that the estimated slope for sons-in-law is 0.548, only slightly lower than the 0.586 figure for sons. In other words, a given differential in wives' background carries nearly as much weight in predicting the success of sons-in-law as is true of the relation between sons and their own parents. When the education of daughters (and sons) is added in equations 4 and 5, this eliminates the previous insignificant role of the son-in-law dummy in the estimated net response of economic success to family background. This recursive model indicates that even the small differential in slope indicated for sons-in-law in equation 3 was conveyed indirectly through education. As will be shown later, daughters had a significantly lower education than sons of

56. This is consistent with a tendency also found for daughters to marry men of lower economic status than their brothers.

Table 4-9. Transition Matrices Relating the Economic Status Ranks, in Tenths, of Successive Generations,[a] Cleveland Area Basic Sample, 1965–66

Rank of decedent parent	Rank of son									
	1 (top)	2	3	4	5	6	7	8	9	10
1 (top)	13	6	3	...	1	...	...	...	...	...
2	2	5	8	4	3	1	...	...	...	...
3	1	4	4	...	3	4	1	3	2	1
4	4	1	2	3	...	4	3	1	3	2
5	1	3	1	1	3	5	3	4	3	...
6	...	3	...	4	1	...	4	6	1	4
7	...	...	4	5	2	4	3	2	1	2
8	1	...	...	3	2	3	3	3	4	4
9	1	...	1	2	6	...	3	4	5	1
10	...	1	...	1	3	2	3	2	1	10

Rank of parent-in-law	Rank of son-in-law									
	1 (top)	2	3	4	5	6	7	8	9	10
1 (top)	10	5	3	...	...	1	...	1	...	...
2	6	5	4	3	...	2	...	...	...	...
3	2	...	4	2	2	1	6	...	2	1
4	1	2	3	2	2	...	4	2	2	2
5	...	...	1	1	2	1	4	4	4	3
6	...	3	2	1	4	...	...	2	4	3
7	...	3	1	4	4	3	3	1	1	...
8	1	1	...	5	2	...	1	0	6	4
9	...	...	1	2	3	3	2	6	2	1
10	...	1	...	1	2	5	2	...	3	6

Source: See appendix A.

a. The economic status measure for sons *Croye* is defined in table 2-7. In the case of 199 sons-in-law, the variable could be described alternatively as measuring the economic status of the daughter, since it is her education that is included in the four-variable index. Decedents are ranked by the first principal component of the ten economic status variables used in regressions in table 3-2. The tabulation is based on 231 married sons only, for comparability with the sons-in-law.

the same background. When this is allowed for in equations 4 and 5, the net relationship between success and background becomes virtually identical for sons and sons-in-law. The only difference that persists between the two groups of men is in the level of the relationship: the apparently significant tendency for daughters, other things being equal, to marry men of lower economic status than sons.[57]

57. As estimated in table 4-1, education (and $AGE \cdot ED$) of son or daughter—not son-in-law—conveyed indirectly some 30 to 40 percent of the effects of family background. In this combined sample of sons and sons-in-law (with *SIL* included in the model), this indirect effect of education appears somewhat less; the average coefficient for *BGC* drops from about 0.575 to 0.424 when education is added, implying an indirect effect of 26 percent.

The two intergenerational relationships can also be compared in terms of transition matrices. Table 4-9 uses separately estimated background indexes for sons and sons-in-law. Forty of the wives of the latter group came from the top fifth in socioeconomic status; 26 of those married men who ranked in the top fifth. This was an even higher ratio than the 19 out of 46 sons from the top fifth who ended up there themselves. Greater mobility was found at the bottom, but again there was little difference between sons and sons-in-law in this respect.

The Role of Explicit Background Influences on Sons and Sons-in-Law

The previous section reported no difference between the relation of sons and sons-in-law to the overall background measure (although sons-in-law were lower, other things being equal). It is interesting to ask whether this is true of the relationship with individual background characteristics. Table 4-10 gives results of separate and combined regressions for married sons and sons-in-law. Various economic status measures are regressed on the ten basic background variables. The first thing to note is that the goodness-of-fit of the son-in-law models falls only moderately short of that for sons, and not at all in the case of income.

The $\bar{R}^2$ values for the two income regressions are virtually identical. For sons-in-law they are lower by 5 to 10 percentage points in the case of the other status measures, but they are still highly significant. It is clear that marital selection is almost as far from random as the relation between sons and parents. The differences between the standard errors of estimate in the two samples are relatively smaller than between $\bar{R}^2$ values, and it remains true that the economic status of sons-in-law can be predicted almost as well from the characteristics of their wives' parents as sons can be predicted from their own parents.

Even more striking than the closeness of the $\bar{R}^2$ values is the similarity of the specific relationships in the two samples. The signs agree for all ten variables and are just as hypothesized for the original sample of sons. Although the variables that are significant vary somewhat across samples, very few of the coefficients estimated from these two very large samples differ significantly from each other. As indicated in table 4-10, three estimates of the coefficient for the wealth proxy (testacy) differed significantly, and one each for the Catholic religion and gross estate did too. Since results are given for ten background variables and six status measures for the current generation, sixty coefficients were estimated from

Table 4-10. Regression Results for Married Sons Compared to Those for Sons-in-Law, Basic Set of Ten Background Variables, Cleveland Area Basic Sample, 1965–66

Regression statistic	Economic status measure[a]					
	RATE	OCC	LOGY	Croy	Croye	(ED)[b]
Sample size						
Sons	248	241	239	231	231	247
Sons-in-law	224	218	204	199	199	224
Both	472	465	443	430	430	471
$\bar{R}^2$						
Sons	0.257	0.278	0.239	0.417	0.442	0.280
Sons-in-law	0.188	0.228	0.243	0.318	0.352	0.212
Both	0.232	0.216	0.252	0.392	0.425	0.269
Variables significant at the 5 percent level						
Sons	GRST SIBS AED3 REL2 RAC2 TES2	All except GRST SIBS	SIBS AED2 AED3 REL3 RAC2	All except GRST	All	GRST SIBS AED2 AED3
Sons-in-law	GRST AED3 RAC2	GRST SIBS AGED AED2 AED3	GRST SIBS AGED AED2 AED3 RAC2	GRST SIBS AGED AED2 AED3 RAC2	All except REL2 TES2	SIBS AED2 AED3 REL3 OCDT
Variables for which son and son-in-law co-efficients differ significantly[c]	REL2[s]	None	$GRST^s$ $TES2^w$	TES^w_2	TES^w_2	None

Sources: Statistics for separate son and son-in-law groups are based on regressions of economic status on the ten independent variables defined in table 3-1. Statistics for the two groups combined are based on regressions containing dummy variables distinguishing the coefficients for sons and sons-in-law.
a. For definitions, see tables 2-2 and 2-7.
b. Educational attainment of son or daughter, not of son-in-law.
c. This is based on the coefficients for variables containing dummies, two-tail test. The difference was called significant if the coefficient on a variable containing a dummy differed significantly from zero at the 5 percent level. The variables for which the coefficients for sons-in-law indicate a stronger (weaker) relationship are indicated by s (w).

each of the two samples. It is remarkable that only five of these sixty differed significantly at the 5 percent level, since chance alone would account for three such significant differences out of sixty.

It was to be expected that the religion and race coefficients for sons-in-law would be similar to those for sons. Assuming minimal intermarriage, the parental characteristics of the son-in-law are generally the same as those of the son. But even among the forty-two coefficients estimated for parental education, family size, occupation, and wealth, there were only four significant differences between results for sons and daughters.[58] Except for these few cases and the constant term, there were no significant differences in the structural relationships for sons and sons-in-law. This confirms the aggregative findings of the last section.

In sum, marital pairing does very little to loosen the link between the economic status of successive generations. The economic status of sons is strongly influenced by that of their parents, and this is almost equally true of daughters.[59] The tendency for daughters to marry men of background and education similar to their own ensures that their ultimate economic status in marriage is almost as closely influenced by their own backgrounds as is the directly achieved economic status of sons.[60] Because of this selection process, wives' background presumably has little independent influence on their husbands' economic status. However, the mating pattern itself ensures that the role of family background in perpetuating inequality operates nearly as strongly on daughters as on sons.

On the Observed Advantage of Sons over Daughters

The similarity of the intergenerational economic relationship for sons and daughters should not cause us to overlook persistent evidence of a differential between the economic status of sons and daughters of given background and education. A detailed comparison of the upward and downward mobility of men and women is beyond the scope of this study.[61] However, in an era of women's liberation it would be inappropriate to ignore completely a differential of this kind. Its apparent existence, in this sample at least, encourages speculation that daughters (whose average year of birth was 1923) had less freedom of marital choice than did the sons and thereby sustained a relative loss in economic status. Although no such general conclusion is drawn here, it seems in order to consider possible explanations of this observed differential.

58. This includes the models explaining education, which is, of course, an independent characteristic of the daughter.
59. For opposing conclusions, see Ivan D. Chase, "A Comparison of Men's and Women's Intergenerational Mobility in the United States," *American Sociological Review,* vol. 40 (August 1975), pp. 483–505; and Blau and Duncan, *American Occupational Structure.*
60. This mating tendency is discussed rather extensively in the literature of sociology as "assortative" mating or "homogamy." See, for example, Blau and Duncan, *American Occupational Structure,* chap. 10.
61. For a new study in this field, see Chase, "A Comparison of Mobility."

The evidence of a relatively poor outcome for daughters compared to sons of equivalent background was reported first in table 4-8. This differential against daughters, measured in terms of the economic status of their husbands, persisted even when the daughter's educational attainment was included in the model.[62] The net relationship (in standardized units) between the composite status measure *Croy* and the socioeconomic background index *BGC*, with daughter's education held constant at the mean, was (figures in parentheses are standard errors):

$$(4\text{-}4) \qquad Croy = 0.419\ BGC - 0.081\ SIL.$$
$$\qquad\qquad\qquad (.055) \qquad\quad (.038)$$

The slope was found to be the same for sons-in-law as for sons, but the negative son-in-law dummy *SIL* indicates that for any given background level, the predicted value of daughter's (son-in-law's) economic status is 0.081 below that of a son with the same background and education as the daughter. This appears to suggest that daughters "marry down," tending to marry men of lower economic status than their brothers.

Table 4-10 showed that coefficients for background variables in models applied to sons and sons-in-law rarely differed significantly. So table 4-11 was devised by pooling the two samples and estimating common background coefficients. Next, the son-in-law variable *SIL* was added as a measure of the differential in ultimate economic status, with background held constant. These dummy variables carry *t*-ratios ranging from 1.86 to 3.18, and those for income, the composite index, and daughter's education show a significant differential against daughters. For example, the predicted family income of daughters (sons-in-law) is about 10 percent below that of sons. The differential for the composite index *Croy* is −0.196, or about one-quarter of a standard deviation in that index. The meaning of this indicated differential against daughters can be illustrated by a comparison with sons whose background and education forecast a median *Croy* index 50 percent from the top. A daughter with the same credentials is predicted to have a husband 60 percent from the top in terms of that index (assuming normality).

A second estimate for the *Croy* index was derived from sibling data in place of explicit background variables. Background was represented in the most complete possible way with family dummies, and the sex differ-

62. It should be stressed that even though the daughter's economic status is identified with that of her husband in the analysis, the measure of educational attainment included as an intermediate variable is always her own, not that of her husband.

Table 4-11. Regressions Estimating the Differential in Economic Status between Sons and Sons-in-Law of Equal Background and Education, Combined Cleveland Area Sample of Married Sons and Daughters, 1965–66

Status measure[a] and standard deviation	Independent variables included in regression[b]	Results from son-in-law dummy SIL		$\bar{R}^2$
		Coefficient	t-ratio	
RATE	FB, SIL	−0.143	1.86	0.222
(0.933)	FB, SIL, ED	−0.130	1.70	0.228
	FB, SIL, AGE·ED	−0.130	1.66	0.230
OCC	FB, SIL	−0.230	1.86	0.266
(1.52)	FB, SIL, ED	−0.100	0.91	0.431
	FB, SIL, AGE·ED	−0.106	0.94	0.394
LOGY	FB, SIL	−0.0433	2.45	0.252
(0.212)	FB, SIL, ED	−0.0345	2.01	0.295
	FB, SIL, AGE·ED	−0.0312	1.85	0.322
Croy	FB, SIL	−0.196	3.18	0.395
(0.808)	FB, SIL, ED	−0.138	2.42	0.485
	FB, SIL, AGE·ED	−0.128	2.23	0.486
	(Family dummies,[c] SIL)	−0.224	2.75	0.460
ED	FB, SIL[d]	−0.206	2.12	0.264
(1.218)				

Source: See appendix A.

a. For definitions, see table 2-2, note a.

b. The abbreviation *FB* refers to the ten basic family background variables used in the regressions in table 3-2. The variable *SIL* is a dummy distinguishing son-in-law. For daughters, the educational attainment variable *ED* is that of the daughter, not of the son-in-law. *AGE·ED* is the product of daughter's age and education.

c. This regression is restricted to married sons and daughters and includes only those in families in which there were at least two siblings. There were 100 such families included, with 285 siblings among them. The composite variable *Croy* was regressed on family dummies and the sex dummy representing sons-in-law.

d. Although the symbol *SIL* designates son-in-law, it is explaining daughter's education in this case and can be regarded as a dummy variable designating daughter.

ential again was highly significant, with a *t*-ratio of 2.75. This amounted to a comparison of the economic status of sons and daughters from the same family, and the daughters were found to have married men of significantly lower status than their brothers.

An attempt was made to explain the apparent differential against women in terms of their disadvantage in education. The last equation in table 4-11 shows that daughters completed significantly fewer years of education than sons of the same background. The coefficient of −0.2 seems rather small, amounting to about four-tenths of a year. However, insofar as women marry men of similar levels of education, this could account for part of the status differential between sons and daughters.

Insertion of educational attainment and the age-education product as intermediate variables in the economic status models did explain part of the sex differential. Table 4-11 shows that an appreciable fraction of the effect of sex on economic status was conveyed indirectly via the daughter's education. For example, the model explaining the composite status shows a drop in the magnitude of the coefficient for the son-in-law variable from −0.196 to an average of −0.133 when education variables are included. Thus, according to the model, about one-third of the differential against daughters is accounted for indirectly through their lower educational attainment.

How is the rest of the sex differential to be accounted for? The question is a puzzling one, since any differential at all appears implausible at the aggregate level. Presumably the only way for it to come about is by the process illustrated schematically for the following five ranked families with one daughter and one son in each:

```
Family rank
    1       D       S
    2       D       S
    3       D       S
    4       D       S
    5       D       S
```

The married daughters and sons are connected by lines, and the unmarried children are circled. The five-family illustration suggests that the tendency for daughters to marry men of lower socioeconomic background than their own must be balanced in the aggregate by a tendency for unmarried daughters to have a relatively low background and for unmarried sons to be of relatively high origins. Since only a slight indication of such a pattern was found, we must search further for the explanation.

It is, of course, possible that women in this particular sample did indeed marry down; this could be readily balanced by some other group in which the women fared better. This is difficult to rationalize, however, and the more likely explanation may be a measurement error deriving from the differing outlook of wives and husbands. Wives (the shoppers) tend to know about prices, and husbands (the workers) know more about earnings. Wives see prices going up but may not be fully aware of offsetting wage increases. Most of the information on sons-in-law in this sample is derived from interviews with their wives (the daughters), whereas the data on sons comes directly from them. A 10 percent lower estimate of family income made by wives than by husbands would not be astonishing. However, a differential response on occupation would seem less plausible, and response error by wives cannot account for the residence differential at all, since the latter was assigned by the interviewer. So we are left with an intriguing phenomenon without an obvious explanation.

Conclusions on Education and Marital Selection

According to this sample and model, something like one-third of the effect of family background on son's economic status appears to have been transmitted indirectly through the intermediate effect of background on educational attainment. Since a man's educational attainment is related to his socioeconomic background, education is, to that extent, inherited. And since education in turn affects the son's economic status, we can say that inherited education accounts for this indirect effect of family background.

The estimated role of inherited education is probably exaggerated by the unavoidable omission from the analysis of other partially inherited characteristics, such as ability and motivation. Work by others that includes ability measures suggest that the ceteris paribus importance of inherited education has indeed been overestimated somewhat here, but its role remains important. No test was possible of the role of motivation, but it is possible that educational attainment is also being given some statistical credit here due in part to inherited motivation. On the other hand, if it had been possible to allow for variations in the quality of education, the estimated role would have been greater than actually found.

Aside from its intermediary function, it was found that educational attainment had an even stronger influence that was entirely independent of measured family background. That is, after family effects were invoked to explain all that they could of the variation in economic status, education then explained from 10 percent to 50 percent of the remainder, depending on the criterion. Insofar as this education effect is also independent of ability and other missing factors, this finding suggests that, despite the substantial influence of his background on a man's chance of economic success, public policies aimed at reducing the inequality of educational attainment would have an independent effect alleviating the inequality of economic status. The potential impact of such a policy is even greater when account is taken (as in chapter 3) of the intergenerational effect of education; that is, a man is affected not only by his own educational attainment, but also by that of his parents.

These findings on the independent effect of educational attainment (like those for inherited education) must be qualified to the extent that they reflect (and take statistical credit for) ability, motivation, and other prior causes that also have a component independent of family background. Insofar as this is true, the estimated effect of education policy is exaggerated. On balance, the literature on this point suggests at least that omission of ability is probably not a major source of bias.

Like education, marital selection may be viewed as having an intermediate role in helping to transmit the power of family background as a perpetuator of inequality. It might be supposed a priori that marital selection by daughters has a larger random component than the relationship between sons and parents; this would be a reasonable expectation, since the link between son-in-law and parent-in-law is one step farther apart than that between son and parents. Since the economic success of daughters must be pragmatically defined as that of the men they marry, a large random component in mate selection would make for a lower family background effect on daughters than on sons. This in turn would be a force working to reduce inequality. Little evidence of such a process was found, however.

The evidence shows that marital selection produces for daughters virtually a carbon copy of the relationship between son and parents. In the first place, the relationship of daughters' economic status (defined as that of the sons-in-law) to their socioeconomic background is almost as close as that between sons and parents. That is, the economic status of men is almost as closely related to their wives' backgrounds as to their own. Apparently assortative mating was going on, with women in this sample tending to marry men with backgrounds very much like their own. In most respects the effect on inequality was virtually the same as if they had married their brothers. Thus, there was little attenuation of this intergenerational economic link due to a relatively large random component in the selection of husbands by daughters.

Not only was the economic status that daughters achieve in marriage closely related to that of their parents, it was virtually as close as the relationship between sons and parents. The statistical relationship to specific parental characteristics rarely differed significantly between daughters and sons. Only with respect to the overall levels attained by daughters and sons was there a consistent difference. The evidence suggested that, given family background (and even the daughter's education), daughters ended up less well off than sons. More specifically, daughters from a given family tended to end up less well off than their brothers. This perplexing finding seems too implausible to be disturbing, and it is hard to believe that this relationship would hold true in the aggregate. Intriguing though it is, it may be in order to write it off as a statistical artifact, or the product of a wife's tendency to underestimate her husband's economic status, especially his income.

appendix A **Data Source**

The data used here were collected for a different purpose a decade ago.[1] The general objective of that study was a thorough analysis of the process by which material wealth is transferred from decedent to survivor. It emphasized the legal process of wealth transmission and the extent to which various parties were satisfied with it. Among the topics included were (1) whether or not a will existed, (2) why and how it was constructed, (3) various interpretations of the "justice" aimed at and delivered by the procedure, (4) the many problems associated with estate settlement, and (5) various evaluations of the entire procedure.

This study required an examination of a large sample of closed estates. The primary sample was a 5 percent systematic selection of 659 decedent estates closed in Cuyahoga County Probate Court between November 9, 1964, and August 8, 1965. The primary data on decedents came from the probate docket; other information on decedents was derived from heirs and death certificates.

Survivors were interviewed during the period February 1, 1965, to May 31, 1966. In addition to data central to the study, detailed information bearing on the economic status of the survivors and decedents was collected, primarily for the purpose of judging the representativeness of the sample. The interviews with survivors appear to have been conducted with remarkable persistence and skill (see especially pp. 45–54). Information of major value included a painstaking coverage of the quality of survivors' residence (see pp. 323–24), an occupation ranking, and information on income and educational attainment. Also available were various control variables, including age and the number of earners per family.

The sample also offers identification of brothers and sisters. This made

1. See Marvin B. Sussman, Judith N. Cates, and David T. Smith, *The Family and Inheritance* (New York: Russell Sage Foundation, 1970), especially pp. 44–54 and app. B, pp. 323–24.

possible the analysis in chapter 2 of this study that did not require background information. Also the data on the decedent parents gathered from the survivor interviews, combined with the probate records and death certificates, produced a very rich profile of socioeconomic background.

appendix B A Comment on the Jencks
Analysis of Brothers

The estimated effects of family background on occupation and income presented in chapter 3 are based on an actual sample of brothers. The relative imprecision of the occupation and income measures analyzed here imparts a downward bias to any estimates of the degree to which economic status is inherited. Even so, the indicated effect of family background on descendants' status is stronger than reported in any known previous study, and it differs most strongly from the highly publicized work of Jencks and colleagues.[1] That study finds differences in income and occupational status among brothers almost as great as those among all men, while the present estimates show inequality among brothers to be far less. A diagnosis of the reasons for this contradiction requires special consideration of the opposite conclusions reached in the Jencks study. It will be necessary to go into some detail to suggest that the weak family background effect found by Jencks is the product of both empirical and methodological difficulties. The low estimate of the degree of inheritance of economic status is traceable in turn to key aspects of their case—the data and their interpretation.

Data Used and Variance Explained

It must be emphasized that the present analysis rests on data gathered from brothers. In contrast, the Jencks study, having no information on brothers, was forced to make inferences from indirect evidence in previous studies, which relate the economic status of males to available evidence on the status of their fathers. The authors rely on these earlier studies to

1. Christopher Jencks and others, *Inequality: A Reassessment of the Effect of Family and Schooling in America* (Basic Books, 1972), especially chaps. 6 and 7.

estimate the fraction of the variance of each status measure that is explained by family background. As in the present study, they interpret this as "all features of the environment that make brothers and sisters alike."[2] Their problem is that they had no reliable way of assessing the effect of all features brothers have in common without information on brothers themselves.

The authors first acknowledge the lacunae in their empirical inventory: "Since we have no data on the correlation between brothers' incomes, we cannot estimate the overall effect of family background on income."[3] But they go on to dismiss the problem by assuming that parental estate size "is the only unmeasured family characteristic that has much direct effect on a son's income."[4]

The authors then settle for the following conclusion on the fraction of income variance that would be explained by background if all relevant features were known and could be included: "Our best guess is that the observed value would be about 0.15. It is certainly no more than 0.20."[5] This figure is sharply lower than the 40 and 44 percent estimates of $\bar{R}_i^2$ from the brothers' data on the logarithm of income reported in table 2-2. In the case of the population from which the Cleveland area sample is drawn, the hypothesis that the actual fraction of income inequality explainable by family background is only 20 percent can be rejected at the 5 percent level on the basis of the basic sample. That is, if the association were actually as weak as the Jencks *upper limit,* the chance of observing a 40 percent or higher explanation in the basic sample is less than one in twenty. The point can be made even more strongly in the case of the extended sample, where the chance of finding a 44 percent explanation or higher is less than 1 percent.[6] The 44 percent estimate carries a 95 per-

2. See, for example, ibid., p. 143.

3. Ibid., p. 345. Note that the "correlation between brothers' incomes" which they would like to have is essentially the "intraclass correlation coefficient," labeled here as $\bar{R}_i^2$. (For the relationship between the concepts of intraclass correlation and the fraction of variance explained by background, see Ronald A. Fisher, *Statistical Methods for Research Workers* [12th ed., London: Oliver and Boyd], chap. 7, especially pp. 223ff.)

4. Jencks and others, *Inequality,* p. 345. The reference to direct effect here is not clear. As is discussed in chapter 4, the effect of the various background variables is partly direct and partly indirect through intermediate variables such as the son's own education. Whatever the relative importance of the direct and indirect components, the degree of inheritance depends upon both.

5. Ibid., p. 239, note 36.

6. These significance tests are based on the F-distribution on the assumption of normality.

cent confidence interval of 0.26–0.58, impressive evidence of a far higher family effect on son's income than suggested by Jencks.

The Cleveland sample shows a degree of intergenerational transmission of income inequality much too far in excess of the Jencks guess to be explained by sampling variability, or by such minor differences as the logarithmic transformation used here. It has already been argued that the Cleveland sample is unlikely to exaggerate the degree of inheritance of status. It seems likely, then, that the absence of income data for brothers has caused Jencks to underestimate substantially the effect of family background. It was impossible for the authors to specify and measure all features brothers have in common; their inferences from regressions on a few explicit background dimensions, although often reported as actual empirical evidence on brothers, are no substitute for actual information.[7]

Conclusions in the Jencks study concerning the fraction of variation in occupational status explained by family background come much closer to the present findings than do the income results. The two new estimates in table 2-2 are 34 and 41 percent—not far above the Jencks assumption of 32 percent.[8] However, the average difference between the occupation classification of pairs of brothers is put by Jencks at 82 percent of that for all men.[9] As will be seen, this figure was derived from an estimated ratio of standard deviations. Despite the closeness of the R^2 figures, this 82 percent ratio is substantially higher than the 62 to 68 percent figures reported in table 2-2. Unlike the case of income, there was little difference between the Jencks R^2 estimates and the basic sample result in table 2-2. This suggests that the source of the discrepancy concerning occupational differences among brothers must be sought primarily in the statistical methodology with respect to average differences, rather than being attributed solely to Jencks's lack of explicit information.

Inferences Concerning Average Differences among Brothers

Not only did the Jencks study rely on few indicators to estimate the overall family background effect, but it also built on these hypothetical

7. See, for example, the unqualified conclusion of the introductory chapter: "Indeed, there is nearly as much economic inequality among brothers raised in the same homes as in the general population" (*Inequality,* pp. 7–8).

8. See ibid., p. 201, note 16. The similarity of estimates is probably due in part to the crudity of the occupation classification in the Cleveland area sample.

9. Ibid., p. 179.

regression results to infer average status differences between brothers. The authors start with the proposition that for a normally distributed variable the average absolute difference between random pairs of individuals is 1.13 standard deviations.[10] Assuming normality, it follows that the ratio of the average difference within families to the overall average difference is the same as the ratio of the standard deviations. Having assumed that family background explains at most 20 percent of income variance, the authors infer that "the within-family standard deviation will be $\sqrt{1 - 0.20} = 90$ percent of the population standard deviation."[11] This result follows from the following standard definition of R^2 in terms of "between," "within," and "total" variance components:

$$R^2 = s_{bu}^2/s_{tu}^2 = 1 - s_{wu}^2/s_{tu}^2,$$

where the subscript u indicates that the variances are unadjusted for degrees of freedom consumed in estimation. From this it follows that:

(B-1) $s_{wu}/s_{tu} = (1 - R^2)^{1/2}.$

The trouble with this reasoning, of course, is that it takes no account of degrees of freedom used up in the computation of R^2. The assumption that 20 percent of income variance can be explained by family background is equivalent to assuming that 20 percent could be explained by a regression of income on dummy variables representing families. Since the number of families is inevitably rather large relative to the total number of observations, this correction for degrees of freedom consumed is essential and is embodied in the $\bar{R}_i^2$ estimates presented in table 2-2. For that reason relation B-1 cannot be applied to these estimates in order to infer the ratio of standard deviations in which Jencks and colleagues are interested. However, it is appropriate to ask what standard deviations are indeed implied by table 2-2. The estimates of $\bar{R}_i^2$ in that table were computed by standard small-sample formulas from the analysis of variance. However, very accurate large-sample approximations facilitate comparison with results from regression analysis. For k sets of brothers in a total sample size of N, the relation in terms of adjusted variances is:

(B-2) $\bar{R}_i^2 = \dfrac{s_b^2 - s_w^2}{s_b^2 + [N/(k - 1)]\, s_w^2},$

where the subscript i attached to $\bar{R}^2$ indicates its equivalence to the intraclass correlation coefficient.[12]

10. Ibid., p. 354.
11. Ibid., note 36, pp. 239–40.
12. This is identical with the result obtainable from a conventional adjustment of R^2 for degrees of freedom used: $\bar{R}^2 = 1 - [N/(N - k)]\,(1 - R^2)$.

It is apparent from B-2 that Jencks's objective of relating the within-family standard deviation to the overall standard deviation cannot be achieved here. Not only is the total variance missing from the relationship, but the appropriately defined variances are not additive; in other words, the estimated fraction of income variance explained by family of origin would be inconsistent with the fraction *not* explained.[13] So we are reduced to making the usual comparison between s_b^2 and s_w^2 via the F-ratio, s_b^2/s_w^2. Ratios significantly greater than unity indicate that inequality among brothers is significantly less than inequality across families. These F-ratios are tabulated in table 2-2 and are all highly significant. The lowest is the 2.2 ratio for occupation in the basic sample, but even that is significant at the 0.1 percent level. In the case of income, for which Jencks found inequality among brothers to be very close to that among all men, the F-ratios of 2.56 and 2.76 show inequality among brothers to be substantially overshadowed by that among families.

It would be illuminating to compare the s_w/s_t ratios to the 90 percent and 82 percent figures Jencks indicates for income and occupation, respectively, but the inconsistency of s_b, s_w and s_t effectively rules that out.[14] Instead, the s_w/s_b ratios implied by the F-ratio were given in table 2-2. These inheritance measures show markedly greater homogeneity of economic status among brothers than indicated by Jencks. The basic sample results for occupation in table 2-2 are especially revealing: despite an $\overline{R}^2$ value virtually identical to that used by Jencks, the standard deviation ratio found here is 68 percent, compared to the Jencks ratio of 82 percent. Although the 68 percent figure is the weakest inheritance measure obtained in this study, it is nearly twice as far as the Jencks measure from the zero-inheritance benchmark of unity. Since the $\overline{R}^2$ values on which these estimates were based are about the same, the difference appears to be due to the contrasting treatment of degrees of freedom, as discussed above. Although the discrepancy between the present estimates for occupation and those of Jencks is less than in the case of income, it remains important for any appraisal of socioeconomic mobility.

13. The number of degrees of freedom for the entire sample is defined as $N - 1$ (along with $k - 1$ "between" and $N - k$ "within"); so estimates of all three variances are available. However, either component can exceed total variance; hence the analysis of variance conventionally excludes total variance in favor of a comparison of within and between variances.

14. For example, in the case of the logarithm of income in the basic sample, the appropriate ratios are $s_b^2/s_t^2 = 1.53$, and $s_w^2/s_t^2 = 0.60$, so the appropriately adjusted components produce fractions of total variance explained and unexplained that exceed 100 percent.

Finally, how are we to interpret the striking discrepancies between the standard deviation ratios recorded in table 2-2 and the much higher inferences by Jencks? The results for income can be used to recapitulate the two basic components of the discrepancy. In the first place, Jencks was compelled to rely on other studies based on incomplete sets of explanatory variables; these were used to guess the fraction of income variance that would be explained by family background if they could have observed all dimensions of the latter. Their conclusion again: "Our best guess is that the observed value would be about 0.15. It is certainly no more than 0.20."[15] The authors' confidence in this inference appears misplaced in light of the 0.40–0.44 estimates in table 2-2, which are based on the incomes of actual brothers. Claims of certainty will be avoided here, but the 95 percent confidence intervals in table 2-2 suggest that it is highly unlikely that the actual value of $\overline{R}_i^2$ is as low as 0.20.[16]

The second main component of the discrepancy between the 60 to 63 percent standard deviation ratio in table 2-2 and the 90 percent guess by Jencks is methodological. Not only did the Jencks study start with a surprisingly low estimate of the effect of family background on income, but their follow-up inferences concerning the ratio of the standard deviation among brothers to the overall standard deviation are questionable. Their 20 percent guess for the fraction of income variance explained by family background is put forward as the maximum that would emerge if data on brothers were available. What would have been the implications if this 20 percent figure had actually been observed on the basis of an analysis of brothers? An acceptable estimate would presumably require a standard analysis of variance, or equivalent regression on dummy variables representing families. Certainly the analysis could not have ignored degrees of freedom consumed in making the estimate. It is therefore misleading to infer, as Jencks and colleagues did, relationships among standard deviations on the basis of relation B-1 as though their 20 percent were a raw R^2 without consideration of degrees of freedom. The appropriate relation for making such inferences has been given here as B-2. Unfortunately, this relation does not imply the general solution for s_w/s_t desired by Jencks; it provides only for a comparison of the within and between stan-

15. Ibid., p. 239.
16. It must be reiterated that the present figures are based on a single sample, but it is at least large enough to yield a fairly tight confidence interval. The general reliability of relationships inferred from this sample has already been argued. It should be added that the logarithmic transformation preferred here seems unlikely to be a major source of the discrepancy in estimates; indeed, results without the transformation were not markedly different.

dard deviations, s_w and s_b. For example, manipulation of relation B-2 leads to

$$(B-3) \qquad s_w/s_b = \left(1 + \frac{N\bar{R}_i^2}{k(1 - \bar{R}_i^2)}\right)^{-1/2}.$$

This shows how the ratio of the within-family standard deviation to the between-family standard deviation depends not only on $\bar{R}_i^2$, but also on N/k, the number of brothers per family in the sample from which the statistic 0.20 was derived. Moreover, it was necessary for estimation purposes that N be greater than k, since the number of family categories would otherwise consume all the degrees of freedom and leave no estimate of family effects. Note, however, that in the limiting case in which $N/k = 1$, B-3 reduces to:

$$(B-4) \qquad s_w/s_b = s_w/s_t = (1 - \bar{R}_i^2)^{1/2}.$$

At this extreme, s_b would equal s_t, since each family includes only one individual; s_w and $\bar{R}_i^2$ are not defined. Yet B-4 is equivalent to B-1, the relation applied by Jencks to interpret the implications of his hypothetical $R^2 = 0.20$. Therefore, in addition to the effect of his low guess concerning R^2, Jencks's interpretation of the 0.20 clearly underestimates the standard deviation ratio. For any assumed $\bar{R}_i^2$, relation B-3 shows that the ratio s_w/s_b must be lower than indicated by Jencks, since N/k must have been greater than unity for any estimates to be obtained at all.[17]

In sum, the Jencks study has underestimated at two levels the ratio of income and occupational inequality among brothers to that for all men. First, its indirect empirical assessment of the effect of family background, especially on income, appears very low in light of the present findings. Second, these low estimates are downgraded even further in Jencks's inferences concerning the ratio of within-family inequality to the overall inequality of status. On both empirical and methodological counts, the estimates of the standard deviation ratio in table 2-2 appear much closer to the mark than Jencks's estimates of 90 percent for income and 82 percent for occupational status.

17. The ratio s_w/s_b is tabulated below for various average family sizes and given hypothetical values of $\bar{R}_i^2$:

$\bar{R}_i^2$	$N/K = 1.5$	$N/k = 2.0$	$N/k = 3.0$
0.2	0.85	0.82	0.76
0.4	0.71	0.65	0.58
0.6	0.55	0.65	0.43

The larger the average family size, the lower the implied ratio of within-family to between-family standard deviations. The difference is not great in the case of Jencks's assumed $\bar{R}_i^2$ of 0.2, and the figures are not far below his extreme assumption of 0.90.

appendix C **A Comparison of the Larger Samples**

Chapter 3 considered the practical meaning of the estimated coefficients for model 3-2, as applied to married sons only. This sample is compared here to others for consistency and accuracy in order to provide a basis for selecting one set of estimates for interpretation. Efforts to explain the economic status of *all* sons in the basic sample were hampered somewhat by two methodological problems. First, as has generally been recognized in income distribution studies, the economic status of the unmarried men (making up roughly one-tenth of the sample) was generally lower and more erratic than that of married men. It thus seemed likely that the accuracy of the estimates could be enhanced by dropping the single sons.[1] Second, the general uselessness of the occupation classification of female decedents has been crudely finessed by assigning them the mean occupation of male decedents. Since this leaves the occupation variable with no explanatory power whatever for sons of female decedents, it was to be expected that concentration on sons of male decedents might provide more accurate estimates.

Table C-1 presents regressions for all sons in the basic sample, for comparison with the earlier results for married sons in table 3-3. Table C-2 indicates the goodness of fit of the basic family background model 3-2 for six economic status measures and three samples. The first sample is the basic one of all sons underlying table C-1. The next sample excludes single sons, improving the fits somewhat for all six status measures. Then the next step, excluding sons of female decedents, again improves the fit in all six cases. Despite a substantial loss of degrees of freedom, the two exclusions together raise the adjusted fraction of status variation explained by about one-tenth to one-quarter, depending on the measure.

---

1. A marital status dummy improved the fit, but omitting the few single sons seemed more efficient.

174

The degree of explanation of the logarithm of income is about 26 percent, a fairly respectable showing against the 40 to 44 percent gross explanation achieved by the analysis of brothers in table 2-2. It was accomplished without the aid of important explanatory background variables such as the second parent's education and parental income.[2] In short, the present estimates suggest that the 40 to 44 percent overall explanation of income variation by family background (table 2-2) is quite plausible. Moreover, when two or three more economic status measures are combined with income to form the indexes *Croy* and *Croye,* the ten explicit family background variables account for more than 44 and 46 percent, respectively, of the variation in these two status indexes. This is a very high fraction in a cross-section model that is obviously missing important explanatory variables.

In terms of accuracy of estimates of the coefficients, the sample of married sons of male decedents is less satisfactory. The sharp cut in sample size swamps the favorable effect of the two data omissions analyzed in table C-2, resulting in generally higher standard errors and fewer significant coefficients, especially for the composite status indexes. However, the regressions for married sons (reported earlier in table 3-3) fared much better. The accuracy of coefficient estimates in this intermediate sample is not much different from that found in the analysis of all sons in table C-1, and the coefficient estimates themselves were remarkably similar for all three overlapping samples. As in table C-1, all signs of significant coefficients and virtually all those of insignificant coefficients were as hypothesized.

Two variations of the basic background model 3-2 seemed to perform at least as well. The inclusion of decedent's education in years instead of the three dummies tended to yield at least as good a fit, but the dummies were retained for the a priori reasons mentioned in chapter 2. Decedent's occupation and gross estate were of no more than marginal explanatory importance throughout, and in many cases the fit of the model could often have been improved by their removal. However, they were kept because of their a priori importance and frequent contribution to the explanation of composite indexes of status achievement.

2. As indicated in table C-1, decedent's education is consistently the strongest explanatory variable. Parental income has revealed its importance in various studies. See, for example, William H. Sewell and Robert M. Hauser, "Causes and Consequences of Higher Education: Models of the Status Attainment Process," *American Journal of Agricultural Economics,* vol. 54 (December 1972), pp. 851–61.

Table C-1. Regression Coefficients Relating Economic Status of All Sons to Explicit Family Background Variables, Cleveland Area Basic Sample,ᵃ 1965–66

Parental variableᵇ	Variable or statistic	Measure of son's economic statusᶜ					
		RATE	OCC	LOGY	Croy	(Croye)	(ED)
...	Constant	4.17* (8.14)	1.20 (1.44)	0.760* (6.54)	−1.23* (3.12)	−1.02* (2.76)	4.23* (6.12)
Age and education	AGED	0.03 (0.46)	0.31* (3.19)	0.024* (1.82)	0.14* (3.06)	0.10* (2.23)	−0.11 (1.35)
	AED2	0.01 (0.59)	0.07* (1.88)	0.013* (2.59)	0.04* (2.43)	0.04* (2.84)	0.09* (2.97)
	AED3	0.06* (2.02)	0.17* (3.71)	0.029* (4.36)	0.10* (4.74)	0.11* (5.71)	0.19* (4.98)
Occupation	OCDT	0.08 (1.54)	0.21* (2.50)	0.006 (0.52)	0.10* (2.53)	0.10* (2.55)	0.10 (1.38)
Family size	SIBS	−0.10* (3.23)	−0.07 (1.54)	−0.018 (2.53)	−0.08* (3.56)	−0.08* (3.58)	−0.07* (1.74)
Race	RAC2	−1.71* (5.10)	−1.54* (2.82)	−0.176* (2.09)	−1.03* (3.83)	−0.90* (3.53)	−0.80* (1.75)
Religion	REL2	−0.28* (2.27)	−0.25 (1.28)	−0.033 (1.17)	−0.19 (2.07)	−0.15* (1.75)	−0.14 (0.83)
	REL3	0.11 (0.45)	0.66* (1.77)	0.077 (1.39)	0.37 (2.07)	0.37* (2.22)	0.42 (1.30)
Wealth	GRST	0.11 (0.81)	0.29 (1.22)	0.031 (0.95)	0.15 (1.31)	0.20* (1.91)	0.54* (2.83)
	TES2	−0.27* (2.04)	−0.35* (1.66)	−0.036 (1.19)	−0.22* (2.24)	−0.20* (2.16)	−0.16 (0.89)
...	Number of sons	280	267	263	253	253	279
...	$\bar{R}^2$	0.230	0.265	0.199	0.394	0.424	0.267

Source: See appendix A.

a. The basic sample is defined in table 2-2, note b.

b. These indicators of parental status are defined in table 3-1; where responses by siblings conflicted, these responses were averaged.

c. Measures of economic status are defined in table 2-2, note a, except composite Croye, which adds son's education to Croy. The numbers in parentheses are t-ratios.

* Regression coefficient significant at the 5 percent level on the one-tail test.

Table C-2. Comparison of Explanatory Power ($\bar{R}^2$) of the Basic Family Background Model 3-2 for Subgroups of Sons in Cleveland Area Basic Sample,[a] 1965–66

Sample	RATE	OCC	LOGY	Croy	(Croye)	(ED)
			Measure of economic status[b]			
All sons						
Number	280	267	263	253	253	279
$\bar{R}^2$	0.230	0.265	0.199	0.394	0.424	0.267
Married sons						
Number	248	241	239	231	231	247
$\bar{R}^2$	0.257	0.278	0.239	0.417	0.442	0.280
Married sons of male decedents						
Number	150	149	147	144	144	150
$\bar{R}^2$	0.292	0.278	0.253	0.437	0.448	0.287

Source: See appendix A.

a. The basic sample is defined in table 2-2, note b.

b. Measures of economic status are as defined in table 2-2, except that *Croye* has been added; this measure combines son's education with the status measures in *Croy*.

In sum, it appears that from the point of view of the goodness of fit, the size of the coefficients, and the accuracy of estimation, the different samples and variants of the basic model yielded fairly consistent indications of the influence of education and all the other explanatory variables.

The sample of all sons offered a lower degree of status explanation than the others, but the estimated coefficients there were typical, and the indicated accuracy of their estimation was as good as any. For brevity, it was essential to focus on one sample, even though the choice between them seemed a toss-up. Since the later analysis of daughters must be restricted to married daughters, the married son sample was chosen for comparability and will be utilized from here on. Thus table 3-3 served as the basis for tentative interpretation of the role of background influences in determination of economic status.[3] Since the practical importance of the individual background factors is to be found in the coefficients and their standard errors, table 3-3 seems as good a source as any.

3. The interpretation had to be rough and tentative because background income, the education of one parent, and other important factors are missing; inevitably the available explanatory variables will get credit for some influence due to other predetermined variables with which they are correlated.

appendix D **Parental Occupation, Family Size, Religion, Race, and Wealth as Predictors of Son's Status**

Parental education as a predictor was considered in chapter 3. The five other available background variables are also of interest in their own right, although some have been conventionally regarded as control variables in attempts to isolate the effects of the son's own education. All the qualifications discussed in chapter 3, such as bias due to unobserved variables, pertain also to the discussion here of the predictive power of these individual background characteristics.

The indicated effects of the other five family background characteristics in table 3-6 are more directly apparent than the age-complicated effects of parental education. The occupation of the son was significantly related to that of his parent, but a difference of one grade in the latter appears to be worth less than one-fifth of a grade to the son.[1] It is useful to illustrate the effects of the same degree of background contrast as specified in table 3-4. For example, parents with occupational ranks about 5 percent from the top and bottom, respectively, differ by about 4.1 grades. Other things being equal, their sons are predicted to differ by about three-quarters of a grade—less than half a standard deviation. Even the maximum difference in occupational rank between two decedents calls for a predicted difference between sons' occupation of 1.28—still below one standard deviation. The two composite success indexes were also significantly related to parental occupation, but again the predicted differential is unimpressive. If the son of an unskilled worker and the son of a major business executive differ in no other (measured) way, then the predicted

1. It should be repeated that parent's occupation was not a promising explanatory variable, since its values for women are necessarily neutralized by substitution of the mean for men. However, the variable was no more effective when the sample was restricted to sons of male decedents.

difference in their composite indexes is 0.48—only about six-tenths of
one standard deviation of that index. If the prediction for the first son
were a composite index at the fiftieth percentile, the executive's son would
be expected to rank at about the thirty-second percentile from the top. It
should be reiterated that the uselessness of female occupational data may
have helped produce this indication of a relatively minor influence of
parent's occupation on son's success.

Family size has a significant effect on all success measures for the sons
except occupational rank. The illustrative contrast in table 3-4 called for
a difference in size of 5.4 between the large and small family. The greatest predicted differential in son's success is in residence rating, which is
depressed 0.7 standard deviations by large family size. However, the income differential is also appreciable as well as significant: sons from the
smaller family tend to average 21 percent more.

The coefficients for religion present a fairly consistent picture. Even if
their backgrounds are alike in the other five respects, sons of Catholics
rank significantly lower than sons of Protestants in residence quality, occupation, and the composite economic success measures. Sons from a
Jewish background fared significantly better than Protestants in occupation, income, and the composite indexes. The educational attainment of
the sons appears considerably less closely related to religion.[2]

The differentials in son's success related to religion appear somewhat
greater than those associated with parental occupation and family size.
A son with a Jewish heritage is expected to have a *Croy* standing 0.71
(0.89 standard deviations) higher than a Catholic son. This predicted
differential can be given practical meaning in terms of observed values of
this success index. For example, an average value of *Croy* would apply to
a son with residence and occupational ranks slightly below average at
four, and income above average, in the $9,600–$12,000 class (about
equivalent to $19,200–$24,000 in 1976). If a Catholic son had this economic success profile, a Jewish son differing in no other way than religion
could achieve his expected rating differential by scoring one notch higher
on all three counts—residence and occupational grades of 5 percent, and
income in the $12,000–$18,000 class ($24,000–$36,000 in 1976).

Economic success of the sons was related more erratically to the two

2. Table 3-3 suggests that the Jewish sons are significantly better off than Catholics on all six counts, including education, but the *t*-ratios in table 3-3 do not offer
this comparison directly.

available indicators of parental material wealth.[3] The estate size was marginally significant in explaining the son's residence quality, but it showed no influence on his occupation, income, or the combination of the three. The contrasting hypothetical large and small estates specified in table 3-4 ($63,000 and $2,300) would lead to a prediction of a residential differential of only about one-third of a grade. A more important effect indicated for this estate size differential was on educational attainment—about 1.7 years, but still only about six-tenths of a standard deviation.

The proxy wealth indicator, testacy, was more consistently significant than estate size, but its indicated influence was also small. Other things being equal, the son of a testate parent is predicted to have a 0.22 advantage in residence, 0.40 in occupation, and 12 percent in income. If the testate decedent also had the advantage in estate size specified above, these estimates become 0.56, 0.77, and 18 percent—still small compared to the indicated influence of parental education.

The measured effect of race on son's success is strong, even though there are only five nonwhites in the sample. It is the only one of the six family background characteristics that rivals age-education in its apparent influence. On the basis of this sample, a white son, identical to a nonwhite in all five other respects, including parental education, is expected to be better off by 1.27 grades in residence, 1.34 in occupation, 75 percent in income, and 1.12 (or 1.4 standard deviations) in the index combining those three. Only with respect to the intermediate variable, years of education, does race appear to make little difference in the prospects for the sons. For the three basic success measures, the indicated statistical significance of the coefficients is generally higher than that of any other background factor except parental college education. However, even though the standard errors of these estimates take account of sample size and the variance-of-race variable, the results should be received with caution. Suspicion inevitably attaches to results from so small a sample, even though the probability interpretation of these t-ratios of around three or four is no different from any others.

If this pattern could be confirmed by a much larger sample, what would that mean? There are two reinforcing explanations. First, since family background has been substantially controlled in this analysis, the apparent racial lag suggests a strong degree of discrimination against nonwhite

3. Technical weaknesses of the available material wealth indicators as explanatory variables were discussed in the text.

sons and sons-in-law. This discrimination is *over and beyond* whatever handicap is conferred by an otherwise disadvantaged background which may also be due to race.[4] Second, a finding of this substantial depression of economic success by race without any accompanying depression of education—a key means to success—suggests that the measure of educational attainment in years (without correction for quality) may be masking further discrimination in the form of the nonwhite son's low-quality education. In the same way parental education may also be effectively overstated for nonwhites, therefore giving too high a status prediction in the first place.[5]

4. The possibility cannot be ruled out that part of the indicated effect of race is due to missing variables uncorrelated with the other background variables. One hypothesis is that IQ could play this role, but it is hard to believe that it would be only weakly correlated with the nine other variables in the model. (This controversy is touched on in chapter 4.)

5. See Finis Welch, "Measurement of the Quality of Schooling," *American Economic Review*, vol. 56 (May 1966, *Papers and Proceedings, 1965*), pp. 379–92; and idem, "Black-White Differences in Returns to Schooling" (National Bureau of Economic Research, 1972; processed).

Index

Ability of sons, 148–50
Advantaged sons, economic success predictions for, 93–96
Age, 10; and education, 77–80; effect of, 50, 70; and income, 78–80; of parent, 18–19; 117–9; of parents at death, 20, 78, 99
Anastasi, Anne, 81n

Background characteristics, 74; and hypotheses of analysis of brothers, 18–19
Background influences, 74, 140–43, 146, 148–49, 156–58; strength of, 19–20; unexplained, 26
Becker, Gary S., 152n
Behrman, J., 73n
Belmont, Lillian, 71n, 83n
Bequests, 7, 29–30, 83–84
Bishop, Yvonne M. M., 39n, 82n
Blau, Peter M., 2, 3n, 81n, 125n, 158n
Bowles, Samuel, 3n, 145n, 151n

Carnegie, Andrew, 7
Caste societies, 10
Cates, Judith N., 13n
Chamberlain, Gary, 36n, 73n, 130n
Chase, Ivan D., 158n
Cleveland sample compared to national samples, 44, 54–5, 89–92
Cooper, George, 6n
Corcoran, Mary, 36n, 54n, 89n
Corry, Bernard, 9n

Daughters, 74; background, 153; economic status of, 24, 113, 114, 124; vs. sons in status, 27–28
Demographic characteristics of sample, 40–46
Disadvantaged sons, economic success predictions for, 93–96

Discrimination, 10–12; by employers, 10–11
Duncan, Beverly, 92n, 119n
Duncan, Otis Dudley, 2, 3n, 39n, 73n, 81n, 92n, 119n, 125n, 158n

Economic mobility: intergenerational, 22–23, 105; patterns, 115–116; upward vs. downward, 113–15
Economic status: basic model of, 84; characteristics, 17–23; composite measures, 53–54, 63–65; defined, 35n; inheritance of, 12–17; measures and meanings, 15–17; measuring degree of inheritance of, 46–47; of parents, index, 106–16; predicting sons', 17–23; predictions of advantaged and disadvantaged sons, 93–96; of sample, 43; of sons, 77; stability of, 35
Education, 2, 3, 28, 85–87, 123, 135, 148–51, 154–55, 162–63; and age, 77–80; of brothers, and income of family, 52–53; of brothers vs. sisters, 159–61; as conveyer of economic status across generations, 126–40; and earning power, 123–24, 144–45; effect of, 125–26; of family, 132–33, 162; and income, 61–67; independent effects of, 25–26, 140–52; inheritance of, 16–17, 26; and marital selection, 162–64; and occupation, 102; of parents, 18–19, 96–105, 119, 150; of parents, estimated effects, 20–21, 33; of parents, and son's income, 30; policies toward, 33–34; role in inheritance of status, 23–28, 146–52; of sample, 43–44; of son in intergenerational transmission of economic status, 124–26; as transmitter of specific background influences, 133–40
Environmental vs. genetic components of parental influence, 2